"Shutup You Animals!!!!"
The Pope is Dead

Photo by Chester Simpson

A book about Dirk Dirksen by Dirk Dirksen

Edited by Ron Turner and James Stark
Cover by James Stark • Cover Photo by Chester Simpson

A Rememberance of Dirk Dirksen

Photographs and Text Documenting Dirk Dirksen by Dirk Dirksen
Edited by Ron Turner and James Stark

Published by
Last Gasp of San Francisco
Ronald E. Turner, Publisher

777 Florida Street
San Francisco, CA 94110

www.lastgasp.com

This edition ©2021
Published by Last Gasp
ISBN: 978-0-86719-874-4

6   5   4   3   2

Table of Contents

Introduction

I spotted Dirk prowling around the church building that housed the Intersection on Union Street, around the corner from the Washington Square Bar and Grill. Karl Cohen was

Ron Turner at 111 Minna.

threading his projector with Betty Boop cartoons and various women from the Free Store collective of Cotati and SF's comedy troupe Les Nicklettes were assembling for the Sunday night performances. Dirk was on the hunt for talent at the Mabuhay on Broadway. His co host was Ness Aquino who I had met when a rock in one of his filipino rice dishes broke my tooth at the original spot on Kearney next to the International Hotel. Ness didn't offer any dental repair. This casual meet up blossomed into a long friendship. We even hawked Zippy the Pinhead t shirts and a Zippy actor Jim Turner on Dirk's television show broadcast out of a tiny shack on the side of San Bruno Mountain. For many years after the close of the Mabuhay Dirk was supposed to be writing his story for publication. Every couple months it was:..."just about done, could I have a little advance?" The last time I saw him for fun was we went to hear Kathy Peck back with the Contractions. Then he came by and wanted a little more advance and the book was almost done, and he died three weeks later. Of course, he had only written a small part of the first chapter. So, we must depend on all his friends to accurately describe him. Please enjoy this tale of how a little Jewish boy from Nazi Germany became the Pope of Punk.

Ron Turner.

Acknowledgements

This book began with Dirk Dirksen wanting to secure his place in history unfortunately he passed before it could be completed. Peter Claudus who assembled the dates and bands that played The Mab took over the project but he had to many other projects and passed it off to Ron and Last Gasp who had agreed to publish it. Ron Turner then brought James Stark on board to assist with the editing and layout.

Several people submitted stories of their experiences, see Table of Contents page, and what The Mab met to them and there are some good ones. Posters came from several collections including: Dirksen Archives, Bryan Ray Turcotte, Regi Mentle, Kareem Kaddad, Kathy Peck, James Stark, Marc Olmstead, Ken Cameron, James Ellis and Vale. We gave credit where we knew the artist but a lot of this information has been lost to time.

Kathy Peck, who produced a couple of benefits for Dirk before and after his passing, was a big help in providing material for the final chapter. Writer Micheal Goldberg for the Jennifer Egan interview sharing her story of her days at The Mab which showed up in her book "A Visit from the Goon Squad" which she got so right. Chester Simpson for the cover photo which he didn't know was his. And those people who made The Mab happen and San Francisco a better place to live.

Dirk Dirksen Interviews Himself

Hello. I've been called "The Pope of Punk," but my real name is Dirk Dirksen. I do whatever I do in the City of San Francisco. I'm not a native. I came here in the early '70s and

opened a venue at a place called "The Mabuhay Gardens." We nicknamed our nightclub 'The Fab Mab' because "Mabuhay Gardens" was the name of the Filipino supper club and piano bar that operated by day in the same space.

I wanted to have a venue that could offer an open forum for ideas to performers and acts, musicians, dancers, comedians, you name it — anyone who uses a stage to do their thing — and to those people they usually attract: writers, photographers, filmmakers, engineers for recording and video, lighting people, and choreographers. The idea was to assemble the greatest cast possible. I had projected that we'd need about 20,000 people to do the experiment I had in mind, which was to witness the genesis of creation — to be there at the moment when it happens for a person who wants to

Photo courtesy of family

express himself, or who has ideas that they want the public to see. I think we succeeded in that, and allowed a lot of people who otherwise would have been considered outlaws in the arts to have a stage on which to do their thing.

"The Fab Mab" started on Mondays and Tuesdays, which were the dark nights at the Mabuhay. I had approached the owner with the offer, "We'll guarantee you $175.00 per night at the bar, if you let us have the venue to do our shows." And we wanted no interference from the management. We said, "We will not get you into any problems with your (liquor) license. However, you will have no ability to say, 'You can't play this,' or 'You can't play that..'"

The formula was quite simple. We'd ask people to send us a tape so that we could identify their genre of music, and a picture so that we could see what they looked like; their name, address, age and instrumentation or, if they were a comedian or a dancer, a description of what they did. One of the reasons we didn't want to know exactly what the music would be, or the lyrics, was that (in the legal sense) we didn't want to practice prior restraint — meaning that if they advocated something that was illegal — drug use or whatever, or if it had nudity in it— we didn't want to know about it until it happened on stage. That cleared the way for spontaneity.

Now, we attracted a great cross-section of everyone: rockers, dancers, heavy metal people, transsexuals, transgenders, bisexuals — you name it — it was all sort of a melting pot. And we had a great audience. The audience was part of the show. I took a page

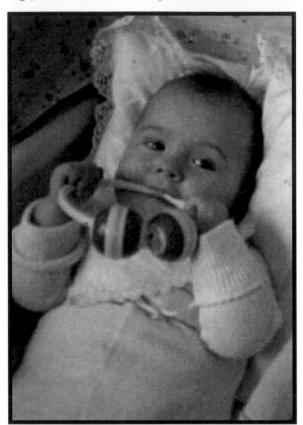

Baby Dirk. Photo courtesy Dirksen Archives

out of the history of show business from Toulouse-Lautrec, the famous French artist, — it so impressed me to see his pictures of all the different people at the Moulin Rouge. There were the pimps and the prostitutes, there was the royalty, there were the aristocrats, the writers, the intellectuals of the area, in the audience at the Moulin Rouge, and I said, "I'm going to try to document a scene like that through technology. I don't want to be the guy behind the camera, necessarily, but I want to document as many people as possible and then track them and see the progression, through the years, of the folks that are performing." I had figured we'd need about ten years to get through 20,000 people — indeed, we got through 22,000+ performers and artists. Out of those, there would probably be about 200 people that would bubble up to the top. That projection, too, was very accurate. I mean, out of that theory – and through that venue — came Henry Rollins, Jello Biafra, Jim Carroll, Billy Idol, Robin Williams, Penelope Houston — and all sorts of other people who now have mainstream name recognition and are having an impact on society.

We offered an open forum. I was a little bit older than many of the people that worked with me, and I had management experience from working as associate producer on a number of shows —network shows and a number of local TV shows——in Hawaii. So we took the door receipts and the bar owner took the proceeds from the bar. We administered, or acted as stewards for the artists. We gave the artists 65% of the evening's receipts, and took 35% for the lights, the audio, the advertising, the insurance and the security. Many of our staffers were people who were also involved in the arts, and there was a wonderful mix of everybody working together. There's something unique about San Francisco: because of its compact area, you keep bumping into the same people. The artistic community is, perhaps, somewhat incestuous because of that: somebody who is a guitarist in one band will be doing the lights for someone else, and his girlfriend, maybe, will be a dancer who's also a choreographer, or a writer, or a photographer — so there's a wonderful melting pot of all the different professions that work in the arts, and we had a really wonderful, tight community.

When you believe, as I do, in booking a multitude of different kinds of things, you realize that just because your audience likes punk rock, you don't have to have an entire bill of punk. You can throw in jazz, country, or comedy, and it makes the whole show a happening. That's what we tried to create. I always felt that you need variety — like Ed Sullivan said: "Take one piece that someone may like and someone else may detest, and if you make it short enough — the person that detests it isn't going to leave you. He or she'll stick around for the next act that they enjoy." And that's what we tried to do.

One problem we had was that a theater was above us, above the Mabuhay. The theater operated from 8 o'clock 'til about 10:30, and we couldn't trespass on their sound, so we had to start at 11 o'clock. That meant we had from 11 until 2 o'clock — because the bars have to close at two—and we crammed three acts into three hours. We had comedians, fire eaters, dancers—you name it— in between the bands. To this day Robin Williams, who did stand-up comedy opening for the Ramones, calls the Mabuhay "the nightclub from hell". He just had a tough time getting that audience — the Ramones audience. And the late comedian, Jane Dornacker, once said, "Well, he

Dirk as a child with siblings in Germany circa 1940

took a place which was rated for 99 people and crammed in 500. That's why it became a hot place: because we were all together in a sauna bath." That was really true. It was a sauna bath of the arts.

There was a great feeling of fellowship among the art community during this period, and we constantly tried to involve the rest of the community. In the ten years we were in existence, we did over 500 benefits. For instance, there was a musician who had fallen off a window ledge — the young woman had lost her keys, so she climbed up three stories and was making her way into the back window when she slipped and ended up in a body cast — and we had a benefit for her. We held some of the first benefits for AIDS victims. We had benefits for political causes like the Nixon Six, which was against the right-wing attempt to fire teachers who were gay. And, also, out of this came the Jello Biafra Mayoral Campaign. He wanted to show the hypocrisy in politics, and he mentioned it to a couple of people. One of them was Brad Lapin of Damage Magazine. Brad said, "Oh, this would be great! If he runs for Mayor, it'll give him a platform for his political concepts ..." We took it a step further, and we made it street theater. But we didn't make it violent street theater. I helped in his mayoral campaign, and we became good friends Here's someone who spent $127 on his campaign, and he came in fourth out of a field of about twelve. And many of the folks who came in behind him spent thirty, forty and fifty thousand dollars. It's interesting that the California Senate Legislature actually made it a law that you have to use your real name when running for office because of Biafra and the Sisters of Perpetual Indulgence (one of them ran for the Board of Supervisors); and (State Senator) Quentin Kopp, who had sent a congratulatory telegram on the night of Biafra's defeat, sponsored that law. So, we did have an impact. I think we made people aware that you should have a sense of humor, even in politics; and that you shouldn't get so polarized that you have to beat up on each other. We always tried to show a sense of humor about things. And the community would always rally, whether it was to raise money for somebody who'd gotten hurt or to come together and say, "This behavior doesn't cut it."

A particular example of unified action occurred during an Avengers concert. It was a Saturday night, the place probably had 500 people in it, and a group of thugs from Martinez or Fresno had come down and they were terrorizing Broadway. They had beaten people

Dirk as a young man. Photo courtesy Dirksen Archives

up and broken windows, they forced their way past our door personnel, and I became aware that they were attacking people on the dance floor. So, as Penelope was wrapping up the song that the Avengers were playing, I took over the mike and said, "Folks, we have a situation here. People are being picked off, one at a time, and if you don't stand together, they're going to get a lot of you. You've got to act as a unit." And before I got the word "unit" out, the crowd just fell silent, they turned on the offending group, and those guys were driven out within five minutes. Up to that point, they had been injuring people; we sent several to the hospital with cut scalps or broken jaws. In the process, I got my nose broken and had a chair broken over my head. There's a wonderful series of photographs by Chester Simpson, the rock 'n' roll photographer, who was working for Rolling Stone at the time: he had a high-speed shutter, and he was clicking all along. He got about 16 photos of people getting cold-cocked, and there is a sequence of me confronting the guy, and being grabbed by the lapels or by the shirt. In the next shot, you see me with a trickle of blood. The chair breaking over my head was not caught on film; it actually hit me on the shoulders — both of the blades— so it never really got me....

I had not conceived the Fab Mab as a punk venue. I had conceived it as an open forum. The punk rockers, because they were banned almost everywhere else, flocked to our forum, and I booked them because that was part of the Fab Mab philosophy. But the notoriety of the place as a punk venue did cause certain problems. Occasionally, people who didn't understand the pseudo-violence on stage or couldn't cope with it would get the wrong idea. I looked at what was occurring on stage and I saw that people in the audience would sometimes get upset and chuck beer bottles. So, I thought, "We've got to somehow defuse that." Well, we got these big barrels— 55-gallon drums— and put popcorn in them so the patrons could gorge on it, and I started telling the audience, "Hey, you little rats: we salt the popcorn really heavily so that you'll drink more. Eat up, folks, because then you'll buy more drinks and we'll make more money off you." The whole bit was designed to make me seem like the personification of a really miserable, scummy, greedy club owner. I used to wear a penis nose with these big black glasses We ran a clear plastic tube along the lining, and I had a squeeze ball in my pocket where we'd put Sea and Ski sun-tan lotion, which has a sort of putrid, yellow-white appearance. And I'd constantly be drooling out of my nose this — this awful fluid. I'd be wiping my nose while introducing the acts, and I'd say, "You know, we haven't hit the bottom of the barrel with this act: we're breaking up the barrel! But you guys out there, you have no taste, so this should be right up your alley!" I tried to bring the audience and the performers together in mutual hate for the club owner. Then, the moment I pulled the glasses off, I could become myself again. Unfortunately, some people

couldn't quite see the distinction. I guess maybe it wasn't strong enough..... .

The L.A. punk rockers were definitely different from the home breed in many ways. First came the Screamers and the Drums, and they were followed by Black Flag, the Circle Jerks, and the Descendants. All of them were equally intense, but some of them had different

Dirk directing "At the Palace" T.V. show, circa 1976. Photo courtesy Dirksen Archives

social consciences and they attracted different audiences. They created different challenges for us to deal with. I had a number of problems with the Circle Jerks, for example, when their fans would come up from L.A. There was a case where there had been rumors that they were planning to trash some people, and, indeed, after the show, one of them was involved in a murder of somebody on Polk Street. It's sort of sad to pour one's soul, and one's very existence and economics, into doing shows, and then to have negative results like that. But, on the whole, I don't regret anything that went on. I ended up with, I think, my

nose broken six or seven times. Both ankles got broken. Both of my knees got screwed up because during a — well, I can't remember who the band was, but we were doing a

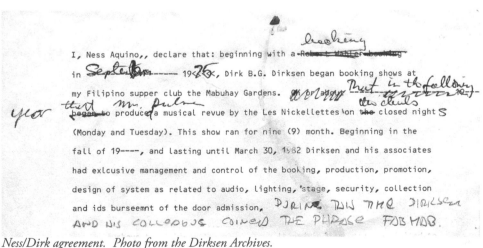

I, Ness Aquino,, declare that: beginning with a ~~Robert Mahler booking~~ *booking* in ~~September~~ 19~~76~~*ƒ*ⓧ, Dirk B.G. Dirksen began booking shows at my Filipino supper club the Mabuhay Gardens. *That in the following* ~~began to produce~~ *m̲r̲. p̲u̲l̲s̲e̲n̲* a musical revue by the Les Nickellettes 'on ~~the~~ *the clubs* closed nightS (Monday and Tuesday). This show ran for nine (9) month. Beginning in the fall of 19----, and lasting until March 30, 1982 Dirksen and his associates had exlcusive management and control of the booking, production, promotion, design of system as related to audio, lighting, 'stage, security, collection and ids burseemnt of the door admission, *DURING THIS TIME DIRKSEN AND HIS COLLEAGUES COINED THE PHRASE FAB MAB.*

Ness/Dirk agreement. Photo from the Dirksen Archives.

daytime show over in Berkeley and somebody tackled me. I saw this football player come charging and he hit me, and that screwed up the knees. But I think it was worth it because, as Voltaire said— I'm probably misquoting him, but, "I'll die defending your right to disagree with me."

That reminds me of Jello Biafra and his famous 'distribution of matter harmful to minors,' when he included the Swiss surrealist's, Giger, famous penis-landscape in his album's art work. Biafra felt that it was the perfect metaphor for the people in society screwing each other over. The painting, for those of you who are not familiar with it, allegedly shows ten or twelve dismembered penises entering some sort of orifice. One reporter who represented an agricultural paper said, "Oh, no, that's seeds sprouting. That's -that's — you guys, you've got it all wrong." So, it's in the mind of the beholder, but to Biafra, it was the perfect example of twelve people screwing each other over, and he included it in an album. Originally, he had envisioned putting it

Dirk at Jello Biafra's wedding with Dick Nose. Photo courtesy Dirksen Archives

on the outside cover, but all the members of the group, and others, including myself, said, "Well, it's a little bit strong." Anyway, that led to the State of California — when they saw the offending picture, they sent it to the City Attorney in Los Angeles, who ended up filing charges against Biafra for distribution of matter harmful to minors. Biafra called me one night and said, "I've heard rumors that they're going to try to arrest me and charge me for the poster." And then, the next day, they did break into his apartment, seized evidence and served him with a warrant. Looking at him and looking at that scene, I felt that there was no choice but to support him, whether or not I believed in that particular piece of art, so that people could have the choice to buy it or not to buy it. When we got into the trial, it was interesting seeing all the 'duck and cover.' And to see all the others who came out in support of us.

Whatever the physical or economic pain, they were well worthwhile because we had a great impact, and helped a lot of creative, talented people to evolve and to grow. And it's wonderful to see those people now, involved in projects, whether it's music or performance or films or books, and to know that in some small way I had a part in encouraging them to explore themselves. I'm continuing to do that with books on the subject, and with a number of very successful videos. The Dead Kennedys is probably one of the most successful punk rock videos. It recently went from MCA over to Warner Brothers — and we're now coming out in DVD format with it and with DOA: The End — on tape. Both of those are one hour or hour-and-a-half concerts that were shot with video cameras, broad-

Dirk wih his dog, Dummy" at the Mabuhay Gardens, 1978. Photo by Chester Simpson

cast quality, three and four cameras. In the case of DOA, it was actually shot at the DNA Lounge, which is a venue South of Market – or was at the time. Brian, who booked it in, was one of the DJs that we originally supported. We were very supportive of DJs on the air, because that was a way to get our audience built in.

We gathered and published the statistical records which tracked airplay and the audiences' preferences for different artists: we called it the Rotten Record Chart. We had, I believe, 11 sources reporting every week, and we would mail out 500 copies all across the world, showing where San Francisco's unique bands and L.A. bands were visiting — how they stood on airplay versus major label airplay by 'new wave' bands of the time. I think that performed a really great service, and it was the brain child of a San Francisco songwriter by the name of Ralph Eno, Freaky Ralph, who for a short time was a roommate of Biafra's. Unfortunately, he died by setting himself on fire because he was depressed with his career. And we all owe a real great debt to Freaky Ralph, because he was a great guy, who took his own money — (he was a clerk at the bank) — to pay for the mailings. For two years —

Freaky Ralph. Dirksen archives

religiously, he mailed these things, and put all of his own money, that he earned — into the mailing of those record charts.

I had a wonderful conversation recently with Flea (of Red Hot Chili Peppers). He was telling me about when he first came to the Fab Mab, when it was still a Filipino supper club and we used to feed the artists the menu of the day, like Adobo Chicken and all those sort-of-exotic Filipino dishes. So, he's 14 years old, he comes in with his bass guitar — he was playing for Fear — and he has the dinner. I think he was high on LSD or something — whatever, I don't know—maybe aspirin and Coca-Cola. In any event, we had an act where they had planted three victims in the audience… so it looks like they've kidnapped a woman who's pregnant, supposedly a member of the audience, and then they do a Charlie Manson on her and rip out this baby (which was a plastic doll with entrails wrapped around it) while Flea was eating his dinner. And seeing this, he said, "Convinced me I wanted to be in show biz!" That was great! I think it must have had an influence on him, because he's definitely a showman in his rock 'n' roll. The Fab Mab, the avant garde rock 'n' roll theatre!

When I moved up here in early '74 I saw a need because, to me, the scene was dull and very self-indulgent after the end of the psychedelic era, with the long guitar or drum solos, and then with that insipid disco music. I felt that we were right to create this venue and say, "We want these four walls to insulate a conducive environment where performers can do their thing, whatever it may be." And we succeeded far more, in many ways, than I ever expected. It has led to my being involved, to this day, with music and books and videos. My partner, Damon Malloy, and I do a lot of advocacy work for Americans With Disabilities, as well as help-ing on two projects that Mikhail Gorbachev is involved in: one is World Without Wars and the other is Missiles to Sunflowers, which is about the abolition of all nuclear weapons. These are all advocacy programs that we spend our own money on. They're not grant-funded or paid for by the government. And, from our free spaghetti dinners, I've moved on to doing a cooking class here in the Mission District at the Parks and Recreation Building across the street from our office. We

Dirk receiving his Dummy Award, August 5, 2006.
Photo courtesy Dirksen Archives.

teach kids from ages five to fourteen to prepare good, nourishing meals, and we purchase it all from Canned Foods, the dented-can food place, and local farmers' markets and such, so we can do it on a budget of twenty bucks. And we feed about 20 or 25 young kids on Wednesday nights. They have a great time chopping up onions, and crying, and learning how to make cookies. And here's the pope of punk becoming a cook, with the help of some student chefs from the California Food Academy.

So, I feel I've got a very rich life. I'm pleased with what has gone on and I have no regrets for, let's say, never getting involved with the corporate world of the arts. I look at myself in comparison to my brother, who is a physicist, who said, "I'm never going to work in the war industry," after being draft-ed at age 14 and fighting for Germany on the Russian Front. He became a worker in a Lockheed think tank, working on Weapons System 2015 — meaning that he would help figure out how if the Russians did this, then we would counter with that, and they would counter it — playing those games. That's what he spent his time on. And I look at what may seem, to some people, to be such a frivolous, stupid thing as punk rock or stand-up comedy, and I think it's a much better way to conduct my life, exploring those things.

Dirk Dirksen

Scene/Arts

San Francisco Examiner
July 27, 1980   ★ Scene Page 1

A section of the San Francisco
Sunday Examiner and Chronicle

The Pope of Punk

By Burr Snider

THE POPE OF PUNK has a dog with a breath to peel the paint off walls, to stop a railroad train dead in its tracks. Dummy is the noxious mutt's name, and, lucky me, he wants to be friends. Ever since I sat down on the couch in the Pope of Punk's smallish Nob Hill apartment, Dummy has been cagily edging over towards me, and now he's preparing for his big move. He wants to get right up in my face and unleash a frontal attack, is what Dummy wants to do, but it's hardly necessary.

Already those foul and fetid fumes of swamp gas steaming from his maw are about to cause me to retch. I'm moving towards my end of the couch as discreetly as I can while I try to keep up with the Pope of Punk's machine gun pace rap and jot notes at the same time, but just as I am at the point of being rendered comatose by Dummy's mephitic emanations, I decide it's time to take a stand.

"You are a very cute dog," I say to the Pope of Punk's pooch — a bald lie on its face, of course, but I am as capable of social phoniness as the next fellow. "But you are simply going to have to move it along here or else I am going to flash all over you."

This totally cracks the Pope of Punk up. He dissolves into a witchy state of laughter somewhere between a snicker and a cackle. "Consider yourself lucky," he says when he pulls himself together. "Dummy peed all over Don Rickles once."

The Pope of Punk, if you don't know, is a feisty, 40ish, provocative fellow name of Dirk Dirksen. Dirksen might also be called The Nabob of New Wave, since he all but singlehandedly created the Punk scene in San Francisco five years ago when he took over late-night operations at a down-and-out Filipino nightclub on lower Broadway and threw open the proceedings to avant-garde rock and decidedly exotic behavior.

And you can believe that if Dummy the dog didn't actually micturate on Don Rickles, Dirk Dirksen himself might well have. Dirksen's stock-in trade at the Mabuhay Gardens, his Punk H.Q., is a sort of institutional nastiness. He's nasty to his punkish patrons, he's nasty to the bands that wheel on and off his stage at a dizzying pace every night of the year, and when he shaves around his little Inspector Closeau whiskbroom mustache in the mirror in the morning, he is no doubt nasty to himself. You can tell when Dirk Dirksen is having a good time by the scowl on his face.

Of course like so much of punkdom, it's mostly a pose, life being the cabaret that it is, old chum. Dirksen plays to provoke the punks, for whom posing is in itself an art form. Punks cultivate a sullen outrageousness as a way of existence. It's a statement about something or other, but never mind that. The point is, as Dirksen well knows, that the cardinal sin in punk theology is to be boring. You can be weird, goofy, alienated or atrophied, but don't be dull. The *world* is dull, for God's sake, but don't you be. So Dirk Dirksen sets himself up deliberately as an outrageously snotty onstage straw man for his crowds to focus a little venom on during those longish stage waits between bands. He calls the interaction participatory theater and considers his clientele to be as much a part of the act as the bands themselves. It can get to be a little chaotic, but as Dirksen freely admits, it's all as carefully structured as ballet.

There's nothing terribly new about all this, of course — outrageousness, real or fabricated, has a time-honored history, as manifested by the Fauves, the Dadaists, the flappers, the beatniks and the Yippies. It just that the punks, Bomb Babies that they are, have added a bit of a bitter edge to it, that's all, and Dirksen is most adroit and artful about manipulating that tension. You know all about The Sex Pistols and the safety pins in the cheeks and Johnny Rotten's charming habits of spitting, bleeding and puking on his audiences. You know about sullen Sid Vicious and the dismally drawn-out but ultimately successful *Todentanz* he played out smack in the glare of the media. You know about the rooster haircuts and the tight leopard-skin pants and the sci-fi sunglasses and the fluorescent tans. All that stuff, the punk paraphernalia, has been around long enough to have seeped into the collective consciousness, but the thing is, you kept hoping it would go away, and it hasn't. It keeps evolving. But though New Wave is no longer a new item, much of it still strives to be as functionally obnoxious as ever. It's the whole point of the exercise.

"Am I really the world's greatest a—hole?" As the Pope of Punk, Dirk Dirksen poses the question rhetorically, knowing the answer doesn't matter nearly as much as the projected image and the vile dialogue it helps him to sustain between himself and his patrons. 'Yes and no," he replies to his own question. "I am creating theater, and at the same time I do have a perverted sense of humor. My persona dictates that I am going to be called an a—hole, and of course it plays right into the punk audience's game. To wit, how much can they harass me?"

Quite a little bit, evidently, since by Dirksen's own tabulation in the five years since he set up in the punk biz, he's had his nose broken six times, had eight pairs of glasses shattered, his ribs kicked in and an ankle dislocated. He's

— See Page 3, Col. 1

13

Punk producer thought everyone could be a star
They buried the pope of punk over the weekend.

Many of the neighbors who rose to eulogize Dirk Dirksen, the 69-year-old former operator of the Mabuhay Gardens, the historic San Francisco punk rock club, knew him only as the crinkly eyed character who gave cooking lessons to the kids on the block at the rec center across the street from where he lived and who died in his sleep two weeks ago.

"He had a way of touching so many different people in so many different walks of life,"

Dirksen as MC. Photo by Chester Simpson

said retired Fire Department Capt. Bob Manning, who worked with Dirksen as a community organizer in the Mission District and knew nothing of his past life as the snarling, sarcastic ringmaster of a circus of the damned that ran seven nights a week, 52 weeks a year for 10 years.

A decidedly ruly mob overflowed an antiseptic funeral chapel in the Outer Mission on Saturday morning. They filled the pews, lined the walls and stood out in the lobby, craning necks over shoulders, saying goodbye to the somewhat strange but rather

wonderful man who always urged them to live their lives "onward and upward."

"He was a man in a penis nose telling us it was better to throw popcorn than beer bottles," said his friend Ron Jones. "Dirk knew everybody had a place on the stage of life — as long as you went on and off on time. You had to remember there were other acts waiting, even if they suck."

Filmmaker Bruce Connor read some of Dirksen's trademark stage announcements: "Tonight's band may not be the best, but you are one of our lesser audiences ... Is that the best you can do to get attention? ... Quiet, animals."

Dirksen was one of the people who really made San Francisco San Francisco. He presided over the Fab Mab, as it was known to one and all, with the bemused tolerance of a cranky uncle who had seen it all and was surprised by nothing.

He saw his little corner of Broadway as a reincarnation of a Berlin cabaret or Montmartre theater. He wasn't just selling over-priced drinks to the unwashed masses; he was making theater and everybody was in the cast.

"He loved you for who you were and who you wanted to be," Jones said.

Night after night, four bands trooped across the tiny stage in the seedy former Philippine supper club. As many as 10,000 bands may have played the Mabuhay.

It was where Neil Young jammed with Devo and Robin Williams opened for the Ramones. It was the high point of their career to thousands more, who never went any further up the ranks than the stage at the Mabuhay.

From the very beginning, when he started presenting late-night performances by the female comedy theatrical troupes, Les Nickelettes in 1974, Dirksen envisioned his enterprise as a television show waiting to be broadcast.

He videotaped every performance, long before videotape was routinely available. But he started in show business as the producer of a famous early live television experiment in Los Angeles, "Rocket To Stardom" — a 12-hour live remote broadcast from a car dealer-

Dirk Dirksen. Photo courtesy of the Dirksen Archives.

ship featuring amateur and semi-professional talent — and he never really stopped thinking of himself as a television producer.

He and his lifelong partner, Damon Molloy, have operated a video service, Dirksen-Molloy Productions, ever since he left the nightclub business, that has produced storytelling videos on everything from a third-grade girls' basketball team to poetry readings by handicapped adults to senior swimmers' water ballet. Dirksen thought everybody should star in their own movie. He wanted to be the producer.

He was recalled as the man who taught the Latino neighborhood kids cooking in weekly classes at the Recreational Center for the Handicapped.

His older sister remembered him as a young boy in war-torn Germany, playing in his neighborhood after air raids left the street destroyed, making castles out of craters with his imagination.

Another friend, Winston Smith, recalled Dirksen encouraging him to finish his book by phoning him every morning. "I'm going to work this morning — what are you doing?" he would say.

It wasn't a crowd full of big time music scenesters and there wasn't a lot of musical star power at the memorial, unless you count an impromptu reunion of the all-female punk rockers, the Contractions, guitarist Mary Kelley seated on a chair, drummer Debbie Hopkins playing softly on a modified kit and vocalist Kathy Peck sobbing her way through the sing-along folk song, "Down In the Valley."

Peck previously recalled Dirksen coming over every day, after her pet Chihuahua was diagnosed with diabetes, to give the pooch its shot because Peck couldn't quite handle it herself.

He was a surly curmudgeon all right, until he got around animals or small children.

In the end, he couldn't even afford to pay for his own funeral. Benefits are in the process of being organized to help pay his debts. But Dirksen was an honest man and they rarely do well in the music business. But, of course, his video and life partner Molloy made sure it was all caught on tape.

"No one is ever going to do anything like that for you ever again," Molloy told them.

Joel Selvin, Chronicle Senior Pop Music Critic

Dirk's Last Day

On November 19, 2006 in the early afternoon I called Dirk to see of he wanted to go to Fisherman's Wharf with me. He "asked a favor of me" to take him back to his apt. He had left his partial behind and wanted to have it so he could stop by a party, "The Mutants" were giving at Lennon Studio's.

When I picked him up Dirk, was apologetic (which was unusual). This for him had been the week from hell. The car broke down, he has had to rely on public transit and as usual with MUNI there were 40-minute delays. The water heater broke which added to the never-ending problems of money and finances. These put the daily stress of living had taken their toll on him.

As it was Dirk didn't have a strong heart. He seemed very weak and exhausted. Denise; he said on a number of occasions that day "stress is going to kill me". As we drove to the Wharf, Dirk talked about how frustrated and tired he was with the way things were working out. He was very annoyed with 3 people who were close to him. Feeling they had the means and talents to make things happen but they were just spinning their wheels. We chatted about the Mab days and how exciting they were and what pain in the ass we both were. The topic came up about the possibility of another Fab Mab reunion and when he would finish his book.

We finally reached Lennon Studios for the Mutants party. The band was playing minus Sally and Sue, The guys sounded great and I could see Dirks immediately perk up. He was enjoying sitting around chatting with different folks. When it was time to leave Dirk's exit was actually heart warming Mike Dingle escorted him to the door. The Band stopped and folks bid him good-bye. There was air of love and respect for Dirk and Dirk for the folks is the room.

On our ride back to his place we talked about how much he liked the band. The Mutants were his favorite band. He liked their style of entertainment; camp, outrageous and entertaining.

As we approached his place I asked again when was he going to finish his book. As usual to avoid answering the question he got on my case for not sending him my story. I dropped him off at his place. We talked about what nice day we hand and that I had better start writing. He made me promise that to finished my story by Friday. We acknowledge what a good day we had together. As I was about to take off he reminded me about how "the stress would kill him", and we said good-bye.

The Next day I stopped home while running errands. The phone rang it was the voice of Dirk's partner Damon Molloy, "Dirk Dead" could I please come over to Dirks Apartment. In that moment of silent shock; I told Damon I'd be right over. Damon just kept repeating to please come over. When I arrived the cops were all ready there and Damon was sitting on the steps waiting for the coroners. He was surprised how fast I got here. I have no memory of the drive there. I asked of I could go in and was explicitly told by the cop not to touch the corpse. (Creepy). I went in to his apartment and there was Dirk lying on his side sleeping, the deep sleep. I of course touched him Yep! He was dead.

When the corners came I asked if they would clean him up and give us a moment with Dirk so we could say goodbye. When they finished their exam Damon and I went in and there was Dirk on the floor in an unzipped body bag. Damon freaked and I stood there and managed to come up with some words befitting of the moment. My vague memory recalls saying a prayer and something like. Here lies Dirk Dirksen "The Pope of Punk" who life touched family, friends and many artist here in San Francisco. Rest in peace Dirk.

denise demise dunne

At The Palace T.V. Show

By Margo Skinner

In olden times there were afternoon musicales in the glittering Garden Court of the Palace Hotel, where the nobs and celebrities met to sip tea and listen to light classics played by orchestras led by Cy Trobbe and Albert White. Those days have come again, with regular "Symphonette" programs currently recreating an old San Francisco tradition.

And soon there will be an "At the Palace" network television show. Now in the works, it's described as "a visual mood piece, inspired by the concert music." The series will use music as frame to show San Francisco at various periods, starting with 1900, and ending, after 12 one-hour programs, with the sound of today. Major musical performers and stars will be shown in live con-certs, and young stars Carl Raymond and Virginia Owen will furnish love interest, with Bay Area entertainment writer George ("Cocoa") Walter adding fun as Uncle Oscar, described as "a gluttonous, charming, rogueish, dirty old man." The show will be directed and produced locally in the Garden Court by Dirk B. Dirksen, and should be both a visual and musical delight.

Photo By Ron Kessler

"At The Palace" T.V. producer-director Dirk Dirksen with leads Carol Raymond and Virginia Owen and make-up artist Andrew Kemper looking on as recreation of 1910 period scene is about to go before location camera at Golden Gate Park Conservatory.

Dirk Dirksen was the first man in show business to give me a break. I was 18, lied and told Dirk I was 23 and had a college degree from Santa Cruz, and he hired me as a doorman at Mabuhay Gardens in 1977. Then he let me migrate into the "Sound Department" where I learned to mix sound from Urex Reed Ashby, and Audrey Judd who's now a VP of Marketing at CBS. I used to run "The Mabuhay Road show" for Dirk, it would be me, sometimes Dirk & Howie Klein taking Mabuhay Bands like The Offs, The Avengers, The Dils and others to places like the Brickyard in Stockton, The Cabaret in Cotati and The Civic in Santa Cruz. Dirk figured the kids there who couldn't make it into S.F. should get a taste of The Fab Mab in their own backyards. The bands always got paid, but Dirk didn't make a penny off of the gigs.

Dirk was color-blind, he didn't care who you were or what you looked like, if you put together a press package and a tape with a 8x10 glossy (they seldom were looked at and never were listened to) he'd give you a chance on stage. Dirk just wanted kids to get used to going through the motions they would eventually have to go through later in their careers. This gave them a jump start.

I remember the first time DEVO played, there were 40 people in the audience. The next time they played there were over 400. I screwed up once, real bad, but Dirk gave me a second chance when he didn't have to:" Well Ted, everyone deserves a second chance, even me!" he said. If you didn't like Dirk, you didn't get Dirk. Everything he did was theater. He could smoke you under the table too: One night late, our doorman Harmon Shragge and I were at Dirk's apartment when Dirk was telling us his plans for the future, Harmon fell asleep. Dirk yelled at him to wake him up: "Hey I'm trying to tell you my plans for the future and you're falling asleep!" Harmon groggily said "But, ...what is the future?" Dirk barked back at him "For You? No Future". How punk is that?

Dirk provided a backdrop and an environment that allowed many of us to develop careers. The first time D.O.A. came down from Canada, they only had a snare drum and one guitar because the Royal Canadian Mounted Police wouldn't let them bring the rest of their equipment into the USA. Dirk called all the bands he knew and arranged for them to lend their amps, guitars and drums to D.O.A. Their roadie, Zippy had holes in the back of his jeans and no underwear on, so Dirk took them all clothes shopping and fed them at Clown Alley.

Dirk was also as tough as nails. It wasn't unusual for someone to try to barge their way in to the club and Dirk would tackle them and fight them until they were out of the club. He was small, but he could fight anyone and kick their ass. I think in the first year I worked the door at Mabuhay Gardens, Dirk had his nose broken 3 times. Dirk was the first person who taught me to stick up for myself. Dirk hated to see weak people or weak-minded people, he'd tell me: "That's the mentality that allows people like Hitler to take power!"

When I left Mabuhay Gardens for TV Broadcasting School, Dirk encouraged me and let me shoot videos of the bands at The Mab. Dirk was my first mentor. Dirk was the first to give a lot of people a break in the business, Robin Williams, Whoopie Goldberg, Chris Isaac, The Dead Kennedys. The first night the Dead Kennedy's were scheduled to play, Dirk said to me "They'll never go anywhere with that name". Few people know that when Dirk was a TV Producer in Hollywood, he was the first person to put Lenny Bruce on camera. He also produced the TV Commercials for The Shoop Shoop Hula Hoop, The Whammo Frisbee, Super Ball and other toys.

At a time when music had gone commercial and saccharine, Dirk came in, took over The S.F. Punk Scene and made it and new music happen. The Mab became the Headquarters for a new sub-culture. Three bands a night, Seven Days a Week for 10 Years. No other music promoter in San Francisco can match that record

Ted Oliphant, Mabuhay Gardens 1977-1982

Ness Aquino

Ness Aquino, native of the village of San Juan on the island of Luzon, left the Philippines in 1962 for San Francisco to obtain an education and pursue a business career. For three years he was consulting director for the Mission District Poverty Program. In 1969 he opened the first Mabuhay Gardens in the International Hotel on Kearny Street to serve the Filipinos community.

From an interview by James Stark in February 1989 with Ness Aquino

Ness Aquino and Dirk Dirksen. Photo from Dirksen Arcives

The Mabuhay Gardens was open in March of 1972 and for the first few months it was a open as a first class Filipino restaurant. After two or three months people were coming and asking why we weren't having entertainment since we were located on Broadway and that was the entertainment center of San Francisco so I started having dancing and floor shows. We would have Floor Shows at 9:30 and 1:30 with dancing in between and that was the format until around 1977. Since we were a Filipino ethnic we were mostly show casing Filipino talent. When Marcos declared Marshal Law in 1972 the Filipino's became nationalistic and build a lot of hotels in the Philipines and by 1975, it was getting difficult for me to get fresh talent from the Philippines because the talent I needed was in demand there. In the early part of 1976, I started to show other types of acts on Mondays and Tuesdays when the Mabuhay was closed for the ethnic Filipino shows. I used to book some rock 'n roll bands and notice that even on Monday or Tuesday nights they were able to draw a fair amount of people. So then I made that a permanent format of operation. Monday and Tuesday Rock 'n roll and the rest of the week Filipino supper club shows.

Since I wasn't able to get fresh talent for the ethnic shows and the crowd was getting bigger for the rock 'n roll shows, in February of 1977 I decided to strictly go into rock 'n roll. At that time, punk rock was in vogue, so naturally I started to showcase punk rock. Initially, I had a booking person named Jerry Paulson, who at that time published a newspaper called Psyclone, so he was very knowledgable of the trends in new music. He knew some of the acts that were very popular doing punk rock-type of shows. Before Jerry, I also booked bands on my own. They were not called punk bands then. The first one I booked was the Nuns. They were very popular in the beginning, and then I booked Crime.

After three months. Jerry Paulson started doing the booking. He was very successful, but I think success went to his head. He started acting very weird, so to speak, drinking too much and so forth. I had to make a change. All along I had befriended Dirk Dirksen, who used to manage a folk singer whom I had booked at the Mabuhay.

Mabuhay Gardens front. Photo from Dirksen Archives.

When Jerry Paulson left, I asked Dirk if he wanted to do the booking and he did that until 1981 or 1982. During the time he was there, of course, he was able to book bands that are now household names, so to speak: Devo, Blondie, Madness, Robert Fripp, Ramones, and dozens of others."

I guess the Nuns saw some posters of shows at the Mabuhay so they came by to see about booking a show on a Monday night. I booked them but at the time I didn't have a proper sound system so they got the Dils to open for them because they had a good sound system. The Nuns drew a good crowd and other bands heard about it and Crime came and booked a night in January of 1977. I remember the first Crime poster, it was very unusual, there was a picture of a woman from a French fashion magazine and the photographer showed up.

When I first met Dirk he was managing folk singer named Jerri Grainger. When I booked her it wasn't on a Monday or Tuesday night she was part of my regular shows for the mainly Filipino clientele. She was good and our customers liked them. While she was playing at the Mabuhay she also played on the Johnny Carson show and we got a lot of publicity from that.

When Dirk starting doing his own shows at the Mabuhay our business relationship was that Dirk took the door and I took the bar. Mary Monday was very influenceal in getting us started because when she was doing her show on Mondays and Tuesdays she brought in Jerry Paulson and that when I met him. I also had presented the Mary Monday Show on the regular supper club nights. I had a Christmas party for some military officers from the Persdio and I booked Mary Monday for that party. Mary did have a very unsual show, a lot makeup, props and costumes. We had about thirty Army officers and throughout the show they were very quite but she got some applase after a while. They said, "this is very unusual experience, we're not use to this kind of entertainment, what is it."

Howie Kline was also very helpful in getting some of the touring bands because he was a rock and roll writer he had contacts to these acts. He was responabile for helping to get bands like Dammed, Blondie, Ramones and Devo. People would contact Howie and he would pass the information to Jerry Paulson and latter Dirk and they would book the bands.

The first bands which later became what has become know as Punk had played previously. The first was The Nuns in December of 1976 and Crime in January of 1977. These shows and others were booked by the bands who worked directly with Ness Aquino, later Jerry Palson who published a magazine called Psyclone booked the late night shows at the Mabuhay. Dirk had been presenting shows at the Mab for a couple of years mostly on Mondays and they were more of a Cabaret/Variety type of show he took over booking the Mab full time in June of 1977. The following list was prepared by Peter Claudis from Dirk Dirksen's files. The majority of the posters come from the collections of: Kareem Kaddad, Bryan Ray Turcotte, Kathy Peck, Dirk Dirksen, Regi Mentle and James Stark.

Poster by James Stark

Poster by James Stark

DECEMBER 1976

20 Nuns

JANUARY 1977

10 Crime

FEBRUARY 1977

7 Premier
   Magister Ludi

8 Kid Courage

14 Leida & The
   Snakes

15 Head

21 Arm N' Hammer

22 Backroad

28 Cornell Herd &
   His Mondo Hot
   Pants Orchestra

MARCH 1977

1 Nuns

2 Blondie
   Crime

3 Blondie
   Crime

7 Pegasus

8 Alta
   Killerwatt

9 Premier
   Hoi Polloi

10 Kid Courage

14 Crime
   Punk

15 Backroad
   Rimbaud's Leg

16 Nuns
   Crime

Psyclone Presents:
THE NERVES
APRIL 5
6

MABUHAY Gardens
443 BROADWAY
SAN FRANCISCO
CALIFORNIA

Poster by Jerry Paulson

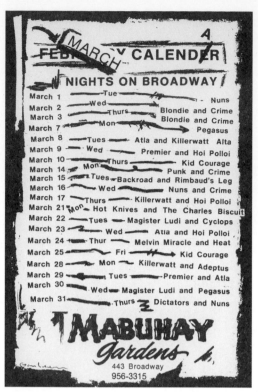

FEBRUARY MARCH CALENDER
NIGHTS ON BROADWAY

March 1	Tue	Nuns
March 2	Wed	
March 3	Thurs	Blondie and Crime
March 7	Mon	Blondie and Crime Pegasus
March 8	Tues	Atla and Killerwatt Alta
March 9	Wed	Premier and Hoi Polloi
March 10	Thurs	Kid Courage
March 14	Mon	Punk and Crime
March 15	Tues	Backroad and Rimbaud's Leg
March 16	Wed	Nuns and Crime
March 17	Thurs	Killerwatt and Hoi Polloi
March 21	Mon	Hot Knives and The Charles Biscuit
March 22	Tues	Magister Ludi and Cyclops
March 23	Wed	Atla and Hoi Polloi
March 24	Thur	Melvin Miracle and Heat
March 25	Fri	Kid Courage
March 28	Mon	Killerwatt and Adeptus
March 29	Tues	Premier and Atla
March 30	Wed	Magister Ludi and Pegasus
March 31	Thurs	Dictators and Nuns

MABUHAY gardens
443 Broadway
956-3315

Poster by Jerry Paulson

Psyclone Presents:
APRIL 7
the diCtAtOrS
AAA
FFF
EEE
K
JKL
NNN
&
MAGISTER LUDI

MABUHAY gardens
443 Broadway
956-3315

Poster by Jerry Paulson

17 Killer watt
Hoi Polloi

21 Hot Knives
Charles Bisquit
Band

22 Magister Ludi
Cyclops

23 Atla
Hoi Polloi

24 Melvin Miracles
Heat

25 Kid Courage

27 Psyclone Party

28 Killerwatt
Adeptus

29 Premier
Atla

30 Magister Ludi
Pegasus

31 The Dictators
The Nuns

APRIL 1977

1 Amphion
Faze

2 Bobby Gonzales

3 C.P.Salt
Cordial

4 Revolver
Ozzie

5 Nerves
Nuclear Valdez

6 Nerves
The Nuns

7 Dictators
Magister Ludi

8 Television
Top Cat

9 Television
Top Cat

11 Killerwatt
Water Baby

12 Amphion
Alexus

13 **Mary Monday**
   Surkus

14 **Eddie Money**
   Premier

15 **Eddie Money**
   Killerwatt

16 **Margie Baker &**
   George Namepen
   Quartet

18 **Ozzie**
   Hoi Polloi

19 **Adeptus**
   Idiot

20 **The Dammed**
   Cyclops

21 **The Dammed**
   Crime

22 **Magister Ludi**
   Dragon

24 **Leila & the**
   Snakes
   Rick & Ruby
   Naomi
   Eiseberg
   & The Dadas

25 **Pegasus**
   Water Baby

26 **Kid Courage**
   Overland Freight

27 **Charles Biscuit**
   Vincent Mason

28 **Kid America**
   Adeptus

Poster by Edwin Heaven

Poster by T. Williams

29 **Mile High**
   Michael Spears

MAY 1977

1 **Dan Dhala**
   Sons of Creation

2 **Rock Band**

3 **The Dogs**

4 **The Dogs**

5 **The Nerves**

6 **The Nerves**

Poster by Judy Steccone

7 **Bobby Gonzales**

9 **Crime**
   Novak

10 **Nuclear Valdez**

11 **Milk & Cookies**

12 **Milk & Cookies**
   St. Punk

13 **The Nuns**
   Novak

14 **Kid Courage**

16 **La Rue**

Poster by Judy Steccone

Poster by Judy Steccone

Poster by Judy Steccone

What can I say, you have gone "Onward and Upward". What a great friend you have been to me. I must have dumped all my problems on you a hundred times yet you never stopped me or said you had to go or get off the phone. You listened (a trait a lot of us don't have) and at the end of all my BS, you always had a great "Positive Spin". No wonder you were involved with a TV show of the same name. Eating breakfast with you and Kathy 25 or 30 times over the last few months was such a great time — breaking up the daily routine with chow and talk. Of course all that verbal abuse I had to take from you, "The Don Rickles of Punk" (was pure joy). When we talked about the Mab and it's reputation of being the "Punk Capital "of the north west you mentioned to me that your real goal was not just "Punk Music", but any one with "Outspoken Ideas" that wanted to be heard and that brought new meaning to the term " Alternative Tentacles" for me.

You and Damon Molloy were such a great team and it seemed no matter what event was happening with the local Community, you both were there filming and documenting, then finding ways for people to see and hear important issues that could affect our lives. And as for "Cosmos", what a fine gem to stumble across with the TV remote on channel 26.

I am so grateful for all the advice, support and help you have given my wife Kathy Peck in her personal life and with "HEAR" over the last quarter century.

My one man musical monologue "Marie, 21 and Flying" is about to be performed in theaters and I owe it all to you for the inspiration and encouragement to do so. I will end every performance on stage from now on with your always thoughtful close of "Onward and Upward". You are sadly missed my friend.

David Denny

■■

I was a teenager when I started hanging out at the Mab. I was only 16, creeping out on the weekends on the pretense of spending the night at my high school friends houses while I was actually working on my moves at the Mab. I eventually ran away from home after being busted for my shenanigans. I never went back. My mother however, in an attempt to save my soul no doubt, informed Dirk and Ness of my juvenile status and I was forbade to enter the club no matter how I begged and promised to behave. I don't know what made Dirk cave in but he let me back in after a few months. I just wanted to see the bands and be part of the scene. I wasn't a bad kid just a little wild child. Probably being a nubile wild child is part of why I was let back in, surely not bad for business. Who knows. After a couple of years I was a denizen if not a fixture. Many nights both Dirk and Ness would check to see if I had eaten and make sure that I got some spaghetti if there was any still around. One night

Hot child in the ity,
Maria Mitchell.

I was standing at the front area (there was still a pinball machine in front as well a Galaxian game...I think) when Dirk came up to me and said "I want to thank you for never making me regret letting you back in here. You have always behaved like a lady and I appreciate that" I was stunned and of course delighted. That was a wonderful feeling to know that he felt that way. I know a lot of people never saw his kind and generous side but it was a big part why he was so successful. I saw Dirk a few years ago when they had the first Mab reunion party. He hadn't aged a bit. I went up to him and asked him if he remembered me and he said " Maria, how could I forget" He actually knew my name 25 years later!!!! Dirk was one of a kind and my life was ever richer for having known him and surely for being allowed to spend much of my truly formative years in world he helped create. I was honored to have known Dirk Dirksen and he is very much missed.

Maria Mitchell
■■■■■■■■■■■■■■■■■■■■■■■■■■■■■■■■■■■■■■

Gary Gutter, Klaus Flouride and Dirk Dirksen, Cocodire for Mab reunion circa 2000. (Photo curiosity Gary Gutter)

Dirk Dirkson was a really good man, he gave me a job and a place to live when I was homeless, working at the On Broadway in 1981 and I was able to see all the best punk rock bands at the time. The pictures that I took of him are from the Mabuhay Gardens reunion show that Dirk put on at the Cocodrie on 5/20/2000 .

Gary Gutter
■■■■■■■■■■■■■■■■■■■■■■■■■■■■■

Ness/Mab story

Ness Aquino, native of the village of San Juan on the island of Luzon, left the Philippines in 1962 for San Francisco to obtain an education and pursue a business career. For three years he was consulting director for the Mission District Poverty Program. In 1969 he opened the first Mabuhay Gardens in the International Hotel on Kearny Street to serve the Filipinos community.

In the spring of 1972 Ness opened the second version of the Mabuhay Gardens in San Francisco's North Beach at 443 Broadway. In the beginning there was a Piano bar and served Filipino cuisine. Later Ness expanded featuring dinner and cocktail performances by Filipino entertainers bring some of them from the Philippine Islands. .Amapola, Eddie Mesa, Celia and the Golden Goodies, Conchito and Norma Balagtas doing gigs there swelled a peak. Amapola was probably the most successful, she and Ness co-hosted a weekly TV program on channel 20 KEMO-TV "The Amapola presents show' which was produced by Dirk Dirksen. This one of the early collaborations between Dirk and Ness.

Later Ness had trouble finding new talent and lost many of his top performers. In 1976 Ness closed the restaurant portion on Monday and Tuesday nights and open as a show case for performers of various genres. By February of 1977 Ness changed his format completely. The restaurant opened at 7pm with more American food items and from 8:30 to

10pm was available as a theatre for legit plays.

In December of 1976 Ness let Jeff Olener of the Nuns book his band on a Monday night charging him $75.00. Crime played played their first show the next month, Monday January 10, 1977, and this was the beginning of the Mabuhay becoming the top punk venue on the West Coast. For the first few months Jerry Paulsen, publisher of Psyclone Magazine, booked the shows with Dirk Dirksen taking over the booking about mid-year continuing until 1982.

■■

Dirk Dirksen saw a Les Nickelettes show at Karl Cohen's vintage movies and vaudeville Sunday night series at the Intersection in late 1974. He recruited the group for a video he was making for public access channel 6. Although Dirk described himself as a hot shot L.A. producer recently relocated to the Bay Area we thought his Gorilla Video was awful. And it went nowhere despite his grandiose promises. Nevertheless, in

Les Nickeletts. Photo by Karl Cohen

1975 Vince Stanich (an unofficial agent for Les Nickelettes) teamed up with Dirk to search for a nightclub venue for the Nicks. Dirk combed Broadway and landed at the Mabuhay Gardens, a Pilipino supper club. He learned that the club was struggling to survive, and that the owner, Ness Aquino was open to new ideas. Dirk made a deal for Les Nickelettes to perform every Monday and Tuesday for an unlimited run. The shows brought in a different crowd.

Problems began when Dirk tried to direct Les Nickelettes – a group of liberated women with strong opinions of what they wanted to do. It didn't go well. We hated his ideas. He wanted to make the group more like a Vegas act – the more he tried to change our material the less we trusted him. Les Nickelettes' run at the club lasted for six months (May – October, 1975) and during that time Dirk never changed as the epitome of the obnoxious impresario. However, this was perfect training for his next role as the "pope of punk." Les Nickelettes were happy to leave Dirk behind as they moved on from the Mabuhay Gardens to produce musical comedy plays. Dirk, of course, stayed and began recruiting punk bands. It didn't take long for the style at Mabuhay Gardens to transform from island décor of tropical trees and flowers to that of slash and burn punk, and be renamed, The Fab Mab.

An Rafferty

The first time I went to the Mabuhay was for the march 20th "coal miner's benefit" in 1978...my mom had let me take my 10 year old foster brother, Mike Munoz, with me to go see the Sex Pistols in January...we had become aware that there were punk shows around town, & wanted to go...the night we went, we got stopped at the door, as the door man made us wait, then came back out, & motioned us in to Dirks office...he looked at me, & looked at my little brother..."how old are you?" he asked..."10" my brother replied "I just saw the sex pistols"...Dirk pondered, then said, "well, if you saw the Sex Pistols, you should come & see this, too!" and stamped our hands...he was grinning at us, and said "NO BEER!" as we went out of the office, & into the dark club...we saw the Dogmatics, and I remember Ricky Williams microphone coming apart in his hands, as he stood there, looking puzzled, while I screwed it back together for him...it was an awesome night!...no pushing, shoving, or heavy crowds...the band right in front of you,...so close, you could touch them...we became regulars there...people would get peeved when they were left out standing, while my 10 year old foster brother went right in..."hey! what makes HIM so special?"..."HE saw the Sex Pistols!" was Dirks cheeky reply...a few months later, I was drumming for VS, and we were opening for THE NUNS...Dirk smiled when he saw me setting up...I wasn't a spectator anymore...I was part of it....he was teasing us, and after our set, he said "hey! let's hear it for bad taste!" which we thought was funny....he also gave me an extra $50 bucks that night for letting Toni Hotel of Noh Mercy use my drums...!!!...for a 17 year old kid, I was rich!...he was always nice to me, personally, and once, i remember wearing a rugby shirt that was identical to the one dirk was also wearing...Olga said, "look! it's the bobsy twins!" when she saw my shirt, but, dirk didn't see me...when he was announcing the upcoming events before we went on, I snuck up behind him onstage, tugged at his sleeve, & when he turned around, I said "da-da?" as he looked sideways at me, & the crowd laughed!....he tousled my hair, & I leaned on his shoulder...he was a funny guy...I remember he also let another older foster brother of mine live in the crawl space of the Mabuhay ceiling...going up there, hunched over, hanging out...the mab rats...that's what me & my brothers became, loving every minute of it...my second childhood home! :

Jane Weems (AKA "Insane Jane")

■■■■■■■■■■■■■■■■■■■■■■■■■■■■■■■■

After winning the 1977 Hayward battle of the bands which was Roxz first gig ever, Dirk let us play at the Mab. I was only 15 and he made me get a work permit and sit backstage all night. My Ibanez Les Paul was stolen about a week before the gig, so I had to borrow a guitar from Larry Litz. When they announced us to go on we walked onstage and I hit the guitar neck on a mic stand and it broke my high "E" string and we walked off stage to do a string change and felt like total morons. But the crowd was very understanding and cheered us on as we made our way back to the stage. It was that night that a talent scout for Shinko Music approached us. We went from Jan. 17, 1977 battle of the bands to a gig at the Mab to a record deal with Toshiba EMI in November of 1977. I have to thank Dirk for letting us play there even though were were young nobodies and very green.

love Nina Markert, ROXZ

Poster by Judy Steccone

Poster by La Rue

12 Musicians' Switchboard Benefit

13 Atla
The Ratz

14 Freestone
Skids

15 Mistress
Pegasus

16 Premier
Piller of Fire

17 Kid Courage
Main Drive

18 Crime
Skidmarks

19 Hoo Doo Rhythm Devils
Naomi Ruth Eisenberg

20 Nelson Slater

Poster by Judy Steccone

Wild Angels
Pomakai Polyne-sian Show

21 Kid America
Shooting Star
Daddy-O

22 Overland Freight
Bisquit

23 Sisters

24 Sisters

25 Hoi Polloi
Forerunner

26 Magister Ludi
Waterbaby
Unholy Three

27 Berlin Brats

28 Berlin Brats

29 Max Lazzer

30 The Dogs

Poster by Don Everson

Poster by Jerry Paulson

Poster by La Rue

JULY 1977

1 **The Dogs**

2 **La Rue**

3 **The Ratz**
Lyre

4 **Crime**
The Avengers

6 **Atla**
Waterbaby

7 **The Dils**

8 **The Nuns**

9 **The Nuns**

10 **Pop**
Main Drive

11 **Pop**
Main Drive
Ore

12 **Neon**

13 **Premier**
Ginger

14 **Unholy Three**
Cunning Stunts
Freestone

15 **Mink De Ville**
Killerwatt

16 **Mink De Ville**
Premier

17 **Pine Street**
Backroad

18 **Kangaroo**
Ozzie

19 **Nuclear Valdez**
Magister Ludi

20 **Pegasus**
Bad Axe

The Symptoms 1978-1982

Oh we moved up to Thursday Nights WOW!

God love ya Dirk, Cause you hated The Symptoms

So remember back in 1978 that band Crisby Baby with those snappy red burnt union suits and those cute little burnt babies pinned to our chest YOU LOVED EM Dirk. We got to play at the MAB on the weekends opening for some of the big boys. Then we took the suits off cause we thought well maybe that's why people were throwing things at us or what ever. So we returned with a new name the SYMPTOMS a new-wave look and well... it was all down hill from there. Our first night out as the Symptoms I went into your office to collect our $12.95 for the night and you said. What happened to you guys where are the union suits??? What happened to the burnt plastic babies pinned to your chests??? Well Mr. D we felt like fools out there, I said, Dirks response: YOU GUYS ARE FOOLS GET THE HELL OUTTA HERE YOU SHIT HEADS . Then you invited us to that lovely Tuesday Night Spaghetti Dinner at the MAB, where you choose the bands to play for the upcoming month. What fun, the club smelled like ammonia and stale urine great for the appetite. The new bands were so excited and fresh. You would have all the bands put their names in a hat and you would pick out names and assign them their gig nights. You would pull out the Symptoms look at us and put our name back in the hat till it came to filling out those great Monday our Tuesday night gigs. The Symptoms played a lot of Tuesday nights. Howie Klien once wrote," On a rainy Tuesday night those 20 people up front were like 200 to the Symptoms" Thanks Dirk we love you too, we REALY do.

Bobby Imsolucki-Drummer

■ ■

WHEN THE FAB MAB FIRST APPEARED ON THE SCENE. I THOUGHT OH WOW..MY TIME HAD FINALLY COME. THERE WAS FINALLY A PLATFORM AND A NAME FOR WHAT I HAD BEEN DOING FOR YEARS...THE PLATFORM WAS THE FAB MAB.

AND THE NAME WAS"PUNK"..DIRK DIRKSEN WAS THE SWINGALLI THAT MADE IT HAP-PEN IN SAN FRANCISCO. I HAD ALREADY PLAYED THE FILMORE IN 1969..

WENT TO NASHVILLE AND SHOOK UP THAT TOWN IN 1971. TOURED WITH DR.HOOK.. CHUCK BERRY..& STEVIE WONDER IN 1973..

BUT IN 1977 I FOUND THE FAB MAB..THIS WAS HOME.

I STARTED PRODUCING MY OWN TV SHOW IN 1978. GIRL GEORGE & THE SUPERSTARS OF THE FUTURE (IT RAN WEEKLY 78' TO 83'). MOST OF MY BANDS ON THE SHOW CAME FROM THE FAB MAB..PEARL HARBOR & THE EXPLOSIONS...BLUE CHEER..ROY LONEY..MIKE WILHELM (from THE FLAMING GROOVIES & THE CHARLATANS) FAST FLOYD..NAOMI RUTH EISENBERG,NAOMI VICE, JUST TO NAME A FEW.

DIRK HIMSELF CAME ON THE SHOW..GAVE A GREAT INTERVIEW OF HOW HE HAD A TV SHOW IN L.A. THAT EVERYONE WAS ON INCLUDING LENNY BRUCE. I STARTED FILMING MY WEEKLY SHOWS AT THE FAB MAB. EVERY FRI. 7pm TO 9pm. BEFORE THE REG.SHOW STARTED. MY BAND PLAYED AT THE MAB TOO. LOVE THE PLACE. DIRK ASKED ME TO BE THE M.C. FOR THE DUMMY AWARDS. GREAT FUN. WORST BAND..WORST SINGER ETC..I

REMEMBER GINGER COYOTE AND THE PUNK GLOBE. OH WHAT A THRILL TO GET A WRITE UP THERE. I WAS AT THE MAB RIGHT AFTER JOHN LENNON GOT SHOT...THE FLAMING GROOVIE'S WERE DOING A TRIBUTE. THAT WAS THE ONLY PLACE TO BE AT A TIME LIKE THAT. THE MUSIC COMMUNITY WAS SHAKEN AND WE ALL HELD ON TIGHT TO EACH OTHER THAT NITE.

DIRK DIRKSEN MADE IT ALL POSSIBLE..THE FAB MAB WAS HOME.

GIRL GEORGE

■■

The Mab is crowded, howling, the wolves are hungry. My band, DAS BLOK is about to go on. Dirk and I are standing stage right in the shadows. He's looking out at the audience, surveying the surging throng.

"I don't know who they could all be here for." he snaps in that voice; sharp, brittle, dripping with the sarcasm that was Dirk.

He turns his head and, leaning in close, looking me dead in the eye, says, "The shape of the coke bottle is designed to give your mouth pleasure when you take a drink."

Staring at each other, Dirk drops his chin, a sly smile appears on his face and then turning, walks to mic and introduces the band.

Owen Masterson: Das Blok, The Fighting Cocks, Yanks

■■■■■■■■■■■■■■■■■■■■■■■■■■■■■■■■■■■■■■

I spent some afternoon's hanging with Dirk around his office. He'd open his wallet and buy everyone piroshkis..

Chuck Prophet

■■

It was 1982 and I was working in the trades—mostly roofing and painting houses—by day and putting a band together at night. My girlfriend and songwriting partner was a bartender at Hotel Utah where we drank and hung out. The bar manager, Dennis, was going out with Sue Mutant and I met Fritz Mutant there and hired him to help on a big roofing job in Pacific Heights. It was really hard, dirty work and Fritz didn't like it much, lasting just two days before collecting his check.

My band, Arms of Venus played the Mab once that fall or early winter. I still have a tape somewhere we dubbed off the soundboard. It was our very first gig and it was horrible. The mix was all high-end and we were out of tune with our vocals but Dirk, mercifully, wasn't there that night so we didn't get the benefit of his most likely withering critique.

Peter Marti, singer/ keyboards ARMS OF VENUS

Poster by Jerry Paulson

Poster by James Stark

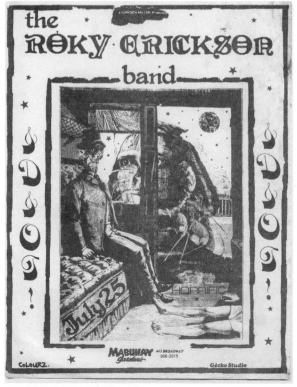

Poster by Gecko Studio

21 Bad Axe
The Dix

22 The Zeros
Weirdos

23 The Zeros
Weirdos

24 Atla
Nimbus

25 Roky Erickson
Idiot

26 Haight Street
Community
Radio Benefit

27 Overland Freight
X-Ray Ted

28 The Screamers
Avengers

29 The Screamers
Street Punks

30 Mary Monday
Leila & the
Snakes

31 Mary Monday
Street Punks

AUGUST 1977

1 Nelson Slater
Cunning Stunts

2 Special Party

3 Killerwatt
Neon
Main Drive

5 Crime
Novak

6 Crime
Avengers

7 Pegasus
Hoi Polloi

8 Waterbrother
Hot Knives
Crystal Rock

9 Neon
Overland Freight
Cross

10 Mile Hi
X-Ray Ted
Shapes of Things

11 Minx
Cunning Stuntz
Sneezer

Poster by Jean Caffine, Will Shatter, Michael Kowalsky

Photo by James Stark

Poster by James Stark

12 **Kid Courage**
   Quayle Brothers

13 **The Ratz**
   Rick & Ruby

14 **Atla**
   Tykus

15 **Atla**
   Premier
   Northstar

16 **Mary Monday**
   The Dix
   Negraphilia

17 **Nuclear Valdez**
   Novak
   Ore

18 **Killerwatt's Free**
   Party for the
   Audience, with
   Magister Ludi
   Cornel Hurd
   Leila & the Snakes

19 **Killerwatt**
   Mile Hi
   Tykus
   Leila & the Snakes

20 **Premier**
   Rick & Ruby
   Leila & the Snakes

21 **Pine Street**
   Rockestra
   Sparkin'
   Leila & the Snakes

22 **Naomi Ruth**
   Eisenberg

23 **Nuclear Valdez**
   Street Punks
   Vincent Mason

24 **Roky Erickson**
   Ozzie

25 **Avengers**
   Street Punks
   X-Ray Ted
   Leila & the Snakes

Photo by Don Everson

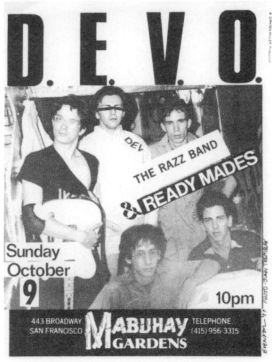

Photo by Stan Trebec Poster by Don Everson

26 La Rue

27 La Rue

28 Slim Productions Party
Leila & the Snakes

29 Waterbaby
Hot Knives
Rockestra

30 Mary Monday
Tommy Dee
Skidmarx

SEPTEMBER 1977

1 Premier
Backroad
Headfirst

2 The Nuns
The Zeros
Leila & the Snakes

3 The Nuns
The Zeros

4 Mile Hi
Pegasus
Leila & the Snakes

5 Nuclear Valdez
X-Ray Ted

6 Overland Freight
Nimbus
Sparkin'

7 Atla
Rage
Rockestra

8 The Nuns
Leila & the Snakes

9 The Nuns
Leila & the Snakes

10 D.E.V.O.
Leila & the Snakes

11 D.E.V.O.
Avengers
Leila & the Snakes

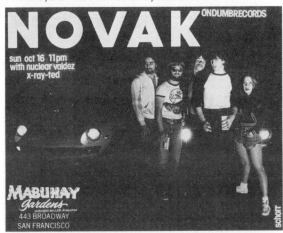

Photo by Schorr

12 Neon
Dark Horse
Cross

13 Killerwatt
Ozzie

14 Mile Hi
Premier
North Star

15 Crime
The Dils
Leila & the Snakes

16 Crime
The Dils
Leila & the Snakes

17 Hoi Polloi
Street Punks
Leila & the Snakes

18 Vincent Mason
Idiot
Leila & the Snakes

19 Mary Monday
X-Ray Ted

Poster by Don Everson

Poster by Don Everson

oster by Anomymous

20 Freestone
Cunning Stuntz
Nitro

21 Waterbaby
Cornel Hurd
Kid America

22 Manx Cross
Leland

23 Kid Courage
Mile Hi

24 Leila & the Snakes

25 Zolar X
Premier
Crystal Rock

26 Nelson Slater
Killerwatt
Fleshtones

27 Zolar X
Hoi Polloi
Quayle Brothers

28 Pine Street
Main Drive
Third Rail

29 Novak
Street Punks
Readymades

30 Atla
Pegasus
Mantyss

OCTOBER 1977

1 Hoi Polloi
Premier
21st Century Blues
Band

2 New Wave Party

3 Rage
Airborne
Crystal Rock

Photo by Jim Jocoy/Poster by Don Everson

Poster by James Stark

Poster byDon Everson

5   **Nibus**
    Waterbaby
    Third Rail

5   **Magister Ludi**
    Quayle Brothers
    Trax

6   **Freestone**
    Cunning Stuntz
    Nitro

7   **Weirdos**

8   **Weirdos**

9   **D.E.V.O.**
    Razz

10 **D.E.V.O.**
    Razz

11 **Atla**
    Sparkin'

12 **Pegasus**
    Exxe
    Michael Spear

13 **Hoi Polloi**
    Mile Hi
    Ore

14 **Hoi Polloi**
    Street Punks
    Readymades

15 **Premier**
    Waterbaby
    Airborne

16 **Novak**
    Nuclear Valdez
    X-Ray Ted

17 **Nelson Slater**
    Melvin Miracle
    Romance

18 **Avengers**
    Whoremones
    Psychotic Pine-
    apple

19 **Magister Ludi**
    Premier
    Cross

20 **The Ratz**
    Cunning Stuntz

21 **Kid Courage**
    Street Punks
    The Rebs

22 **Street Punks**
    Mile Hi
    Magnum

23 **Overland Freight**
    X-Ray Ted
    Nitro

24 **Mary Monday**
    Fleshtones
    Presence

25 **Zolar X**
    Idiot
    Adeptus

26 **Zolar X**
    Sparkin'
    USSA

27 **The Dils**
    Avengers

To me, one of the most memorable encounters I had with Dirk was the very first time I met him. As I recall, it was in the autumn of 1977. The Dils were playing their first gig at the Mabuhay since reforming as a three piece and the first time during the period I'd managed the band. Chip, Tony, and Endre (their first drummer) were all still living near San Diego and I was still living in Hollywood and they'd been invited up to open for the Nuns, based on the friendship previously forged between the two bands.

Peter Urban taking target pratice with Negative Trend on stage
Photo by James Stark

The band had driven up, bringing along Chip's girlfriend Kathy Kato and a girlfriend of hers and I'd flown up to meet them and arrived at the Mab about 10:30 or so.

The Nuns already had a solid following and it was a Friday or Saturday, so the gig was well attended and the Dils won over the audience easily, so I was pretty pleased with how things were going, though I was somewhat annoyed that the Nuns had only offered 15% of the door, which wasn't a lot when you were driving 450 miles each way to get to the show.

I suppose, in part, I was in a particularly good mood when the Dils finished their set, because things were going so well and both the band and I fit into the San Francisco punk scene much better than we did with the punks in Los Angeles, so when the Nuns came on, I joined in the dancing fray of pogoing punks and before long was drenched in beer and sweat. Someone knocked over a table by the dance floor and knocked a candle on the floor and when I picked up a large shard of glass from the broken candle holder and attempted to bury it in the wax to keep others from getting injured, I managed to bring my ring finger down hard onto another shard sticking up and pretty much cut the entire tip of my finger in half. I grabbed a wad of napkins, wrapped my finger in them and returned to dancing with Kathy and her friend in front of the stage.

As the set progressed, I kept bleeding through the wad of napkins, at which point I'd grab more and add them to the ever widening mass of bloody paper wadded around my finger. By the time the set ended, my hair was sort of sticking every which-way, matted with dried beer; I was pale and slightly giddy from blood loss; soaked in sweat; and by that point had this really massive wad of completely blood-soaked napkins wrapped around my finger and sort of held in place with my other hand. It was in that state that I entered Dirk's office, where he was counting money with the Nuns manager, Edwin Heaven, sitting in front of his desk, wearing a three-piece suit, with a tiny, gold safety-pin through his lapel.

I plopped myself into another chair and asked how many paid admissions there had been. I still remember Dirk staring at me in relative disbelief, but he did give me a figure. I quickly did the math in my head and said something like, "That comes to $167.50 for the Dils. Can I get paid now, as we'd like to get out of here."

Apparently, Edwin had been pulling some crap before I'd entered the room and Dirk informs me that Edwin is now saying that the Dils are only going to get 5% of the door. I started to launch into this diatribe about what our agreement had been and the expenses we incurred, but Dirk told me to hang on. He gave Edwin the money for the Nuns, apparently including the additional 10% we'd been promised and Edwin left. Then Dirk turned to me, still with this odd look on his face—I'm pretty certain because of the contrast between the band manager who'd just excited (complete with gold safety pin in lapel) and the one sitting in front of him now, with matted hair, smelling of beer and sweat, more than a little pale, with this ridiculous clump of blood-oozing napkins around his finger, but still calmly computing 15% of the door and prepared to argue with both he and Edwin over the attempt to screw over my band—and told me that the Nuns were the best drawing band he had, so he was compelled to give them what they demanded. Without any word of further argument, however, he told me that he would make up the difference out of his own cut of the door and counted out the full 15% to me. I dealt with Dirk many, many times after that, but I don't ever recall him giving up any of his 35% of the door on any other occasion. But, the other times the Dils, or even the other bands I managed, the Zeros and Negative Trend, never needed to get paid like we needed it that time. Had we gotten screwed out of that 10%, it might have dampened future enthusiasm for driving up from Southern California to play again and the whole course of the Dils career might have been significantly altered and my punks days as well. I like to tell myself there was an element of sympathy generated by how pathetic I must have looked drained of blood, with this mass of gore-stained napkins that prompted Dirk to make up for Edwin's nasty little knife in the Dils' back, but whether I like to admit it or not, it was probably just one demonstration of Dirk actually having a heart, somewhere hidden behind the penis-nose glasses and the obnoxious insults. I have a couple of other stories I'd like to share, but that is my fondest memory of my dealings with Dirk.

Peter Urban

■■■■■■■■■■■■■■■■■■■■■■■■■■■■■■■■■■

Here is a funny Mab Story...My first show at the mab I hitch hiked to the city with a friend from Fremont, I think I was 17 -18 years old. We had tons of Marijuana & Black Beauties on us to sell and make some money to buy booze and take a bus back to fremont. We were in the girls bathroom stall and we noticed the SFPD in the girls room...we got nervous about being underage & having all this stash so we flushed all our stash down the toilet!!! We waited till the SFPD left the room and left the stall! when we walked out into the club.... We realized the SFPD was the Band!! and they went by the name CRIME.... I never realized that in just a short time later I would be in a band (The Next) with Brittley Black playing a show with them or that years later I would be playing with Frankie, Britt & Ripper or would be recording a record with Johnny Strike (TVH)

Jimmy Crucifix

SCREAMERS SCREAMERS

DEC. 10TH & 19TH

AT THE MABUHAY

PIX by YOSHI BRAKHE

Photo by Moshe Brakhe

oster by Anomymous

Poster by Search & Destroy Staff

28 Zeros
   The Dils
   Ozzie

29 Zero
   Pegasus
   Rage

30 Atla
   Pegasus
   Rage

31 Special
   Halloween Party

DECEMBER 1977

1 The Dogs
   Statics

2 Eddie and the Hot
   Rods

4 Zippers
   Pop
   Tremors

5 Zippers
   Pop
   Tremors

6 Nico

7 Party for
   Search & Destroy
   Magazine

8 Nico
   Crime
   Leila & the Snakes

9 Talking Heads

10 Talking Heads

11 Shock
   Skulls

12 Skulls
   Shock

13 Overland Freight
   Main Drive
   Whoremones

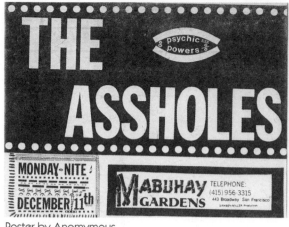

Poster by Anomymous

oster by Anomymous

14 **Nuclear Valdez**
   UXA
   Bandaloons

15 **Hoi Polloi**
   Quayle Bros.
   Exxe

16 **Kid Courage**
   Wate
   Sparkin'

17 **Crime**
   plus special
   guests

18 **The Screamers**
   The Deadbeats

19 **The Screamers**
   The Deadbeats
   Ogden Edsel
   Mondo Bizzaro

20 **X-Ray Ted**
   The Mutants
   Seizure
   Redwood Players

21 **Magister Ludi**
   Quayle Bros.
   Trax
   Bandaloons

22 **The Readymades**
   The Liars
   Tuxedo Moon
   Brown & Coffey

23 **Premier**
   Street Punks

24 **Special Christmas**
   Party

25 **DIX**
   Sleepers (1st.
   show)

26 **Punk Christmas**
   Party

27 **Melvin Miracle**
   Lazar
   Fast Floyd

28 **Rage**
   Rock Island

29 **Freestone**
   Cunning Stuntz
   Nitro

30 **Avengers**
   The Readymades
   The Liars

Poster by James Stark

Poster by Don Everson

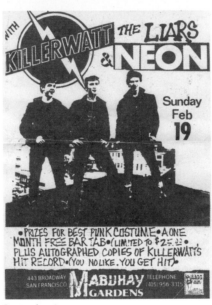

Poster by Anomymous

Poster by James Stark

14 Premier
Neon

17 Novak
Nuclear Valdez
Negative Trend

18 Magister Ludi
Whoremones
Lazor

19 The Readymades
Street Punks
Zolar X

20 Crime
UXA
The Speepers

21 Crime
Negative Trend
The Sleepers

22 Enemy
The Feelings
The Mentors

23 Enemy
The Feelings
The Mentors

24 The Mutants
Permanent Wave
Rocky Sullivan

25 X-Ray Ted
Overland Freight
Crystal Rock

26 Killerwatt
Ozzie
Tuxedo Moon

27 Magnum
The Sleepers
Fast

31 New Year's Eve
Party
Nimbus
Mile Hi

JANUARY 1978

1 The Dogs
Statics

3 Suicide
Nick Gilder
Negative Trend

5 Special Birthday
Dyan Buckelew
Stars
Killowatt

8 Razz Band
Back Stage Pass
X-Statics

9 Razz Band
Back Stage Pass
X-Statics

10 Freestone

Exxe
The Tricks

11 Killerwatt
Rock Island

12 Rage
Magnum
Next

13 Weirdos
Leila & the Snakes
The Dix

When I first met Dirk I really did not care for him much, although I thought some of his banter to the crowd at The Mabuhay was hilarious. My dislike would rise when he directed his jabs in my direction. However. it did not take long before Dirk became a friend and a father like figure to me. I had left home in the Midwest and was in need of a "real" family. One that showed love and support. I had moved to SF right after getting a Drivers License and never looked back. I soon found my "family " at The Mabuhay Gardens. It was from those days, that I found people who have remained loyal and true friends . Yes, my "REAL" family...

When I first started doing Punk Globe it was Dirk who urged me to continue doing it. At times I would get depressed and wanna stop doing it. But it was his foresight that made me continue. He would tell me that although it seemed like at the time people did not really appreciate my labor of love at the time . In the future it would be my work with Punk Globe that would garner me a lot of respect. He offered the Mabuhay Gardens and On Broadway as a venues so I could throw benefits to continue printing the Punk Globe. He also introduced me to Roger Reyes who worked with Dirk doing graphics for DMP. Every month we would gather at Roger's Van Ness Apartment which he shared with KUSF Dee Jay -Denise Demise. We would put together the final layouts for Punk Globe. Dirk would always stop by before he went to The Mabuhay with

Ginger at Dirkfest. Photo by James Stark

Pizza for us. People like Julie Stein, Danielle Bardazzi, Anna Pirhana, George Epileptic, Spence Coppens and myself would all be there doing the old cut and paste to complete the next issue. It was through Dirk that we were all able to get together and get the work done but also have fun doing it. These monthly get togethers be came a monthly ritual and would continue until Roger became ill . I look back at those times as some of my best.

In the early 80's I had been at Copymat on Polk Street. I had in my bag some rubber cement, the blue print pages and a pair of scissors. This particular day the cops were doing a sting on Polk Street and I was stopped and arrested for carrying a concealed weapon. The scissors were less than six inches long but the Vice Cop who picked me up assured me this was not a joke. I was handcuffed and thrown into a paddy wagon. Luckily Marilyn McIntosh who worked at The Palms had seen the arrest and her first instinct was to call Dirk. Dirk and Gary Erhke contacted Ness to put the Mabuhay up as collateral with a Bail Bondsman so by the time I was taken to Bryant Street my bail was in process. It was not

PUNK GLOBE
JANUARY
1980
$1

Early Punk Globe cover

until I was actually booked that the amount of money that would be needed.. My bail was $2,000 which with a bail bondsman it was 10%. Another supporter of Punk Rock and a true friend Lenore "Real Cool Chick" Cautrelle who was then in her late 60's contacted Herb Caen and on the day of my court date the head story in his column in the Chronicle was about my arrest. He indicated that I was on my way to a sewing bee and was pulled over by the cops because I had Purple Hair. The case was dropped and I remember after comin home after my court date that I had a message from Dirk letting me know he was thinking about me. Dirk had a talent in joining people together for a cause.

He asked me to be involved with his Birthday at The Mabuhay Gardens when he was shot out of a cannon and we staged me picking up his hand. I remember that f Stop Fitzgerald was there taking photo's and Dirk pouring a half a bottle of catsup over my arm and me holding a severed hand of Dirks. Little did I know this picture would appear in numerous publication including Punk Globe..

I remember that he was responsible for putting together a crew for the "Jello Biafra for Mayor" Campaign that was as diverse as the crowd at The Mabuhay Gardens. We had myself, Olga de Volga, Chi Chi, Lenore Cautrelle, Gloria Harrison, Dirk, Barbar Helbert, Brad Lapin, Roger Reyes and a few others.. I remember that we all gathered at a location in Nob Hill to support Biafra in his Mayoral Debate which included Dianne Feinstein.. I remember Ms. Feinstein greeting Lenore Cautrelle who immediately informed her that she was there in support of Biafra. After the Mabuhay closed I would stay in touch with Dirk and would always get his annual Holiday Card.. After I moved south to Hollywood he would call and check in with me and when I had shows with The White Trash Debutantes in the Bay Area he would come out and see us or we would get together with Kathy Peck and David Denny for brunch. We had a bond that was there for life. I remember getting first an email in November from the Wonderful Ruby Ray letting me know Dirk had passed and then

THIS ISSUE:
Dirk "UNVEILED"
GINGER SWORN IN
PUNK GLOBE Top Ten

PUNK GLOBE

FEBRUARY $1.00

Punk Globe (cover curiosity, Kathy Peck)
Photo by Julie Stein

speaking with Kathy Peck and I was numb. We were all in shock. Dirk was the person we all channeled to when anything bad happened within the community. I remember going out with him ,Kathy and David in early October and he was so spry and we were talking about how happy he was that I had started doing the Punk Globe online. I had sent him and interview and was waiting for him to do it. Within a month and a half he was gone.. Kathy Peck pulled herself together immediately to begin work with getting him cremated and a location to place the ashes. She then asked me to help her with organizing a Memorial Show which took a lot of time and energy. There was obstacles that happened that were unneeded but in June 2007 we gave Dirk Dirksen the send off he so highly deserved. The two shows paying tribute was mainly done with Kathy Peck's guidance and strength. But it was the whole PUNK COMMUNITY who got together for these events. Special Shouts out to Kathy Peck, The Audiences, All The Bands that played both shows, The DJ's, Emcee's, Sound and Camera Crew, The Roadies, Damon Malloy, Dirk's Sister and Immediate Family, The Photographers, Dawn Holiday, Great American Music Hall and Slims staff, the Radio and Media support, Lennon Studio's .. We all help make history. And now through the fearless efforts of Kathy Peck- we now have the alley way right next to 443 Broadway that will bear his name. DIRK DIRKSEN WAY!!

Ginger Coyote, Punk Globe

■■■■■■■■■■■■■■■■■■■■■■■■■■■■■■■■■■■■■■

Memories of the Mab

I cleaved my way through the throng of people crowding around the door, past the line waiting to enter, and stopped where the bouncer stood holding a rope across the entrance to the club. He never acknowledged that he recognized me. He stood there, big, immobile, impassable.

I turned to Dirk Dirksen, a few feet away at his podium. I knew Dirk had seen me, but he didn't look up. He continued counting out money to someone who was buying a ticket to get in. Then he suspended the transaction and looked over my way, lowering his head slightly to peer over the rim of his glasses. We stared at each other for a moment. He knew I wanted in for free. I knew he was waiting to see if I would accept intimidation and pay. "Come on," I said finally, smiling, "tell your thug to let me pass."

Dirk smiled too, but in a malicious sort of way. "So you think it's that easy, huh?" Meanwhile, a line of people waiting to buy their tickets were staring at me. No one I knew was in that line. I looked past the bouncer into the club and recognized lots of people. A tall, dark-haired guy wearing leather pants and Beatle boots came over to say hi. We chatted over the rope, while Dirk turned back to his transaction. I knew this might take time.

The bouncer let several people with tickets pass. I waited. Dirk continued to sell tickets, watching me out of the corner of his eye. I wasn't begging. I was cool. Dirk knew as well as I did that he would eventually let me in.

"Okay," Dirk called over, and made a gesture with his head to the bouncer, motioning for him to let me pass. I glided past the rope without any apparent eagerness. Cool.

The Mabuhay "Gardens" felt more underwater than above-ground: exotic tropicals, garish clothes and neon faces swimming through the Polynesian decor, palm trees and bamboo, op-art bodies in leather mini-skirts, pretty faces, strange faces weaving among pillars and potted plants.

45

Loud music, really loud music. I anchored myself at the bar, glass in hand, watching the faces come bobbing up for drinks then wander back into the tank....

My first booking meeting was as manager of my boyfriend's band, the Fleshapoids. They were a new band, unheard of. "The whats?" Dirk asked me when I got up the nerve to speak. We played cat and mouse, and he did give us a night, opening for some small band on some week-day night. I was thrilled, I had managed to get a gig! I remember sitting at those meetings, heart pounding when I needed to ask anything, and wilting under Dirk's sarcastic remarks. I have always held that Dirk prepared me for the rest of my career—after his harsh, sarcastic treatment I could handle anyone or anything else. The tough stance I learned at the Mabuhay served me well in the following years....

The Mab was unique in many ways. It was the first punk club. It was the most stable, outliving many other venues. It was one of the only clubs dedicated entirely to our music. It was where everyone had to start. In some ways, it was like home. It was run by our evil step-mother, Dirk. Who, we all knew, deep down really cared for us.

Annette Jarvie

■ ■

My story is one that Dirk told me

Back in the Mab days, there was some opening band that used a fishing pole to dangle something out in the audience, and they left the pole behind, as well as one of those fisherman baskets that the singer had worn on stage. The pole and basket wound up in Dirk's office, in case some-

Frankie and Dirk at the Mab.   Photo by James Stark

body came back for it. Nobody ever did, but after a Crime show, while the band was being paid off, Frankie from Crime noticed the pole and started talking about how he hadn't been fishing since he was a kid but he remembered it was fun. He looked in the basket and there were some lures and some extra line. Eventually, he talked Dirk into going fishing - that night!

They got in Frankie's car and drove down the Peninsula to the big lake just off 280. Since there was only one pole, Frankie thought it would be extra-cool to tie some line and a lure onto his guitar and try using that. They fished a while without catching anything, then a game warden came along. It turned out that there it was a reservoir and there was no trespassing and no fishing allowed.

The game warden noticed Frankie's uniform (he was still wearing it from the show) and said something like, "I'll just make this a warning, out of professional courtesy."

Maybe you're heard some more details from somebody else. That's all I remember of the story.

Michael Andrews

28 The Avengers
The Dils
UXA

29 The Dils
The Avengers
Negative Trend

31 Waterbaby
Nimbus
The Brains

FEBRUARY 1978

1 Mary Monday
Seizure
Shaun Vail and Salle
Bandaloons

2 Mile Hi
Killerwatt
Nitro
Bandaloons

3 Premier
The Dils
Tuxedo Moon

4 Crime
The Zeros
Tuxedo Moon

5 The Readymades
The Dils
The Zeros
Tuxedo Moon

6 The Readymades
The Dils
The Zeros

7 Premier
Magister Ludi

8 X-Ray Ted
Rocky Sullivan
Fast Floyd

9 Leland
The Liars
Stefan Weizer

10 The Dogs
Terrorists

11 The Dogs
Killerwatt
Nimbus

12 An Evening with
Peter Hammill

13 An Evening with
Peter Hammill

14 Leggs
Tuxedo Moon
The Whoremones

15 Novak
Freestone
The Names

16 The Mutants
The Sleepers
The Names

17 The Readymades
Tuxedo Moon
The Beans

18 Private Party

19 Killerwatt
The Liars
Neon

20 Street Punks
$27 Snap-On Face

21 Rage
Magnum
Lazzor

Poster by Anomymous

Poster by Don Everson

22 Ozzie
Permanent
Wave
The Sleepers

23 Mile Hi
Next

24 The Nuns
Negative Trend

Photo by James Stark / Poster by Don Everson

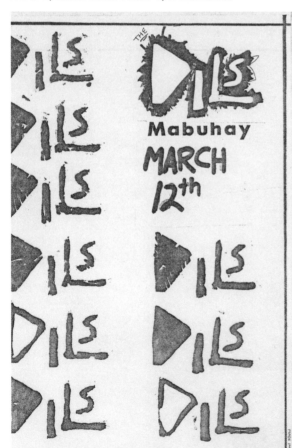

Poster by Penelope Houston

8 Negative Trend
Psychotic Pineapple
SST

9 Premier
Maindrive
The Whoremones

10 Crime
Tuxedo Moon
The Sleepers

11 The Readymades
The Zippers
Fast Floyd

12 The Zippers
UXA

14 Ozzie
The Fleshtones
The Strays

15 The Sleepers

16 Rocky Sullivan
Nimbus
Seizure

17 Killerwatt
Cunning Stuntz

18 The Nuns

19 Sons of Creation

20 Coal Miners Benefit
14 SF Punk
Rock Groups

22 Rage
Exxe
Headrush

23 The Mutants
The Sleepers
Negative Memo

27 Black Randy
The Statics
Ointment

28 UXA
The Mutants
Negative Trend

MARCH 1978

1 Rock'n'Roll
Party:
Free Buffet

2 Cornell Hurd
Overland
Freight
Bandaloons

3 Punk Special

4 Punk Special

5 Rage
Nimbus
Monster

7 The Mutants
The Sleepers

25 The Avengers
Black Randy

26 The Avengers
Black Randy
The Sleepers

SOMETIME 2004 OR 2005—I was stage managing a 4 day conference -ON REFORM-ING THE U.N. in the 21st century at san francisco state— for the unity foundation and bill mccarthy//when a german senator from the european union[and a founding father of eu] was speaking —i gave him the signal, time was up-and he ignored me and continued his 20 minute speech for about 12 or so minutes——and i was fuming—so i walked from the front of the conference room to the back—where damon and dirk were filming the event . so i sat down at the end of the last row—and fumed —when dirk walked over to me and —said stick your hand out—so with a question mark on my face hesitantly I did—[cause you never could tell with dirk what he was up to]—and he then stuck a quarter into my hand—and i looked up to him —like whats that for—i had no idea-what he was up to —then he smirked at me and said- "quarter for your thoughts "—and i just cracked up laughing—cause he saw and knew exactly what was going on —and had the compassion to diffuse my state of mind at just the right moment.//He sat down and then we started regale each other with funny stories/it was a great moment for me////   ITS a SMALL STORY BUT IT WAS INDICATIVE of the dirk i knew——always a wisecrack at the right moment—to diffuse the reality of what was going on————i loved the guy—and we certainly all miss him. he was a heartfelt cantankerous lovable curmudgeon—one of a kind—never be another dirk-!!

Will Dodger

■ ■

Dirk was a total jerk when he was in character, but a true gentleman when not in the public light.

The Psycotic Pineapple was just toweling off after a set opening for The Jim Carroll Band when Dirk came backstage to try to borrow a guitar from us. Since Patti Smith was in town, she was going to come and make a surprise appearance with Jim Carroll, and they needed a guitar for herto "jam" on. We already knew of her reputation for smashing guitars, and no one in the band was willing to sacrifice their trusty saw. We unanimously refused. Dirk came back twice to beg us, but no go. Apparently, Dirk finally found a guitar, because as I watched the set, it was so crowded that I could only see the tops of the heads of the band. Then I saw a guitar come rising up and then down repeatedly until there was noth-ing left. Dirk never held it against us or ever mentioned it again. Any other club manager would have thrown away our phone number.

John Seabury

■ ■

I was a disc jockey at KALX-FM U.C. Berkeley. I was probably the first disc jockey on any radio station who dedicated their complete 4 hour show to punk music. I was also recording punk ,new wave and local punk bands for radio broadcasts on KALX at all of the local ven-ues, Old Waldorf, Keystone Berkeley, Berkeley Square, Pauley Ballroom and yes, the fabulous

Poster by Search & Destroy Staff

APRIL 1978

1 Avengers
Cunning Stunts
Teenage

2 Rage
Killerwatt
Strays

3 Legs
The Imposters

4 The Readymades
Nuclear Valdez
Wildman Fisher

5 The Mutants
The Liars
Teenage Fakes

6 Roky Erickson &
The Aliens
Psychotic Pine
apple

7 Roky Erickson &
The Aliens
Psychotic Pine
apple

8 VOM
Nuclear Valdez
Ozzie

9 VOM
The Sleepers
DV-8

10 Legs
Fleshtones
Lucky Stiffs

11 Tuxedo Moon
The Beans
SST

12 Disaster Party
Leila & The
Snakes
Bandaloons
Tuxedo Moon

13 The Sleepers
UXA
The Assassins

14 Killerwatt
Premier
The Brains

15 The Readymades
Gary Valentine
Crisspy Baby

16 Gary Valentine
Scars
Crisspy Baby

24 Magister Ludi
Freestone

25 Lance Loud's
Mumps
Needles & Pins

26 Thrasher's Ball

27 Needles & Pins
F-Word

28 The Dics (?)
F-Word

29 Enemy
Lazor

30 Enemy
Killerwatt

31 The Avengers
Psychotic Pine
apple
Permanent Wave

Poster by Leo Zulueta

50

Mabuhay Gardens. Dirk and I became good friends and in December I told Dirk about my idea of recording the local punk bands there on a weekly basis to help give them exposure to the radio listeners as well as teens under 21 who could not attend the shows in person. Dirk said that was a wonderful idea and he would clear it with the bands who played there, so that we could record every weekend either on a Friday or Saturday night. On December 8,1979 with the Readymades, a local San Francisco punk, new wave band, I did the first recording of what was to become known as the "Live At The Fab Mab" weekly radio broadcasts. I continued doing these Mabuhay recordings from December through May 1981. I was also the Mabuhay soundman on Sunday & Monday nights, and when Dirk started doing shows upstairs at the On Broadway on Friday & Saturdays, he asked me to be the soundman there as well, which I did through July 1981.For a complete list of the bands that were recorded at the Mab for the "Live At The Fab Mab" radio show you can visit my website at http://www.angelfire.com/oh/liveperformances/livetapes.html

Dirk was a wonderful person and with his passing,I have lost a good friend. I think it's a fitting tribute that the city of San Francisco is renaming the alley next to the Mab, Dirk Dirksen Place and putting a plaque at the alley next to the Mab to remember him by. If Bill Graham can have something named after him, then, Dirk deserves to have something named after him. After all, Dirk did for punk, what Bill Graham did for rock.

Terry Hammer

■■■■■■■■■■■■■■■■■■■■■■■■■■■■■■■■■■■■

I use to go to the Mab with my friends from Hollywood like the Maus Maus, the Dickies, the Circle Jerks, and then just the road trip to have an excuse to go to SF. In Hollywood we had Brendan Mullen, but Dirk was an entirely different animal. As I wasn't in a band in those early days I had no dealings with him (good or bad) he just seemed reallly funny, sarcastic, and older than everyone else. Before I moved to SF I was asked to be in a punk rock version of El Topo written and starring Eric Rad and myself, Dirk let us use the On Broadway stage and with lighting and what not we did a short 8 mm film. That's when I first got to know him as person, he was really sweet and supportive and after filming we all hung out. After I moved to SF and started Housecoat Project he was always around. I can remember being let into his inner chamber upstairs at the on Broadway and having charming conversations. He called me his "bad little step child" and one time when i was supposed to do

Meri St. Meri at the Thrift Shop.
Photo by James Stark

a show (he was MCing) and I didn't show up. I was told he said "well Meri St. Mary was supposed to be here but she got her drugs all mixed up" - I mean that was his kind of humor, I wasn't mad at him. After all the clubs closed and he was doing his TV show with Damon I was riding my bike down Folsom and I saw Dirk with a camera and some folks and I screamed "Dirk Dirksen I love you" - later I called him and told him that was me and he said it was so great because the band he was filming thought he was some kind of big star. I lost touch with him for awhile (I was raising my son and in the east bay) however I called him and he cared to know what I was up to etc. then he would say "hey come on by we'll roast some weenies" he was on Treat Street. Being a close friend of Kathy Peck's I heard of his goings on and the work he that he was doing for the community. At the Fab Mab reunion (I didn't go) Kathy told me Dirk said where is Meri St. Mary? She should be here. We hit it off and I thought of him fondly (still do). I'm proud to have known him and appreciate his kind words whenever I called he never judged me or made me feel bad. I find sarcasm a relief in this world of bullshitters. I miss him and feel honored to have spent time with him. Onward and Upward!!!!

Meri St. Mary

■■■■■■■■■■■■■■■■■■■■■■■■■■■■■■■■■■■

The first time I ran into Dirk was in 1977, one afternoon at the Mabuhay Gardens when I was delivering some sound equipment for the new and unknown band Crime. This was probably around April or May of 1977. I'd been living at Ashbury & Fulton for well over a year since I'd hitched-hiked out to California from Boston where I was working for a couple months (stopping there when I first returned to America after having spent most of the previous 7 years living in Italy since the late 1960s). I had been a roadie for the last couple years back in Italy so when I wound up in San Francisco years later I worked as a "rent-a-roadie" for a studio rental outfit south of Market.

We worked all the big shows and rock acts in around San Francisco in 1976 and '77. I worked with mostly local bands like the Tubes, Santana, Quicksilver, Journey, Crosby, Stills & Nash, etc… but also national acts that came through the City such as the Beach Boys, Taj Mahal, Jackson Browne, Bonnie Raitt and countless others. Our pay was the exploitative sum of $2.25 minimum wage (take home pay was $2.10) but since we didn't have to wear suits or uniforms and since we could choose our own hours, that and certain other fringe benefits made the job tolerable.

One spring day in 1977 I was sent over to the Mabuhay Gardens on Broadway to drop off what was probably the least costly public address equipment we had for rent; two Shure columns and a tiny mixing board. These were usually used for weddings and funerals and not much else. But for Crime, it seemed their budget-minded production people figured it would do just fine.

I recall setting up the speakers and being asked by one of the band members if there were any way I could make the speakers sound louder. I turned them up to their maximum notch (going from one to ten) and even after that he asked me, "yeah, but, uh, can't you just make it louder?" After tweaking everything I could tweak and being asked the same question again I pointed out to him that the volume control went up to 10 and that's as far as the knob would turn. He seemed puzzled that turning the knob any further wouldn't result in loader amplification. I went back to the Studios just scratching my head. (About 7 or 8 years later ---in 1984 or '85--- I saw the film "Spinal Tap" wherein one of the band members is pointing out that their amps are actually louder than any other bands' amps because their volume control knobs "go all the way to 11, not just 10". My jaw dropped when I saw that scene since it wasn't just a joke, it had actually happened to me, only way back in 1977. Art imitates life—and vice versa.

Winston Smith

17 Legs
   UXA
   DV-8

18 Disaster Party
   Exxe
   The Brains

19 Overland Freight
   Fast Floyd
   The Beans

20 Magister Ludi
   Ozzie
   Street Life

21 The Dils
   Rank & File
   UXA

22 The Nuns

23 Lazor

24 Negative Trend
   Max Trash
   The Goats

25 Second Annual
   Free Party
   Killerwatt

26 Neon
   Seizure
   Spies

27 The Avengers

28 The Avengers

29 La Rue

30 Ointment

MAY 1978

1 Legs
   DV-8
   The Maids

Poster by ARP Visuals

Poster by Anomymous

Photo by Marcus Leatherdale

2 Seizure
  Raw Meat
  Blast

3 Roger Carroll's
  Overland Freight
  Crisspy Baby

4 The Sleepers
  Strays
  Now

5 Magister Ludi
  The Dix
  UXA

6 Leila & the Snakes
  Tuxedo Moon
  Psychotic Pineapple

8 Legs
  The Offs
  Avant Garde
  The Assassins

53

Poster by Anomymous

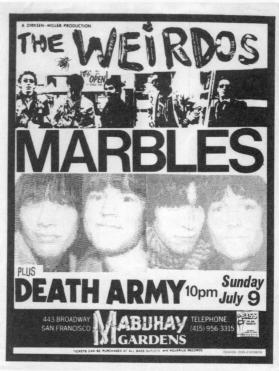

Poster by Don Everson

9 The Teenage
The Brains
The Imposters

10 Permanent Wave
The News
Blast

11 Benefit: Search &
Destroy Magazine
The Avengers
Crime
The Dils
UXA

12 The Dils
The Zeros
The Offs

13 The Screamers
The Zippers
Devy Ants

14 The Screamers
The Zippers
Space Trash

15 Rank & File
Legs
The Imposters
Teenage Fakes

16 Rage
Seizure
Max Trash

17 Psychotic Pine
apple
Fast Floyd
Lucky Stiff

18 Leland

19 The Avengers
"X"

20 The Readymades
"X"
DV-8

21 Benefit for Fol-
som Studios

Poster by Anomymous

22 Rank & File
Dogmatics
Tuxedo Moon
Whoremones
The Gourds

23 UXA
The Offs
Sharp

24 The Mutants
The Beans
No Sisters

25 Benefit for Mak-
ing It
By The Bay

26 The Nuns
The Sleepers
The Offs

27 The Nuns
The Sleepers
The Offs

28 Special Party

29 Street Punks
Magnum
Roxy
Blank

30 Magister Ludi
Bandaloons
The Strays

31 Neon
Spies
Stalworth

NATIONAL ENQUIRER

40¢

January 6, 1981   30586-2   LARGEST CIRCULATION OF ANY PAPER IN AMERICA

NEW YEAR'S EVE
TRAGEDY

Cannon Misfires "Human Cannonball" Snuffed

Ex-Angel
Recovers
'Cannonball'
Arm
         page 13
★ ★ ★

Billy Hawk
Pukes Over
Remains
Of Dirk
         page 13
★ ★ ★

Pyro-Technician
Claims
Innocence
         page 13
★ ★ ★

Audience
Screams
For More
         page 13

SHOCKING

FabMabExecProducerDismembered

FabMab
NEW YEAR'S TRAGEDY

(San Francisco) At midnight New Year's Eve, the audience saw DIRK (The Human Cannonball) DIRKSEN disappear into the gapping 70MM mouth of a fifteen foot long cannon barrel on stage.

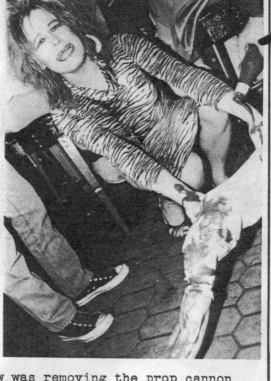

SUDDENLY, disaster struck. Pyrotechnician ROBERT FRYE screwed up. His handywork misfired! Lighting Director KEVIN DOOLAN said, "It was a case of shocking incompetence." The audience kept screaming for more or a refund. As the crew was removing the prop cannon, GINGER COYOTE helped in moving some of the equipment, including the arm of CANNONBALL. Everyone had a great time and said they still want to see DIRK shot out of a cannon.

Photo by: F. Stop Fitzgerald

Photos by F. Stop Fitzgerald

I was as angry as ten snakes in 1970 something, but I just didn't ever get mad at Dirk Dirksen. So Dirk pulled off a real Hat Trick there. At 17, I wanted a sandwich, I might fuck you or spit at you but I didn't necessarily like you. However, I did have to get into the Mabuhay Gardens whenever I could, and hang out in the Ladies Bathroom as long as possible, making life hell for any normal type women who wandered in to piss or do coke.

On a roll, I'd grab people's half empty beers and chug them, faster and faster, until one night I woke up on the floor a few feet from the stage, and my eyes noted a ring of nightclub patrons, giving my body some distance like the bad accident I'd become, mad and confused. Out I went again, until I came to a minute later with Dirk ramming the back of my head into the side of a van parked in the alleyway, yelling in that piercing voice.

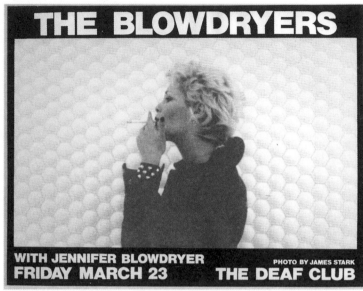

Poster by James Stark

For awhile, I had to stand around outside the Mabuhay Garden with a group home refugee, Mary, due to our underage. One night Dirk emerged waving around a white foam corps sign with "2 Blonde Girls 86ed" on it. I loved it, and started a band, the Blowdryers, just to get in to the Mabuhay and The Stud, another Mecca of antennaed in great music.

"He hated you, and then when he saw you perform, he loved you." Said Brett from Seizure at the after party for Dirk's memorial, over at the Jimmy Crucifix house. Still socially clueless, I had crashed the memorial with an impromptu little speech, unaware of how......pre-planned things like funerals tend to be.

Well maybe Dirk didn't love me, but Brett pointed out that he opened the door just an inch, and that was all I needed.

When the Mab sort of became the On Broadway, next door and up a flight, I made it all the way into Dirk's office. He took a hit, probably a maintenance pot head at that point, and said when he was a German kid going to school in the states, he'd come home with his t-shirt so drenched in blood his mother had to peel it off him. That's how he learned to fight, more specifically to head butt. He wasn't telling exactly to me, but I was there and guess what, I'm the one that remembers it, motherfucker. Watch how you act around the kids, even the ones with the kittens and the fake prison tattoos on their closed off faces. It matters.

Having worked in early television, Dirk knew what he was mocking when he staged a Punk Rock Awards Ceremony, but I only knew in a more formal hence deceitful world I wouldn't have been allowed near the joint. I own a nook at San Francisco's Neptune Society Columbarium. I won't be in the same room as Dirk, because I'm all grown up now and they weren't offering any decent spaces in the coolest buildings. I got the idea from Kris Kross who told me where his picture and ashes were representing. There's a lot of gays, club promoters, alcoholics, firemen and Asians who have their ashes, urns, and knick knacks on display for eternity up there at Anza and Arguello, and soon my mother Lenore and I will join them, the second I can scrape up the additional $500 for our internment, and die. "Finally, a place you can afford in San Francisco" jokes the Columbarium brochure. My kind of people.

Jennifer Blowdryer

Poster by James Stark

Poster by Don Evenson

JUNE 1978

1 The Dogs
Ripper

2 The Dogs
Ripper

3 Leila & the Snakes

4 Crime
The Sleepers
Blast

5 Private Party

6 Lazor
Street Life
Amsterdam

7 Sleepers
Assassins
Death Army

8 Gary Valentine

9 The Readymades
Gary Valentine

10 The Cramps
Permanent Wave
The Offs

11 The Cramps
UXA

12 Rank & File
Legs
Pox

13 Seizure
The Beans
Tommy

14 Psychotic Pine
apple

15 Street Punks
F-Word
Flesh Eaters

16 F-Word
Flesh Eaters

17 The Dils
F-Word
Flesh Eaters

19 The Mutants
Crisspy Baby
Max Trash
6 O'Clock News

20 Tuxedo Moon
Nick Gravenites
Requiem

21 Roger Carroll
The Imposters
The Brains

'Nazi,' 15, Kills Schoolmate Over Taunt

Roger E. Needham
AP Wirephoto

oster by Anomymous

58

22　The Avengers
　　The Dils
　　The Mutants

23　The Avengers
　　The Liars
　　Seizure

24　Crime
　　DV-8
　　Nuclear Valdez

25　The Screamers
　　Street Punks
　　The Offs

26　The Screamers
　　The Mutants
　　The Offs
　　Avante Garde

27　Fast Floyd
　　Seizure
　　The Strays

28　Neon
　　Blast
　　Sharp

29　Permanent Wave
　　The Sleepers
　　U.X.A

30　Alley Cats
　　The Bags
　　The Consumers

JULY 1978

1　Alley Cats
　　The Sleepers
　　The Consumers

2　Benefit: Private
　　Space
　　Shuttle Flight

Poster by John Seabury

3　The Nuns
　　The Hitmakers

4　Suicide Com-
　　mand
　　The Readymades
　　The Liars

5　Suicide Command
　　The Readymades
　　Novak

6　Rage
　　Roxy

7　Kid Courage
　　The Brains
　　Sharp

8　The Marbels
　　The Dils

9　The Weirdos
　　Marbels
　　Death Army

10　The Weirdos
　　UXA
　　Negative Trend

Poster by Don Evenson

11　Ray Campi & the
　　Rockabilly Rebels

12　Roger Carroll
　　Tommy & the Spies

13　The Sleepers
　　Fear

　　The Stags

14　The Mutants
　　Fear
　　Seizure

15　The Screamers
　　Snot Puppies

Oh lord where does one begin. For me it isn't stories so much as images. Dirk had more presence than most the bands that crossed his stage. More character and probably more guts. All the impressions I have are less than stories or vignettes and so much more. It was his love that, in the end, sticks out so much more. I don't think I know too many people that cared more and did it with what actually amounted to a lesser use of ego. Dirk really wanted you to be your best and to be truly honest. Entertaining too if possible.

The images that stick out the most are not the ones that others would mention. Not Dirk on stage, although he completely owned it, not at the front (or back) door where he controlled access and maintained a semblance of democracy, not on the sidewalk where he'd mingle with the wide range of people - cops, street punks, movie and rock stars, the sheriff, passersby, regular club goers, and want to be Mab performers. No, what remains fresh is the small quiet moments where he'd let his mask down and honestly and kindly tell what he thought of your band and it's performance. He'd share years of wisdom of stage craft and promotion. But he usually shared that only with those who he thought were going to be receptive and open. He knew the difference between art and pretense, even though on stage he'd mix the two.

We still love him and miss him dearly.

John VKTM

■■■■■■■■■■■■■■■■■■■■■■■■■■■■■■■■■■■■■

Here's a copy of a note I sent Kathy Peck
at the time of Dirk's passing:

I had a nodding acquaintance with Dirk through my associations with Freaky Ralph Eno, the Pointless Sisters, and Rick & Ruby, but I only played the Mab once, with Theee STUPEDS. Dirk paid me $14, which I had to split five ways with the rest of the band.

(If I were telling this story at today's memorial, at this point I would have tossed a handful of bills in the air and said "I wish I could say that evens the score, but it doesn't come close. For one thing, it's only five bucks.")

Up until the moment he gave me the money, I had only known Dirk in his stage persona; it was at that moment, when he gave me the money without a shred of apology but at the same time with exquisite sympathy, that I realized the asshole was just an act, and the real Dirk was a smart, wise, warm human being. And that second impression has lasted with me for the next 25 years.

He's always been kind to me, greeted me warmly, tossed gigs my way when he could, commiserated with me when he couldn't, and — especially since his heart operation — shown me a vulnerable side that couldn't have been more alien from the asshole image.

In reflecting on him after his death, it finally — finally! — dawns on me that Dirk was an early progenitor of performance art. In 1980 I thought to be in show biz you had to pigeonhole yourself into a pre-formed mold: actor, singer, bass player, cellist. Andy Kaufman got away with what he did by billing himself as a comedian. There was no category of "punk rock promoter slash insulting master of ceremonies". I couldn't see Dirk's art, so I dismissed it as a personality defect.

I realize now that it was his own artistry that enabled him to see the artistry in other kindred spirits: Ralph, Jane Dornacker, Rick & Ruby, and — I'm proud and humble to report — me. In my checkered career I've received many compliments, most of them well-intentioned, but most of them missing their mark: I simply can't hear the words "You're such a good piano player" without thinking of all the myriad pianists who are light-years beyond me. But Dirk's acceptance and respect meant the world to me, and played no small part in giving me the confidence to keep at it, and I know I'm not the only one who could say that. He gave a lot of musicians a venue, but he gave a lot of other artists courage and inspiration as well.

Here's the $14 I owe him, plus a little something for yourself. Keep up the good work.

Very best wishes, jraoul

■■■■■■■■■■■■■■■■■■■■■■■■■■■■■■■■■■■

In 2007, I saw Dirk for the last time. He was announcing the Contractions and Los Microwaves maybe a month before he died. He looked thinner, greyer, but in many ways exactly the same. It brought back a lot of memories of his battery acid wit. Even now, he was brutal, really nasty about Los Microwaves. I liked Los Microwaves, remembering their hit 45 "East Coast/West Coast," which really summed up how a lot of us felt at the time - trying to decide whether to migrate to NYC or not… So Dirk's aesthetic completely mystified me. He was a business man, but he genuinely liked certain acts. You could be a industrial band, a punk band, it defied any category. It never seemed to have any logic.

Marc Olmsted, lead singer of the Job

■■■■■■■■■■■■■■■■■■■■■■■■■■■■■■■■■■

You know, he always had an idea for his band introductions. Once my band the Expressions was waiting to go on. We were a six piece and Dirk came upstairs to the Mab's dressing room with a beer six package with 6 glasses of red wine where the beer would be. We drank the wine before going on and as we came out he said 'they've been upstairs getting drunk and now here they are to entertain the likes of you.' And when my trio Peter Bilt first played he said, 'they've been studying at the music conservatory for the last three years and now they're about to cast pearls before you swine.'

peter bilt
peter dunne, senior producer, antenna audio inc.

16 The Screamers
Middle Class
Snot Puppies

17 Middle Class
6 O'Clock News
Max Trash and
Avante Garde

18 Psychotic Pine-
apple
No Sisters
Roxy

19 The Offs
DV-8
Negative Trend
Dead Kennedys

20 Leila & the Snakes
The Mutants
Lucky Stiffs

21 The Avengers
The Dils
Negative Trend

22 UXA
Man Ka Zam
Seizure

23 The Deadbeats
Man Ka Zam
The Assassins
The Gourds

24 The Deadbeats
Fast Floyd
Amsterdam

25 Neon
Seizure
The Imposters

26 Kid Courage
The Liars
DV-8

27 Crime
The Hitmakers
Blank

28 Crime

The Offs
The Hitmakers

29 Leila & the
Snakes

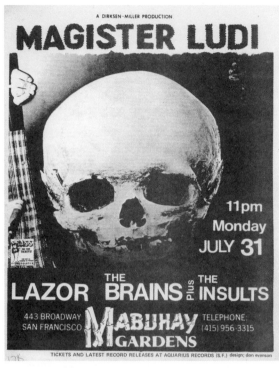

Poster by Don Evenson

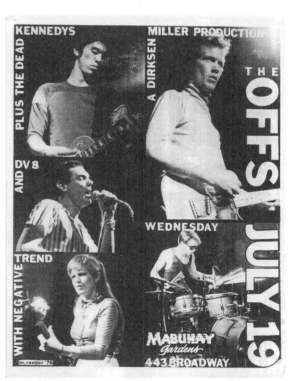

Poster by M Ranger

No Sisters
Neon

30 Avengers
Crisspy Baby
Sleepers

31 Magister Ludi
Lazor
The Brains
The Insults

AUGUST 1978

3 The Weirdos

4 The Weirdos

6 China's Comidos
Kids
Seizure
The Assassins

7 Kids
Sharp
Blast
6 O' Clock News

8 Magister Ludi
The Strays
The Beans

9 The Drains
The Imposters
DV-8

10 Leila & the Snakes
Messiah
X-Ray Ted

11 D.O.A.
ROXZ
Novak

12 Avengers
D.O.A.
The Insults

Poster by Roger Reyes

Poster by Don Evenson

13 **The Offs**
   Dead Kennedys
   Ivy & the Eaters

14 **No Sisters**
   Crisspy Baby
   Teenage Fakes
   Sass
   Blow-Up

15 **Ray Campi & the**
   Rockabilly Rebels
   Roy Loney Band

16 **Rage**
   Dread Scott
   Blow-Up

17 **The Dils**
   The Offs
   Dread Scott

18 **Kid Courage**
   Blow-Up
   The Lewd

19 **Avengers**
   UXA
   The Lewd

20 **The Zeros**
   The Deadbeats
   The Sleepers

21 **DV-8**
   The Zeros
   Flesh Eaters
   The Undersongs

22 **Avengers**
   Negative Trend
   +Flesh Eaters

23 **Psychotic**
   Pineapple
   Imposters
   Lucky Stiffs

24 **Seizure**
   Alleycats
   Blitz

25 **Zippers**
   Alleycats
   The Offs

26 **Leila & the Snakes**
   Zippers
   No Sisters

27 **Tuxedo Moon**
   The Drains
   Timmy

28 **The Dils**
   Negative Trend

29 **Neon**
   ROXZ
   The Hitmakers

30 **Kid Courage**
   Contraband
   Death Army

31 **Crime**
   Novak
   Seizure

SEPTEMBER 1978

1 **Crime**
  The Offs
  Dead Kennedys

2 **The Mutants**
  Yoel
  Dead Kennedys

3 **The Readymades**
  The Imposters
  Novak

4 **The Dils**
  The Mutants, Yoel
  Dead Kennedys,
  Snuky

5 **Leila & the Snakes**
  Rootes of Rasta
  Blair (?) Miller

6 **The Offs**
  Negative Trend
  X-Ray Ted

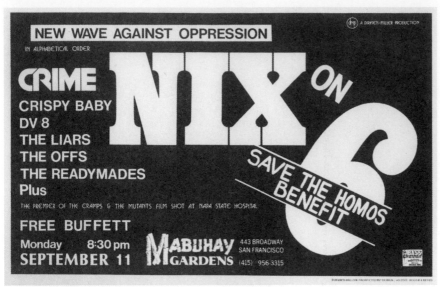

NEW WAVE AGAINST OPPRESSION

IN ALPHABETICAL ORDER

CRIME
CRISPY BABY
DV 8
THE LIARS
THE OFFS
THE READYMADES
Plus

NIX ON **6**

SAVE THE HOMOS BENEFIT

THE PREMIER OF THE CRAMPS & THE MUTANTS FILM SHOT AT NAPA STATE HOSPITAL

FREE BUFFETT
Monday   8:30 pm
SEPTEMBER 11

MABUHAY GARDENS
443 BROADWAY
SAN FRANCISCO
(415) 956-3315

A DIRKSEN-MILLER PRODUCTION

Poster by Roger Eeyes

12 **The Dils**
    The Middle Class
    Negative Trend

13 **Leila & the Snakes**
    The Middle Class
    Roy Loney

14 **The Dickies**
    ROXZ
    Novak

15 **The Dickies**
    Fear and Sharp

Poster by Anomymous

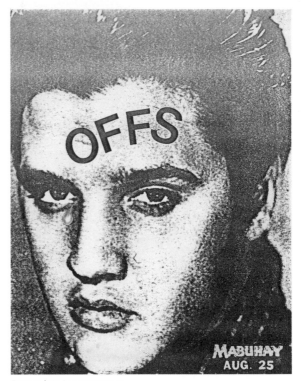

Poster by Anomymous

7   **Weirdos**
    Yoel
    MX-80 Sound
    No Sisters

8   **Weirdos**
    Yoel
    Negative Trend
    Crispy Baby

9   **The Avengers**
    "X"
    MX-80 Sound

10 **The Avengers**
    "X"
    TBA

11 **Nix on 6**
    Crime,

Crispy Baby
The Dils, DV-8,
The Offs, The
Liars
The Readymades
Plus the pre-
miere
of The Cramps &
the Mutants film

16 **Dead Kennedys**
    The Dogs and Fear
    Bobby Gonzales

17 **The Dogs**
    Kid Courage
    The Strays

18 **The Assassins**

with the **ZEROS** & the **FLESHEATERS**
MON. AUG. 21 MABUHAY Gardens
443 Broadway San Francisco
956-3315

Poster by Anomymous

THE NUNS

OCTOBER 20 1978 – OCTOBER 21 1978
Friday   saturday
Imposters   MUTANTS
   WITH   WITH
Olga's Group   No Sisters
            11pm

443 BROADWAY
SAN FRANCISCO
(415) 956-3315
MABUHAY GARDENS

Poster by Roger Reyes

Fast Floyd and
Sharp
The Beans

19 The Heartbreak-
ers
with Johnny
Thunder
DV8
The Liars

20 The Heartbreak-
ers
with Johnny
Thunder
The Imposters
Seizure

21 Roy Loney
Roxz
Bomb Squad

22 The Enemy
The Telepaths
The Mutants

23 Seattle Bird Night
The Enemy
The Telepaths
Dead Kennedys

24 Psychotic Pin-
apple
Dred Scott and
Timmy
Teenage Fakes

25 Birthday Party for
Roxz
Dorian & the De
mons
Trixx
DNA

26 Neon
Dread Scott
Blast

27 Negative Trend
The Plugz
The Lucky Stiffs

28 The Dils
The Plugz
Dead Kennedys

29 The Readymades
The Alley Cats
Ivy & the Eaters

30 Leila & the Snakes
No Sisters
Dorian & the De-
mons

OCTOBER 1978

1 The Mutants
The Alleycats
Young Adults

2 Full Hand
The Liars
Baby Murphy

3 Special Party

4 The Offs
Seizure
JJ 180

5 The Weirdos
Dead Kennedys
The Feederz

6 The Weirdos
The Feederz
Novak

7 Crime
Novak
The Clergymen

8 Zippers
Sharp
The Clergymen

9 Benefit

10 Fast Floyd
MX 80 Sound
The Beans
D.N.A.

bates motel

checked in	checked out
X Oct. 27	
X Oct. 28	

NESS AQUINO's
MABUHAY
Gardens
443 Broadway • San Francisco • 956-3315

Poster by OSTROM

Poster by Anomymous

Poster by Anomymous

11 The Imposters
Psychotic Pineapple
Rockamatics

12 The Liars
Neon
Young Adults

13 The Offs
Coil Head

14 The Mutants

D.O.A.
Yoel

15 D.O.A.
Novak
J.J.180

16 Benefit for Proposition W
Stigma

17 Flight 182
Seizure
Blast

18 Honolulu Dogs
Rage
No Thanks

19 No Sisters
MX-80 Sound
Crisspy Baby

20 The Nuns
The Mutants
Olga's Group
Bay Area Outrageous
Beauty Pageant

21 The Nuns
The Imposters
No Sisters
William Talen

22 Dead Kennedys
Young Adults

23 Sharp
Ivey & the Eaters
The Doktors
The Greek$

24 X-Ray Ted
Skin
The Natives

25 Thrust

26 The Plugz
Roy Loney &
the Lucky Stiffs

27 The Liars
The Plugz
Bates Motel

28 William Talen
Saxophone Yogi-
Psychotic Pine
apple
Bates Motel
On The Rag

29 Shock
The Zeros
The Angry Samoans

30 Shock
DNA
The Insults
Eye Protection

31 Crime
Pearl Harbor &
the Explosions
Dead Kennedys
Brittley Black's
Next

NOVEMBER 1978

1 Sharp
Rage
No Thanks

2 Seizure

3 The Nuns

4 The Nuns

5 Psychotic Pine-
apple
Brainiacs
Thrust

6 The Liars
Lucky Stiffs
Mannequin
Doktors

7 Roxz
Kick
DNA

8 Controllers
Assassins
Snuky

9 Controllers

10 Rockabilly Rebels
 The Imposters
 Neon

11 Rockabilly Rebels
 Roy Loney
 Seizure

12 Controllers
 Fast Floyd
 Eye Protection
 Complete Un-
 knowns

13 X-Ray Ted
 Whoremones
 The Geeks

14 Benefit for Stolen
 Equipment of UXA
 Billy & Lynwood
 (ex-UXA)
 New Bandand
 Negative Trend
 Red Products
 Brittley Black's
 Next
 VS.

15 No Sisters
 The Cramps
 MX-80 Sound

16 The Cramps
 Alleycats
 Rocomatics

17 Avengers
 Alleycats
 Red Products

18 Avengers
 Zeros
 VS.

19 Pearl Harbor & the
 Explosions

Poster by Anomymous

MX-80 Sound
 Highway
 Blair Miller

20 Video & Film Night

21 Blow Up
 Crisspy Baby
 Ivey & the Eaters

22 Dead Kennedys
 Blow Up
 Sub Humans

23 Sub Humans
 Assassins
 Whoremones
 Blair Miller

24 The Mutants
 Sub Humans
 On the Rag
 The Situations

25 The Readymades
 S.V.T.
 Holly & the Ital-
 ians

26 No Sisters
 The Beans
 Undersongs
 Ruby Zebra

27 Snuky Tate's
 Great
 Rebate Benefit
 Billy & Lynwood
 Neon
 Brittley Black's
 Next
 Dead Kennedys
 Eye Protection

28 The Avengers
 Pearl Harbor &
 the Explosions
 Tree

29 KPOO Radio
 Benefit
 Seizure
 Fast Floyd
 The Kick
 KGB
 The Nubs
 The Undersongs

30 The Zeros
 JJ 180
 Mannequin

DECEMBER 1978

1 Flight
 The Offs
 The Liars

2 The Mutants
 Dead Kennedy's
 KGB

3 Contraband
 PBX
 The Doktors
 The Undersongs

4 & 5 Benefit for SF
 Art Institute

6 Tuxedo Moon
 The Humans
 The Beans

7 Pearl Harbor
 & the Explosions

Poster by Leo Zulueta

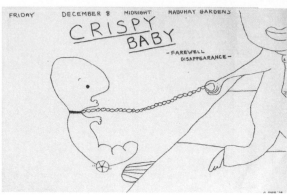

Poster by Anomymous

Roy Loney
& the Rockin' "Z"s
The Imposters

8 Crime
Crispy Baby
VS

9 Crime
The Next
Eye Protection

10 Sharp
Contraband
Blast
The Insults and
Clone

11 Fast Floyd
Blitz
The Complete

Unknowns
The Blitz and
Snuky Tate

12 Honolulu Doggs
Stu Blank Band
Felix The Cat

13 The Runz
The Mondellos

14 Mary Monday

15 The Offs
Dead Kennedys

16 The Readymades
Roy Loney & the
Rockin' 'Z's
X-Ray Ted

17 Vain
Ivy & the Eaters
The Kick

18 Vain
Neon
Big Wow
Glass
Sir.Vivor

19 Seizure
The Mutants
X-Ray Ted
The Untanglers

20 Naomi Ruth
Eisenberg Band
Psychotic Pine-
apple
Don Oliver &
Frenz

21 Rocket Produc
tions
Founding Party

22 SVT
No Sisters
JJ 180

23 The Zippers
Flight
KGB

24 Tuxedo Moon
The Kick

25 Free Christmas
Party

26 Lazar
SAV
The Haze
The Untanglers

27 The Next
The Liars
Novak
Bay Area Outra-
geous Beauty
Pageant

28 The Imposters
Holly & the Italians
Gypsy Dream

29 Premier
Mr. Wonderful
Holly & the Italians

30 The Avengers
The Controllers
The Situations

31 New Year's
Spectacular
VIPs

Translator moved from LA to get away from the music biz (and ironically were signed to 415 a few months later) and 'cause we'd heard from friends that what we were doing might be well received in SF. I don't remember how, but we landed a gig at the Mab very soon after arriving in SF. Our music, which was certainly loud and aggressively played, was more melodic and Beatle-y than was typical at the Mab in 1980, and though the song were short, they often had pretty weird psychedelic bits in the middle. Anyway, I remember that a very punk band played right before us and the kids were going nuts for it – we looked at each other and said 'crap, we're gonna get killed'… but we just got up and played our stuff. Though I remember one kid shouting at Larry "cut your hair," we went over really well. I think just the fact that we unapologetically played our songs and were very 'in your face' about it got us some respect. We even played a ballad ('The End of Their Love') which morphed at the end into a fast, hard version of 'She's Leaving Home.' There was a mosh pit during it…

Then Dirk got up and said "Ok people…in case you missed it, those guys sang in HARMONY. Take a lesson!" Then he told us we could come back any time we wanted. Eventually, years later, we'd played at the Mab and On Broadway so much he called us 'the house band.'

We were all so damn lucky to have had Dirk to give us a place to be. Loved the guy.

Dave Scheff, For Translator (Steve Barton, Larry Dekker, Robert Darlington and me)

■■■■■■■■■■■■■■■■■■■■■■■■■■■■■■■■■■■■■■

We kept playing these grinding weeknight gigs at the Mab. I'm not sure Dirk even noticed us. There are only so many of those a working band can play and stay together. After 3 of these, we stopped booking there.

The best gig at the Mab we ever had was a few years later opening for My Sin at an all-ages show. My Sin has just had a big write-up in the Pink Section* and looked like he (a one-man synth act) was going to make it big. But our guitarist thought an all-ages show was lame and to prove it, went to score heroin. He showed up in the middle of our set, walked up on stage and plugged in. Gary [Schwantes, the sax & keyboard player] was so disgusted he quit and the band collapsed. So the Job officially died at the Mab. We never played again until Gary's 50th birthday party nearly 20 years later.

Marc Olmsted, lLad Singer with Tom Latta, Bass. Photo by KameraZ

Marc Olmsted, lead singer of the Job

The Mabuhay Gardens was a Filipino restaurant at the far end of the Strip. They usually hosted supper club acts for their diners and every now and then we'd go there to see local performers like the Leila and the Snakes (which featured the uniquely wonderful Jane Dornacker) and comedians Rick & Ruby. The food was not so special and the wine was like kool-aid spiked with break fluid but we were there for the acts, not the cuisine or the atmosphere.

Once Dirk Dirksen began hosing regular nights with some very odd acts the doors were flung wide open for Punk and there was no turning back. Dirk managed to pull off staging acts there at the Mabuhay Gardens that were life-changing events. He truly did change the culture of San Francisco, ushering in a "Brave New World" for our local scene, showcasing bands that would probably never get a chance to perform before the insane crowds of raggedy-assed punks and other flotsam and jetsam, testing their "talents" against other local low-life bands and having a blast while doing it.

Winston Smith at Dirk Fest, 2008 Photo by James Stark

Regardless of who was performing, most nights at the Mabuhay were full of rollicking fun and impromptu insanity. As crowded and jammed as it could sometimes get I recall being there for some shows where their were more people on stage in the band (Mutants, Tragic Mulatto, and others) than there were people in the audience. Nevertheless, the show always went on. And Dirk was the mastermind behind it all.

Later when he moved the show up stairs at the On Broadway, the stage got bigger and the bar got longer. There was even a somewhat plush "salon" room and a slightly abbreviated balcony. As with the Mab, the "plumbing facilities" were not always up to most 20th century standards and the less time you had to spend in them the better. A couple years after that the On Broadway closed and most punk bands wanting to perform in North Beach wound up at The Stone, directly across the street. For me it was an especially satisfying era since I never had two pennies to rub together and, thanks to Dirk and the thoughtful members of now long-disappeared bands, I never had to pay to get into any of the shows. (I reckon that Dirk figured the more money left in my pocket the more I would spend at the bar and that's where the club really made money).

Dirk continued to produce punk and underground shows throughout the City for years and, as always, he would take people under his wing and help to foster their careers as artists and performers. For this, all of us are grateful, since without his care and kindness many of us wouldn't have much to even call "careers". And Dirk didn't help people because he thought they were going to be the next big thing or that their unique vision should be marketed to the world, he helped people that he knew were probably not going to ever launch a serious career or wind up devoting their lives to one cause or the other—he did it to help us realize our full potential and find a certain direction in our lives. And many people Dirk worked to help out had little or nothing to do with the Punk scene or Underground art. He was doing this just to be a pal and just to pass on help and advice. Dirk was one of the most sincerely "giving" individuals I've ever known. Most of us didn't deserve his kindness and help. (And he knew that. But he gave it anyway).

I was first introduced to Dirk when Biafra and I dropped by his place on California Street back around 1980 or so. The moment we met and Biafra explained that I was the artist for the Dead Kennedy albums (and had been responsible for the numerous "Fake Band Flyers" which Dirk had been wondering about for a while), Dirk turned and selected a book from his library shelf and handed it to me to check out. In the next moment I was pouring over this very large book all about poster art (incredible works from to Andy Warhol, etc.). Biafra made some puzzled remark questioning why Dirk would show me that book since it had nothing to do with punk rock. Dirk said, "Well, since Winston's an artist and obviously interested in poster art I was pretty sure he'd appreciate having a look at the work in this book". At that moment I knew the man understood me, artist to artist.

In that moment we formed a friendship that became a bond that only grew stronger over time. Dirk often helped me out in many ways over the years but his help was especially appreciated in the early 1990's when he offered to help me prepare my first book as a portfolio of my artwork. Dirk kindly offered to propose the project to Ron Turner of Last Gasp of San Francisco, well known publisher of underground comics and bizarre art books. Ron and I had talked about doing a book for years but not until Dirk took over actually organizing it did it ever happen. Dirk also wrote the foreword to the book. He refused any offer of payment. I was overwhelmed.

Thanks to Dirk believing in my artwork my work was seen by many more people than I could ever have personally reached (and seen by even more people who might see my work only on a few record covers). A book presented profoundly expanded opportunities for me as an artist to not only display my artwork but also to secure commissions from magazines and record company art departments for illustrations and album cover art. I had no idea how important this would be for me, but Dirk knew.

Dirk saw it as a project he was taking on and to see to it that I wouldn't completely blow it by being my usual, lazy, unmotivated self, prone to dissipating my energies and wasting my time (something he knew that I was very good at). Instead, Dirk insisted that I focus my energies and schedule my time to sort through my work and make the selections that would successfully contribute to the project.

I have never been a "Morning Person". My personal chrono-biology is tuned to Hong Kong time. I have always been a night owl and most of my best collage work has been created between 11 p.m. and 5 a.m.. I don't know, maybe I was a vampire in a former life, but getting up before noon for me is like a pre-dawn raid. It takes me hours to come to and even then it's hours later before my creative juices start flowing. When I lived in a tiny 5' by 10' room near the top of Telegraph Hill Dirk would sometimes call me up in the morning, saying, "Good Morning, Winnie! I'm going to work to-day. What are you doing?"

Well, that was usually enough for me to drag my sorry ass out of bed and get on the ball. The guilt trip alone was a good motivational technique. Dirk would also prod me into meeting with him at Suzanne Stefanic's house to scan each page that I had laid out by hand, gluing all pictures and page numbers to cardboard. At that time no computers were used to do the layout except for Suzanne typing up what I'd write and printing it out. Then I would cut it out and paste it up under one of my pictures. This was only barely more high tech than Guttenberg but it did do the trick.

Dirk often took us for trips up to Sonoma for pleasant visits to the country and along the way he would tell us wild and wooly tales of his adventures. He also took me up to the village of Mendocino to introduce me to galleries and friends, several of whom have remained good friends over the years. He even helped arrange a couple of shows for my work in some very classy galleries that I could have never otherwise done work with. Dirk and Damon also taped me for interviews on his television show and advertised my first book continuously. His advise on both personal and private issues was invaluable to me, as I am sure many friends and colleagues could say. Dirk's friendship, generosity and respect was among my most cherished honors and I know that there are numerous others who feel the same way.

One time Dirk was there with us and he happened to mention that he was German and that he was actually born in Berlin. Then he told me one of the most amazing stories I'd ever heard from anyone. He told me that during the 1930s his folks detested Hitler and what he was doing to Germany and planning for the rest of Europe. He said they tried to leave the country a couple times but were stopped because his dad was a physicist and the Nazis wanted him to work on their Atomic research programme to develop a bomb. Though Dirk was only a wee lad during the War he recalled that Himmler and other top Nazi officials visited their home for dinner on several occasions.

The best part was that Dirk said his father's scientific team would make breakthroughs in their research and his father would deliberately steer them into dead-ends so their research would be continuously delayed, thus preventing Hitler from getting the Bomb before the U.S. did. Lots of countries were working on it, even the Imperial Japanese. It was a race, and the best thing Dirk's father could do was to interfere with the Nazis' plans as much as he could. In effect, Dirk's father was one of the unsung heros of the War.

After the Soviets bombed Berlin and the U.S. and Soviet occupation forces were fighting over who would get the top scientists Dirk and his sister and folks were able to emigrate to America. The U.S. officials told Dirk's mother that she had no idea how many times the Nazis were on the brink of sending them all off to a death camp since they knew that they were not supporters of the Third Reich. They said, "Madam, do you realize how close you came to having your entire family sent off to a labor camp because of all the things you said over the telefone?" She had no idea that the SS were tapping all their fone calls due to Dirk's dad being in a high security position and would routinely make remarks about what a disaster Hitler was for Germany and how he should be stopped, etc… Dirk postulated that had his dad's research team ever actually made it to their goal the Gestapo would have dispensed with them as soon as possible. They would have been of no further use to the Reich.

Biafra and I were talking about this once and it occurred to us that Hitler's police state tactics were probably a major influence on Dirk's consciousness and social awareness and helped create in him an aversion to such horrors, and that this may have contributed to Dirk becoming an ardent supporter of Free Speech and the Arts. So, as we figured it, Hitler and his thugs were inadvertently responsible for fostering the underground art scene and Punk movement in San Francisco. Hitler would be spinning in his grave!! This was truly sublime poetic justice!

Winston Smith

Even when he was doing his most insolent, brazen, disdainful "routine"—and it WAS a routine, because Dirk, away from the Mabuhay was one of the sweetest, nicest guys you could ever meet—he showed me and my band, The Nuns, great respect and reverence. After all, to get down to brass tacks, if not for The Nuns punk would never have reached San Francisco as quickly and he and Ness would not have had such a wide window of opportunity. Did Dirk show any favoritism to The Nuns? Hell, yes. Like I said, if not for them (and, let us not forget, Mary Monday) the venue would've perhaps remained as a restaurant with a Filipino Elvis

impersonator. Dirk was there for us, though. In many ways, at many times. When Jane Dornacker (Leila & The Snakes) died in a helicopter crash over New York City (tragically, she died live on the radio), it was Dirk who jumped in with Bill Graham to do a benefit concert. In the famed Friday the 13 poster (see page 23), that's Dirk peeking over the toilet stall.

Edwin Heaven with Nuns Jeff and Al.
Photo by James Stark

He called now and then to tell me his plans for a Punk Rock Festival (even though, as I told him, the word "festival" and "punk" was an oxymoron) and how much he want to put the original Nuns on stage. (Alejandro Escovedo, who is now managed by Jon Landau, Bruce Springsteen's manager, wanted to move forward not backwards, so the original Nuns would never truly reunite; at least not without Al.) Here's a nice little story: when The Nuns were thrown off the bill with Blondie at the Old Waldorf when Michael Kowaski did something to tick off Deborah Harry. I told the owner (Jeffery Pollack) that the guy is not a part of The Nuns, he was just a fan. Didn't matter, next night we were off the bill—even though I had purchased an outdoor billboard across from the Fab Mab advertising The Nuns at this venue. So, I called Dirk, told him The Nuns wanted to do a free show the next night. Dirk said yeah, and Rabbit Jones (RIP) and I climbed the billboard and with red spray paint wrote TO HELL WITH in front of the words THE OLD WALDORF ... and then, below that, a long arrow pointing across the street with the words: FREE CONCERT AT MABUHAY. A photo wound up in the Chronicle the next day along with a blurb in Joel Selvin's column (with our side of the story) and that night a thousand fans lined up Broadway and down Kearny Street, many of whom were turned away. That night at Mr. Pollack's club (which is now The Punch Line), only a handful of people showed up to see Blondie. End of story. (Except a few months later Iggy Pop was playing The Old Waldorf and he had crashed at my apartment on Kearny Street a couple nights and wanted me to go to his show and I told him I was 86'd and he said show up at 8 PM and there was a line outside waiting for the 10 PM show as Ig came out in nothing but black brief's, combat boots, battle helmet, body makeup to accentuate his Yoga muscle tone definition, and marched me right past the owner, who was doing a slow-burn.)

Oh, one more thing. Once Dirk loaned me a gun to use in a short (which I wrote, directed and played a sleazy cop) called Film Noir.

It was a starter gun. Go figure.

Edwin Heaven

Poster by Punk Globe

Poster by Anomymous

JANUARY 1979

1 **KGB**
   Complete Un-
   knowns
   VKTMS
   Ruby Zebra

2 **The Assassins**
   The Situations
   Alex the Cat

3 **Mary Monday**
   MX-80 Sound
   Eye Protection

4 **Honolulu Doggs**
   I Scream
   The Clones
   Nephron
   Fly Babies
   Torque

5 **Kid Courage**
   The Kick
   The Mannequins

6 **Rox**
   Sharp
   Pearlie Gates
   The Imposters

7 **Stray Cats**
   Thrust

8 **Fast Floyd**
   Throw Money
   Beans

9 **Sharp**
   Noise
   Ear Rush

10 **Avaunte Guarde**
   Stars in Paradise
   The Humans
   Blitz

11 **Tuxedo Moon**
   KGB
   Situations

12 **The Offs**

The Mutants
Axzum

13 **Flight**
   Skin
   Mary Monday

14 **Skin**
   MX 80 Sound
   Beans

15 **KGB**
   The Eaters
   Blitz
   Lucky Stiffs
   Hyway

16 **Benefit for the**
   Harvey Milk
   United Fund
   VIPs
   Situations
   SVT
   On The Rag
   KGB

17 **Pearl Harbor & the**
   Explosions
   The Runz
   The Bandaloons

18 **The Kick**
   Mile Hi
   Alley Cats
   Beans

19 **Dead Kennedys**
   The Next
   Alley Cats

20 **Seizure**
   Shock
   Mr. Wonderful

21 **The Alleycats**
   Eye Protection
   Shock

22 **Punk Globe Benefit**
   KGB
   Lady LaRu
   Crime

Poster by Anomymous

Poster by Anomymous

Eye Protection
Bill Fold & Loose
Change
Bambi & Gloria
Pristine Condition

23 **The Symptoms**
Alex the Cat
Thrust

24 **Novak**
The Beans
The Mannequins

25 **VIPs**
The Situations
VKTMS

26 **The Readymades**
Aurora Pushups
The Crawdaddies

27 **Roy Loney & the**
Phantom Movers
Tuxedo Moon
Natasha

28 **The Next**
Crawdaddies
Public Enemies
The Rotters

29 **The Beans**
Whoremones
The Situations

Complete Un-
knowns

30 **Gypsy Dream**
Rage
Avalon Boulevard

31 **Contraband**
The Noize
Ivy & the Eaters

FEBRUARY 1979

1 **The Mutants**
KGB

2 **Crime**
The Situations
VKTMS

3 **Mabuhay Legal**
Defense Fund
Benefit
The Offs
Dead Kennedys
Push Ups

4 **Push Ups**
Ivy & the Eaters
The Mannequins

5 **Assassins**
Golden Dragon
Lady La Rue

MX-80 Sound
The Stigmas

6 **Debutantes &**
Delinquents Ball
The Situations
VS.
Noh Mercy (for-
merly On The
Rag)

7 **Novak**
Kick
The Runz

8 **Mary Monday**
The Subhumans
Alex the Kat

9 **Ray Campi & the**
Rockabilly Rebels
Pearl Harbor &
the Explosions
No Sisters

10 **Ray Campi & the**
Rockabilly Rebels
Pearl Harbor &
the Explosions
Angry Samoans

11 **The Mutants**
Sub Humans
Angry Samoans

12 **KPOO FM Benefit**
Stray Cats
VKTMS
VIPs
Alex the Kat
The Symptoms
Mary Monday

13 **Sharp**
KGB
Whoremones
The Ravens

Poster by Anomymous

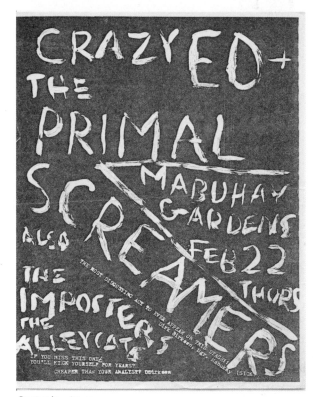

Poster by Anomymous

**14 Bay Area Outra-
geous Beauty
Pageant**

15 The Next

No Sisters
Lazar

**16 The Avengers
Count Five
Psychotic Reation**

**17 Stu Blank Band
Naomi Ruth
Eisenberg
Gypsy Dream**

**18 The Imposters
Brainiacs
KGB
Don Oliver Scott-
Frenz Jazz
Ensemble**

**19 Pearl Harbor &
the Explosions
Roy Loney & the
Phantom Movers
Mary Monday**

**20 Ivy & the Eaters
The Noise
The Symptoms**

**21 Leland
Psychotic Pine-
apple
The Blitz
Outrageous
Beauty Pageant**

**22 Crazy Ed & the
Primal Screamers
The Impostors
Alley Cats**

**23 The Offs
Alley Cats
The Bags**

**24 Dead Kennedys
VIPs
The Runz**

**25 Alley Cats
VS.
Stray Cats**

**26 Complete
Uknowns
Los Microwaves
Tales of Twisted
Romance
Requiem Mass
for Lucky Stiffs**

**27 Hyway
Push Ups
Alex the Kat**

**28 Pearl Harbor &
the Explosions
Contraband
VKTMS
Bay Area Outr-
geous Beauty
Pageant**

MARCH 1979

**1 The Mutants
Dead Kennedys
Yoel**

**2 The Readymades
Roy Loney & the
Phantom Movers**

LaRue was a three-man singer-songwriter team comprised of singer Bob Banks, rhythm guitarist Danny Sego and myself on keyboards, backed by some of the best musicians in the Bay Area, including Larry "L.C." Ellam on lead guitar, Marc Covell on drums and George "Guts" Gearhardt on bass for our Fab Mab gigs, which was our lineup on the first live recording from the Mabuhay Gardens, recorded on August 27th, 1977, engineered by Dave Towers and released on LaRue Records.

Poster by Anomymous

The mobile unit was parked in the alley outside the rear exit. The EP also featured two songs recorded at Filmways/Wally Heider Recording, and a cover photo by Pat Johnson. Liner notes state: "LaRue wishes to extend special thanx, … most of all, to Dirk B.G. Dirksen and Ness Aquino of the MABUHAY GARDENS for their cooperation and good humor."

For our shows at the Mab, we took out extra ads in the pink section and rented klieg lights and stretch limousines, with my dog, Jethro, waiting for us in the passenger seat. After we had finished playing, we would follow Dirk into the office and Danny and Banks would menacingly hover over him to claim our rightful share of the nightly receipts, a ritual I understand was not limited solely to LaRue.

The tireless efforts and encouragement of both Dirk and Ness during these years were invaluable to musicians and fans alike throughout the Bay Area. There was finally a venue for rock and roll, one which didn't charge bands for the privilege of playing and where people could go to have a good time, seven nights a week, and listen to live music, not disco. Merv was slinging the drinks and characters like "Rabbit" and a steady stream of unique security personnel and other local scenery added flavor to the venue and to the shows Dirk was presenting 24/7/366 (even Leap Years). The LaRue-Rock era ended when punk hit San Francisco, with musical genres changing almost overnight. Dirk pounced on this change and began relationships with new bands and performers, providing them with a venue to harness their energies and guaranteeing San Francisco's stature as the most important city in the world's music scene.

My new relationship as the lawyer for Dirk and the club was the equivalent of bringing order to a legal mosh pit. In addition to working with bands, I was playing more defense than Ronnie Lott.* A typical case might feature a young lady from the suburbs who, having made her pilgrimage to the City, had gotten wasted and started a brawl. After being ejected, sustaining bruises to both body and ego, she would hire an attorney and sue the bouncer, Dirk, Ness, and Does One to Ten. Fortunately, once opposing counsel had a chance to objectively assess the evening's activities, these cases would quietly disappear or settle for nuisance value.

Dirk would try to steer as much business my way as possible, and he was very instrumental in helping me develop my practice. In a way, Dirk was a benevolent despot who really wanted musicians and people he liked in the music world to succeed. For example, he spent countless hours with Jello Biafra, and was involved in everything from his mayoral campaign to forming the No More Censorship Legal Defense Fund to help raise funds to defend Biafra against an overzealous prosecutor's attempt to use a DK album insert to

"send a cost-effective message" to the arts community. Being from a family which had fled Europe due to the rise of fascism, Dirk was politically aware of oppressive forces, and was a strong supporter of liberal causes and the State of Israel.

In addition to the legal trench warfare, I collaborated with Dirk on quite a number of video and television projects, ranging from the taping of the last three nights of the On Broadway to producing a video-catalog for San Francisco Law School during which Dirk interviewed the likes of former Governor Edmund G. "Pat" Brown, Assemblyman Milton Marks and many other legal luminaries. Dirk handled these people with extraordinary skill

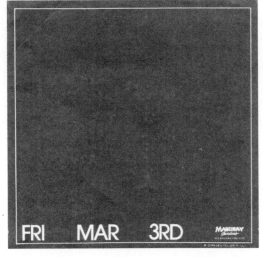

and diplomacy. Other collaborations included an instructional drum video for a client of mine, rock-drummer Bill Lordan of Robin Trower and Sly Stone fame, and a recruiting video for Dr. Bill Shapiro of the UCSF Anesthesiology Department, set to the music of "Every Breath You Take" by Sting, who generously agreed to waive fees for this worthy project. I remember Dirk, and Damon Molloy spending countless hours at the hospital, and later the studio, creating a truly remarkable product. We also produced six, half-hour "Dirk Dirksen Presents" television shows, which aired in San Francisco on Viacom 6. These shows provided an outlet for groups who couldn't get on to MTV, but who had poured a lot of sweat and money into creating some outstanding, non-establishment videos. When a project he liked came his way, you could hear the wheels churning and watch as the ideas started to flow. These projects were a welcome respite from his role as ringmaster at the Mab, and let him stretch out and enjoy himself as a producer/director.

If one person deserves credit as being the sine qua non of the non-Bill Graham music scene in San Francisco, that person is Dirk. He made the Mabuhay Gardens, and later the On Broadway, the centers of the rock, punk and the performing arts universe, and helped start and advance the careers of scores of artists. For San Francisco in its Golden Age of Rock on Broadway, he was the hardest working man in show business.

Bob Moselle

Bob Moselle was keyboardist and songwriter for LaRue, one of San Francisco's best-known rock bands in the era when Rock and Roll reigned supreme in San Francisco and at the Fab Mab, a time before punk would become the dominant musical force. After the passing of the musical torch, Bob graduated from law school and became the lawyer for Dirk, Ness, the Mabuhay Gardens, and, later, the On Broadway Theatre as well as many of the bands, including DKs, MDC, Bomb, Lethal Gospel, Y&T and individual artists from bands such as Crucifix, Flipper, Verbal Abuse and DRI.

* Hall of famer and San Francisco 49er's Football Star.

APRIL 7 saturday 11pm

2nd GENERATION

EX-AVENGERS Craig Westermark New Group

RONDOS

EX-NUNS Jennifer Miro New Group

VIPS

with mechanics

MABUHAY gardens
443 Broadway San Francisco
956-3315

Poster by Roger Reyes

Poster by Scott Ryser

3 The Readymades
The Rondos

4 The Rondos
The Spoilers
TBA

5 The Next
VS.
Blowdryers

6 Mannequins
Imposters
Big Deal

7 Naomi Ruth Eisen-
berg Band
Hyway
The Nubs

8 The Offs

The Rotters
VKTMS

9 Pearl Harbor &
the Explosions
No Sisters
Humans

10 Avengers
The Rotters
Metro

11 Ivy & the Eaters
Neighbors
Owen Maerks
Band
The Aliens

12 KPOO FM Benefit

13 Push Ups
The Undersongs
The Blitz

14 Tuxedo Moon
The Cramps
The Solution

15 VIPs
VS.
The Situations

16 Yesterday and
Today
Mile Hi
The Runz

17 The Mutants
The Cramps
Noh Mercy

18 The Cramps
VKTMS
Highway 1

19 The Beat
Daylights
Trixx
The Insults

20 Gypsy Dream
Los Microwaves
Avalon Boule--
vard

21 Tuxedo Moon
Pink Section
The Units

22 Levi & the Rock-
cats
No Sisters
6 O'Clock News

23 Crime
Levi & the Rockats
X-Ray Ted

24 Kid Courage
Mary Monday
The Sillies

25 The Sillies
The Symptoms
SSI
The Colin Lyndon
Band

26 First Semi-Annual
Musical Dog
Awards

27 Lady LaRue
Death Army

28 Mary Monday
VKTMS
Red Alert

29 Pearl Harbor & the
Explosions
The Vains
Bandaloons

30 Crime
The Vains
Contraband

31 Roy Loney & the
Phantom Movers
VIPs
Novak

APRIL 1979

1 The Next
Pearl Harbor & the
Explosions
The Push Ups
T.M. & Bink
Snort o' Madness

CRIME
LEVI AND THE ROCKCATS
X-RAY TED

©1979 SAD DREAM IMAGE

FRIDAY MAR. 23
MABUHAY GARDENS

Poster by James Stark

NEW YEARS EVE
THE NEXT
APR. 1ST

PEARL HARBOUR
AND THE EXPLOSIONS
THE PUSHUPS

A DIRKSEN-MILLER PRODUCTION
MABUHAY GARDENS
443 BROADWAY
SAN FRANCISCO

Poster by Rabbitt

2 **George & the Super Stars**
Living Daylights
SSI

3 **Los Microwaves**
The Schem, The Outfits
Bob Pittman

4 **Big Deal**
The Symptoms
3rd Wind

5 **KGB**
VS.
The Blowdryers

6 **Dead Kennedys**
The Situations
William Talen & the Edge

7 **VIPs**
Rondos
Mechanics
The Kats

8 **Rondos**
Mechanics
The Humans
The Undersongs

9 **Ivy & the Eaters**
Pressure
The Beat
Blue Cheer

10 **The Impostors**
X-Ray Ted
The Mondellos

11 **Birthday Party for Shaun of Sharp**
VKTMS
The High Beams

12 **The Go Gos**
Mary Monday
Pink Section
Bay Area Outrageous
Beauty Pageant

13 **The Mutants**
90-90s
The Runz

14 **Pearl Harbor & the Explosions**
Skin
Hyway

15 **The Magnetics**
Rockin' Horse
Bluesland Music
Mystery Spot

16 **Owen Maerks Band**
The Suspects
Big Deal
Golden Dragon
Snuky Tate

17 **Angela Bowie's The Front**
William Talen & the Edge
Tattooed Vegetbles
Zev

18 **Mr. Wonderful**
JJ 180
Alex the Kat

19 **No Sisters**
Novak
The Charmers

20 **Ray Campi & the Rockabilly Rebels**
6 O'Clock News

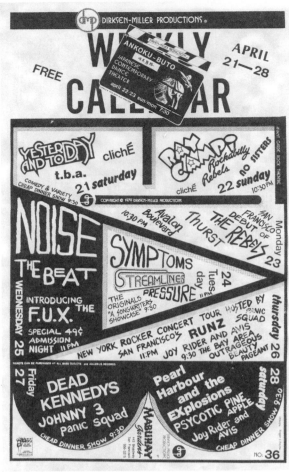

Poster by Roger Reyes

21 **Yesterday and Today**
Shakin' Street
Clichë

22 **Ray Campi & the Rockabilly Rebels**
No Sisters
Clichë

23 **The Rebels**
Thrust
Avalon Boulevard

24 **The Symptoms**
Streamliner
Pressure
The Originals, "A Songwriters Showcase"

25 **Noise**
The Beat
The F.U.X.

26 **The Runz**
Panic Squad
Joy Rider and Avis
Bay Area Outrageous Beauty Pageant

27 **Dead Kennedys**
Johnny 3
Panic Squad

28 **Pearl Harbor & the Explosions**
Psychotic Pineapple
Joy Rider and Avis

29 **Ivy & the Eaters**
Owen Maerks with the Science Patrol
The Fleshapoids

30 **Sharp**
The Stigmas
The Exploding Pintos

Poster by Anomymous

Poster by Anomymous

81

MAY 1979

1 **The Dinosaurs**
Owen Maerks &
the Science Patrol
Surface Music

2 **Lady LaRue and**
Mr. A
VKTMS
The Outfits

3 **UXA**
The Blowdryers
Pressure
Outrageous
Beauty Pageant

4 **Yesterday and**
Today
The Next
Timmy

5 **Roy Loney & the**
Phantom Movers
Psychotic Pine-
apple
The Bandaloons

6 **Shakin' Street**
Jim Carroll
Controllers
Swamp (Japa-
nese dance/
performance)

7 **Punk Globe Benefit**
Metro Police
U.X.A.
Eye Protection
VKTMS
Jah Hovah
The Blowdryers
Double Feature
Harmony, The
Kosmic Cowgirl
Swamp (Japa-

nese dance/
performance)

8 **Noh Mercy**
The Units
Pink Section
The Piccadillos

9 **Big Deal**
JJ 180
3rd Wind

10 **No Sisters**
The Charmers
The Humans

11 **Mile Hi**
Mr. Wonderful
6 O'Clock News

12 **Crime**
The Mutants
Mondellos

13 **The Next**
Mary Monday
The Push Ups
X. Dreamiest

Poster by Anomymous

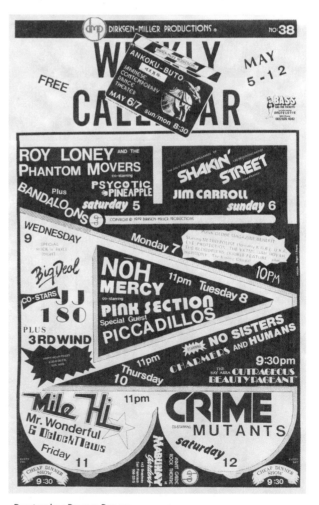

Poster by Roger Reyes

82

ELEKTRA
ASYLUM
NONESUCH
RECORDS

1/12/78

Dear Dirk—

You are an asshole!
I hope the Mabuhay Gardens
burns down with you in it!!

Very Sincerely,

Bruce Shindler

P.S. Don't ever depend on any
Warner-Elektra-Atlantic support
in the future.

962 North LaCienega Blvd., Los Angeles, California 90069 (213) 655-8280
A Division of Warner Communications Inc.

Letter From Bruce Shindler

83

Certificate of Pardon
City and County of San Francisco

To **DIRK DIRKSEN**

WHEREAS, Dirk Dirksen is known far and wide as THE POPE OF PUNK, and

WHEREAS, Dirk has been known to engage in some rather bizzare behavior such as audience torture, sexual assault on a microphone, and contributing to the delinquency of an entire generation, and

WHEREAS, Dirk has encouraged and solicited youthful rebellion, musical anarachy, mohawk haircuts, Jello for Mayor, offensive graffiti, and even staying out after curfew,

THEREFORE, BE IT NOW RESOLVED: That on the extremely sad occasion of the closing of the ON BROADWAY, Dirk Dirksen, who is sure to continue his disruptive influences in other forums, is hereby PARDONED(*) for all past and future sins, improprieties, indescretions and offending behavior.

GOOD LUCK, DIRK --- YOU'LL NEED IT!!

JUNE 16, 1984
Date

Michael Hennessey
Sheriff

(*)void where prohibited by law

84

My favorite remembrances of Dirk (apart from sending punk rockers to my City Hall office when they were in trouble) were his closing time antics at the Mabuhay. The magic hour would arrive, the band would still be playing and Dirk would bull his way to the microphone. He'd tell the band to fuck off and then yell at the crowd, "Get out, you assholes! It's two o'clock and I can't make any more money off you, so get the hell out!" Sometimes this worked and sometimes it didn't. One night, a patron, inspired no doubt by Pete Townsend and his guitar smashing finale, picked up a chair and started bashing it on the floor. Dirk leaped off the low stage, microphone in hand, and clubbed the cretin over the head with the mike. You could hear the amplified beating throughout the club. The crowd dispersed rather quickly that night. Other nights, the last band on the bill wouldn't get on stage until a few minutes before the witching hour and tried to keep playing after Dirk started his shut-down routine. Dirk would yell, "Pull the plug, pull the goddamn plug," and some henchman would find the band's electrical source and quickly transform the group into an acoustic ensemble which was about the worst thing that could happen to a punk group.

San Francisco County Sheriff Mike Hennessey

■■■■■■■■■■■■■■■■■■■■■■■■■■■■■■■■■■■■■■■

Reguarding The Pardon

And, yes, I remember giving Dirk the "Pardon." I gave it to him after the Mabuhay had been closed and he was producing shows upstairs at the "On Broadway." This was sometime in 1984. I had been going to the Fab Mab since around '77 and became friendly with Dirk and Ness Aquino. I'd usually hang around at the front door with whoever was taking admission money and sometimes venture down to the stage if it was a group I liked, like The Avengers or The Mutants or Crime. I started going to the Mab before I was Sheriff. I was a lawyer working on behalf of prisoners in the County Jail. One day I saw a poster for a group called "Crime" and thought that they must be right up my alley, so I went to the Fab Mab and fell in love with the energy and the scene. I became a regular.

So when the On Broadway announced that it was closing I decided to go to that last show and see if I could run into Dirk to give him an official "Pardon." I had printed up some blank Pardon forms several years earlier and gave them to people I liked at their retirement parties or other events. So, I typed one up for Dirk and went over to Broadway. When I got there, there was already a line out the front and around the block down Montgomery Street. I started walking up the line when I ran into Dirk who was cruising the crowd. I gave him the Pardon there on the street. It was rather unceremonious, but it was a personal gesture from me to him anyway. Please note the asterisk: "Void Where Prohibited by Law."

San Francisco County Sheriff Mike Hennessey

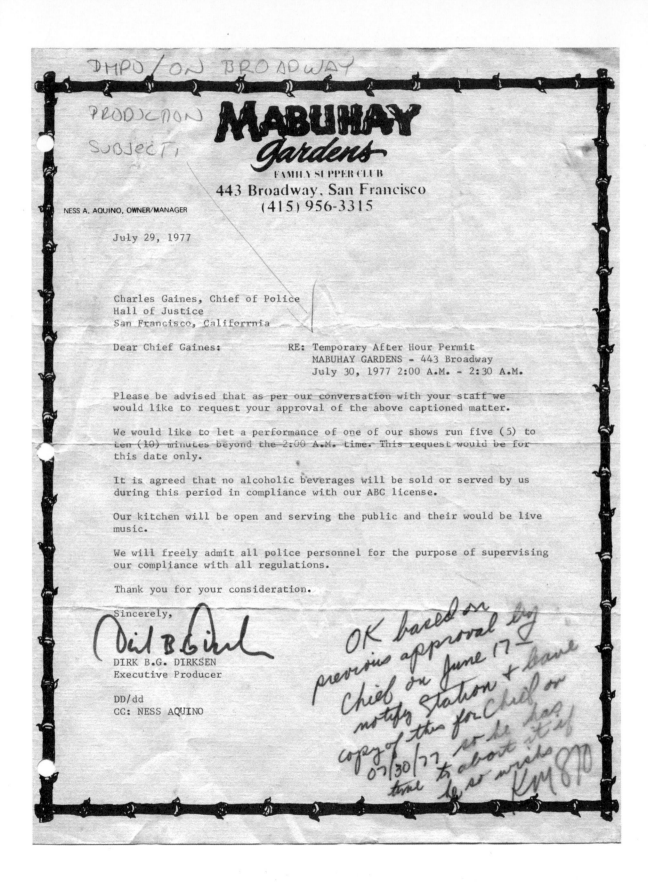

DMPU/ON BROADWAY

PRODUCTION
SUBJECT,

MABUHAY
Gardens
FAMILY SUPPER CLUB
443 Broadway, San Francisco
(415) 956-3315

NESS A. AQUINO, OWNER/MANAGER

July 29, 1977

Charles Gaines, Chief of Police
Hall of Justice
San Francisco, Califorrnia

Dear Chief Gaines: RE: Temporary After Hour Permit
                                  MABUHAY GARDENS - 443 Broadway
                                  July 30, 1977 2:00 A.M. - 2:30 A.M.

Please be advised that as per our conversation with your staff we
would like to request your approval of the above captioned matter.

We would like to let a performance of one of our shows run five (5) to
ten (10) minutes beyond the 2:00 A.M. time. This request would be for
this date only.

It is agreed that no alcoholic beverages will be sold or served by us
during this period in compliance with our ABC license.

Our kitchen will be open and serving the public and their would be live
music.

We will freely admit all police personnel for the purpose of supervising
our compliance with all regulations.

Thank you for your consideration.

Sincerely,

DIRK B.G. DIRKSEN
Executive Producer

DD/dd
CC: NESS AQUINO

OK based on
previous approval by
Chief on June 17 —
notify station + leave
copy of this for Chief on
07/30/77 so he has
time to about it if
he so wishes
KM 870

RED ITALY
A NEW FILM BY ERIC MITCHELL · STARRING ·
JENNIFER MIRO
SPECIAL LATE SHOW
THE VIPS
MAY 23, 24, 25
FILM WILL BE SHOWN AT 8:00 · VIPS AT 11:00
MABUHAY Gardens 443 Broadway
San Francisco Calif.

Poster by James Stark

Poster by Roger Reyes

14 KPOO Radio Benefit
The Noise
The Beans
Los Microwaves
JJ 180
The Beat
The Outfits

15 Pearl Harbor & the
Explosions
Big Deal
Eye Protection

16 V.S.
The Blowdriers
Pink Section

17 The Bags
The Offs
VKTMS

18 Dead Kennedys
The Bags

The Units

19 Tuxedo Moon
Noh Mercy
The Humans

20 Richie Ray
The Beans
The Beat
Don'ts

21 The Real Kids
The Sex Dogs
Lurid Tails

22 The Real Kids
6 O'Clock News
The Cinders

23 The VIPs
Eye Protection
Tatooed Vegetable

24 The VIPs
The Noise
The Hyway

25 The VIPs
No Sisters
The GoGos
The Mondellos

26 The Mutants
The GoGos
The Units

27 The GoGos
The Peccadillos
The Humans
Noh Mercy

28 Nico
Lady La Rue and
Mr. A
The Big Wow
The Suspects
The Dont's
Bob Pittman

29 The Eaters
Big Wow
Eye Protection
The Originals

30 The Symptoms
Los Microwaves
The Beat

Doug Brodoff

31 Dead Kennedys
The Push Ups
Pink Section

JUNE 1979

1 The Offs
The Mutants
Fast Floyd

2 The Offs
Pink Section
The Mummers &
Poppers

3 The Beat
Eye Protection
The Blow Dryers
The Symptoms
The Mondellos
Sharp

4 (Closed for Private
Party)

5 Lady La Rue
Legionaire's Dis-
ease
The Alter Boys

6 The Press
Big Deal

Jennifer Egan's Mabuhay Memories: "An Historically Significant Moment"
By Michael Goldberg

If back in the late '70s you had hung out at the San Francisco punk club, the Mabuhay Gardens, and, as I do, still vividly remember nights when The Avengers or Crime blew the walls out, you might, like me, have been surprised, shocked actually, to find a short story in the March 8, 2010 issue of the *New Yorker*, set, in part, at that small, gritty, graffiti-inscribed club. Shock because even during its heyday, 30-plus years earlier, the Mabuhay was mostly known to only a few thousand punks spread around the Bay Area. The story, "Ask Me If I Care," by novelist Jennifer Egan, turned up a year later, in 2011, as a chapter in her exceptional and Pulitzer winning fourth novel, "A Visit from the Goon Squad."

Reading that *New Yorker* article, I was surprised to find how accurate Egan's description of the club and the bands that played there was, but it turns out there's good reason for that. Beginning in 1977, and for the next two years, Egan, a student at San Francisco's Lowell High School at the time, visited the Mabuhay on a weekly basis.

"It felt like the epicenter of a certain kind of action that was very raw, kind of dangerous, a bit out of control," Egan told me. "I waited years. I always knew I had to find a way to write about it. I just thought 'this is too good.' "

Egan says she was never a punk. In fact, as a teenager she wished she had been born a decade earlier. "My favorite band was the Who," she said. "I grew up wishing I had grown up in the '60s."

Today, Egan lives in Brooklyn with her husband and two sons. Just back from a month-long book tour promoting her fifth novel, "Manhattan Beach," in late June of 2018 the novelist, who says she still digs the punk sounds she listened to as a teenager, took time to reflect on her Mabuhay days.

Jennifer Egan: So I just want to warn you, I definitely wasn't a Mabuhay insider. So I'm gonna give you kind of the high school student's perspective.

Michael Goldberg: I'm wondering why you chose to use the Mabuhay as a setting in a chapter of your book. You could have made up the name of a club, but you used a very specific place.

Egan: It's a good question. I make things up if the real thing doesn't exist to my specifications, but I think in a way this was sort of the opposite. I had been wanting for years to find a way to write about that moment in San Francisco, even though I was not an insider. I think just even as a witness, it was a very striking thing to behold and I did have a friend who got very deeply into it and actually got addicted to heroin and all kinds of crazy things. Actually I had two friends who sort of disappeared into it, so I felt its power and also the striking way in which it repudiated the moment of San Francisco history that I was really fixated on, which was the 1960s. So it just didn't make sense to make up another club. I mean the Mabuhay really was the middle of all that, and I think I actually wanted to write about that, about it [the Mabuhay] specifically.

Goldberg: So did you go to the Mabuhay as a teenager?

Egan: Yes, a lot. The way I remember it is that I went pretty much every weekend with my friends. Even though we weren't punks, we dressed up to fit in. We were all under-age, but everyone had the fake ID. I got mine on Broadway actually, and yeah, it was a really fascinating place, just to be at, and a fascinating place to witness.

Goldberg: What made it so interesting?

Egan: The scene itself was very gritty, and extreme and the Mabuhay was basically very small and kind of scrappy. You were cheek by jowl with all these, first of all, all these amazing musicians. How good were they really, I don't know. It was a small club, and when we went there I would be dancing directly in front of the stage when the Dead Kennedys, or The Sleepers were playing. I felt like I was quite approximate to a rather – it felt like a historically significant moment. I felt that even as a know-nothing high school student. And it was just great people watching. It was just a fascinating scene to behold. It felt like the epicenter of a certain kind of action that was very raw, kind of dangerous, a bit out of control and yet accessible in this rather limited way to anyone who wanted to come on in. And as a pretty high school student one never had to suffer long before gaining admittance where ever one wanted. It was an accessible and exciting milieu.

Rick Williams: Sleepers. Photo by James Stark

Goldberg: What years did you go to the Mabuhay? The punk shows started there in 1976 and '77-'80 were the heyday years.

Egan: The year I'm writing about [in "A Visit from the Goon Squad"] is 1979. Those kids [in the book] are a year older than I am; they were the class of '79, the ones I wrote about. Probably '78 and '79 would have been two years when I was there the most. Mostly my junior and senior years. I had a friend, a good friend from high school who dated the bassist for Flipper, I can't remember his name [Bruce Loose], but I ended up hanging out a lot with them, and we would go to shows at Target Video and all over the place. She was a real insider and then I had another friend who dated Ricky Sleeper [Ricky Williams, singer for The Sleepers], and she was the one who really got sucked in.

But through them I had more access than just your average high school student paying the door fee. It would have been '77-'78, '78-'79, those kind of school years would have been when I was there.

Goldberg: In your book, the teenage girl Rhea asks herself, "When does a fake Mohawk become a real Mohawk? Who decides? How do you know if it's happened?" Did you feel like that? I mean this whole issue of fake punk versus real punk?

Egan: I totally felt like that, I mean I was absolutely—I was a fake, although I wasn't even really a fake punk because I didn't really cross over in any serious way. There was a whole kind of scene that my friend, the friend who dated Ricky Sleeper, got involved in and they were all heroin addicts and I remember meeting her at her apartment, and they were all shooting up and they were all sharing needles. 'Cause this is of course right before AIDS was named, and she offered me some and it was like out of the question that I would

Jennifer Miro: Nuns. Photo by James Stark

do that. I mean there was just no way even though I was curious enough, and this is the journalist in me. I want to see *everything*. I was curious enough to want to get that close, but there was no way. There was some kind of rudder in me that absolutely would not allow me to cross a certain line. And that was the way in which I was fake because it was a pretty hardcore scene. A lot of my friends' friends were making porn movies to support their habits. I mean, it was really, as I'm sure you know, it was pretty hardcore and a lot of people didn't make it out. There was excitement about those extremes, but clearly also a lot of real pain around that. All of that was really exciting to me.

Goldberg: There's this other aspect of punk. This positive aspect. There's that dark side of punk, which obviously didn't just happen in San Francisco, but there's also another side. For one thing, the idea that anyone could get up on that stage and in fact anyone did. Jello Biafra was in the audience for quite a while before they formed the Dead Kennedys and the same with Debora Iyall before Romeo Void. So it was basically refuting what had gone on for so long, which is: there are the rock stars that are on the stage and then there's the audience.

Egan: Right.

Goldberg: And that boundary, for a certain period of time, was erased. So that was one really positive thing that was going on at the time. There was also the whole DIY movement which came out of punk, which I think continues to this day, which also was there, and then San Francisco was the most political punk city.

Egan: Yeah, Jello [Biafra, of The Dead Kennedys] ran for mayor.

Goldberg: And when the city was evicting Chinese-Americans from apartment buildings where they lived so the buildings could be torn down and replaced, punks would join in the protests.

Egan: I have to say, frankly, I was kind of unaware of the political aspects of it but I just – I think that may be another measure of the degree to which I was sort of outside. I didn't really know that those conversations were even happening. But it's fascinating to hear that.

Goldberg: What bands did you see?

Egan: I would look every week at the club listings and the bands in my book [The Sleepers, Crime, The Nuns, the Avengers, The Mutants, Negative Trend], those are names that stick in my memory. I remember seeing X at one point. I remember the Dead Kennedys, because Jello Biafra was a very striking figure, but some of the others didn't have someone like that and they do kind of blend together. I also went to the People's Temple. There were other clubs, but the Mabuhay was really the epicenter.

I think I did see The Nuns, and actually the lead singer of The Nuns got in touch with me. She died a couple of years ago [of cancer on December 16, 2011]. Jennifer Miro [Jennifer Anderson] got in touch after my book came out, and we exchanged some emails. She was very alienated from everyone from that time. I'm not quite sure why. And she was living in New York, and we actually talked about getting together. It never happened. She was very striking, a very striking-looking person. I would see Iggy a lot, I adored Iggy, but he was at bigger venues. He was amazing. And I loved Patti Smith but she was at bigger clubs.

Goldberg: At the Mabuhay, did it mean more than music to you?

Egan: Yes, absolutely, because again, musically, well I have to say Flipper had a very distinct sound. They were amazing. Some of them – the DIY aspect, of course, had its results on stage. But I would say *strongly* that the feeling of the music was what really mattered to me and some of it I really loved. I thought The Sleepers were great. They had a couple of really beautiful songs and, again, Ricky Sleeper was a very compelling figure, very sort of wan and fragile and clearly very troubled, that was very evident. But the anger, the pace, the energy and the sort of rage were all incredibly compelling to me as a sort of troubled teen. I could not get enough of it.

And I listened to it at home, too. It was hard to get records of a lot of these people. Obviously, so long pre-internet. I loved the Sex Pistols, The Stranglers, I loved it. I mean I genuinely loved the music. I still do, I have to say, when I hear some of this stuff, it's not just that it brings back a time. I feel like they were doing something that was really an important and interesting step.

Goldberg: Do you think the Mabuhay had an impact in some way? On our culture?

Egan: It may be my bias, but I would say yes, because it was an epicenter. In terms of San Francisco punk rock, it not only enabled it but I think it really was kind of an essential component of it. It was a kind of community at the center and that was obvious even to someone who had no part in the community, really, except very peripherally.

Dirk Dirksen was a fascinating figure, a very strange gentleman. Very present, a very palpable part of that experience. And I just feel like it was all a really integrated sort of, what's the word I want, not a support system, it was like a sort of lab where this music was allowed to explode onto the scene and it was pretty unique, and the fact that a Lowell High

School student like me and her friends, who, I mean we took drugs but we were basically pretty straight arrows, could go there and enjoy it was part of the magic, really, because in that way it did more than just encourage artists to fulfill their own visions whatever those consisted of, but it really did help that moment to penetrate the larger culture, which would be me, just a pretty ordinary high school student, a public high school student in San Francisco, who was looking for action with her friends.

Michael Kowalsky with Dirk Dirksen at the Mab.   Photo by James Stark

I was impacted by that scene, and I don't know if I would have been without the Mabuhay. I waited years. I always knew I had to find a way to write about it. I just thought "this is too good," and it's not like my whole book is about [the Mabuhay] by any means, but I kept feeling like "no one has really done this exactly," and I'm sure someone could do a more thorough going job and I'm not that person, but it was so original. It really felt like a little piece of cultural history that I had the good luck to bumble into.

Goldberg: You mentioned Dirk Dirksen. What did you think of Dirk Dirksen at the time?

Egan: It seemed to me that he was the guy everyone loved to hate. I recall people actually throwing things at him. And he would be on stage too long. He was very insulting to the bands, but I think that that was all posturing in retrospect. It was sort of a role that he played. He definitely, in my memory, played the role of the sourpuss, the sort of skeptical, over it, weary and bored dad who had to oversee all this mayhem. I don't know why I have this impression but I feel like later, and I haven't really read extensively at all about any of this, but I somehow came to the conclusion, and I think he passed away quite a while ago …

Goldberg: Yeah, he did, in 2006.

Egan: … I came to the conclusion that, in fact, he was a much more essential part of all of it, and that that was probably a [important] role that he played. He was a sort of odd figure because he seemed like a total straight arrow – the way he looked, even. He was very nerdy. He wasn't a punk at all, certainly not in his attire. He had a sneering aspect, but not the kind of punk sneer, more like the dad who thinks this is all stupid, kind of sneer. So everyone would scream and yell and wanted him to shut up and get on with the music and that was fun, and that's why I think it was a role.

Goldberg: At the time did you think he was playing a role?

Egan: No. I just thought he was a jerk, I thought he was just a tiresome, needling presence who didn't get what we were doing.

Goldberg: There are people who had never heard of the Mabuhay until they read about it in your book or when your chapter was in the *New Yorker.*

Egan: It's interesting.

Goldberg: Earlier this year, there was a Bruce Conner exhibit in the Philippines for the first time and as part of that, they held a "Mabuhay Gardens Punk Party."

Egan: [laughs] Funny!

Goldberg: So it seems like the Mabuhay is living on. You think about it, a lot of years have gone by since that small club closed in 1986.

Egan: Yeah. Well, now I have to tell you, I agree with you. I didn't realize that myself until I started doing—I didn't do a ton of research, I really was relying a lot on memory to write that chapter, but I wanted to awaken my own impressions. So, I looked a lot on YouTube, and I watched a ton of videos, which was very strange and kind of moving because of course, that was really before the age of videos. We didn't record every move we made then, and yet someone *was* recording because there's a lot of it that you can see. And that was really amazing to watch The Sleepers, to hear a song I remembered. It was amazing. But I also noticed that there's a Facebook group for the Mabuhay and that all existed when I was writing the stuff which was like 2007 - 2008. And I was amazed by how many people reached out to me about the club after the book came out. Not because they had never heard of it before, but because they also had strong memories and feelings about it. So I think it really was a more important place than it or any of its patrons realized at the time.

And the fact that so many people from that time have passed away, not just from drugs, but from AIDS. This was a critical moment in San Francisco history and anyone who was there remembers. And the other reason I really remember it is that my job, the job I had then – the reason I was able to go to clubs or do anything – I worked [after school] at a café, Kiss My Sweet, on Haight Street for like three years. Kiss My Sweet was run completely by leather boys and they all had been persecuted in their hometowns and they were thrilled to be in San Francisco and to be out. They were insanely promiscuous and no one knew about AIDS, I mean no one had ever heard of it.

And yet there were these people who were persistently sick by the end of that decade. By 1980 there were people who were getting sick a lot and no one knew why. I think in a way the Mabuhay may – because that scene too was very promiscuous in terms of drug use, and needles, which again, I saw with my own eyes even as a person who was not part of it. I think it may have had a little bit the aura of the innocence of not knowing what was about to happen and in fact, was already happening. And I think that adds to the nostalgia. We didn't know. Luckily for me, I said "no" to that needle but who knows how my life might have changed if I had said "yes."

Goldberg: There were a lot of women in San Francisco punk bands. Was that important?

Egan: I'm sure it was, although I have to say, it didn't feel like an especially feminist scene to my eye, and I think that may just be my own particular – the accident of my own involvement. The only girls I knew who were connected to that [scene] were largely connected by their dating of guys in bands. But it's true that if I think about the kind of aesthetic of all of it, the guys were very effeminate actually. Like Ricky [Williams]. I don't know, the Flipper squad was a little different, but there were these kind of fragile, sort of feminine-seeming guys who were super sexy as part of these bands, so the sensibility was a little more feminine, actually, and maybe there was some connection between that and the fact that there were so many female artists.

Goldberg: You told me you thought the location of the Mabuhay was important.

Egan: The highway that collapsed in the earthquake changed the whole configuration of how people drive through San Francisco, as I'm sure you know. Before that highway collapsed in 1989, many people who were getting on the highway or getting off the highway drove along Broadway. It was a huge thoroughfare and that was a really important feature of

Don Vinyl in the women's bathroom at the Mab. Photo by James Stark

that street. It was just packed with cars, and so you just felt like you were in the middle of something even when I just went to dinner at Vanessi's [a now defunct restaurant that was on Broadway on the opposite side of the street from the Mabuhay] with my parents. I could look out the window and I could see all the punks walking by and all the traffic and it just felt like, "Oh my god, this is right at the heart of something." And all the strip clubs. I guess there are still a few strip clubs, but they were much more active then and there was a lot of overlap because, again, a lot of [punk] women who were addicted to drugs were doing sex work to support their habits. So there was again a sense of this odd symbiosis among these various businesses and institutions along Broadway. There were all these arcades where you would go to play pinball and do that kind of stuff, and there was an amazing store called The Magic Eye, kind of a hangover from the '60s counterculture, it sold all kinds of powders and potions, and dried herbs and had all kinds of pyramids and pentagons. That was kitty-corner from the Mabuhay. I think it's important to note how much other stuff was converging within just a few little blocks. People trying to get on the highway, honking their horns and the people running between the cars talking to people in the cars. And that's always exciting when different sorts of groups and people, doing all different things, converge in a particular place. It just makes that place very kind of hot and exciting.

Goldberg: Is there any specific time you went to the Mabuhay that stands out for some reason

Egan: This weird thing happens when I write about things, which is that the things I've written become like my own memories. It's very strange. Ontologically, in the end, there's not much difference between memory and imagination, so it's a little hard. I feel like I was there a couple of times when serious fights happened even to the point where we may have all been evicted because sometimes the scene in front of the stage was insane. I kind of liked that, but people would be basically throwing each other around, and I feel like there was some time, but it is just very wispy and I don't trust memory, but I feel like there was some time when Dirk had had enough and basically, I definitely... actually, it's coming back to me. I definitely witnessed some sort of fight where bottles were getting thrown and where people started bleeding copiously and I believe that Dirk shut it down and we all had to leave. I couldn't swear to that, but I'm sure that had to have happened, where the boisterous slam dancing just got too intense.

One other thing I would just mention is that the bathroom was crazy, the ladies' room or the girls' room. I just remember it being madness, people snorting coke right out in the open. The walls were just embedded with graffiti. I remember meeting people and exchanging phone numbers with people, with other girls, and thinking, "Oh yeah, we're gonna be friends now," just that kind of communal feeling that would happen sometimes. And it never went anywhere. When I woke up the next day, it was like I was a high school student again and no I was not gonna be hanging out with these people.

But interestingly, as I said before, two of my peers, they didn't go to Lowell, they went to other high schools, two of them actually did cross over and get very deeply into the scene. And I think probably that may be what stays with me the most, and I think it really impacted the rest of their lives. In the case of one of them, very negatively. She was arrested, she was shooting drugs, it was terrible. I think she's okay. I know she didn't get AIDS, which is a miracle. For me it was just an interesting thing to have witnessed, but I think that, as you say, it was a porous scene in the sense that an audience member could become an artist, but also a witness to it could very easily cross over and become of it and it was a pretty gritty, rather, in some ways, kind of dangerous environment because of all the drugs. And we're now on round two of the opioid epidemic so as a culture, we understand better than ever how intractable that problem can be, and how it really does change your life if you get hooked on it in the sense that the specter of that will always be there. So in that way, it really was dangerous, and we were just kids full of excitement and admiration. It took a strong backbone to define the limits to which one would go and most of us had that but not everyone.

So that is probably what stays with me the most, and just a memory of the raw kind of joyfully raging aesthetic, which was so different. My favorite band was the Who. I grew up wishing I had grown up in the '60s. None of that is in my novel, 'cause I don't really like to write about myself. I was writing about people for whom this was the be all end all. That wasn't true for me at all. I wanted to have been born 10 years earlier, but it was so thrilling and just bracing to see these people whose every aesthetic choice was about repudiating everything that that decade [the '60s] had stood for, that the counterculture had stood for. And even though my heart was still with the '60s counterculture it was just enthralling to see this new way of thinking and acting and singing.

I guess probably another reason I was so drawn to it is because even though it wasn't really my music or my scene, it was something new, and the thing that had bothered me so much about missing the '60s was that I had missed what clearly had been an absolutely riveting cultural explosion and even though this new one had nothing but contempt for the one that I revered and had almost nothing in common with it aesthetically, it was just inherently exciting to be present when something new exploded into being and I still feel lucky, that I got to see it.

Poster by Roger Reyes

Poster by Anomymous

6 O'Clock News
The Charmers

7 UXA
Legionaire's Dis-
ease
VKTMS

8 Roy Loney
Big Deal

9 Pearl Harbor & the
Explosions
The Simpletones
The Mondellos

10 The Simpletones
Tattooed Vegetable
The Beans

11 Tal Pheno & the

Twitchers
Lurid Tails

12 Tuxedo Moon
The VIPs
The Mondellos

13 Pressure
Owen Maerks
&   the Science
Patrol
MX 80 Sound

14 Mary Monday
The Beat
Eddie & the Sub-
titles
Bay Area Outra-
geous.Beauty
Pageant

15 Yesterday and
Today
Sharp
Nitro

16 SVT
Eye Protection
The Mon-
dellos

17 The Symptoms
The Units
The Blow Dryers

18 F.U.X.
Shaun Good
Golden Dragon
The Exploding
Pinto

19 Pearl Harbor &

the Explosions
Eye Protection
Thriller

20 Noh Mercy
Pink Section
The Touch Tones

21 No Sisters
Psychotic Pine-
apple
Big Deal

22 The Readymades
The Kats
The Mondellos

23 The Avengers
The Fillmore Struts
The Roomates

24 **The Kats**
VIPs
The Suspects

25 **Tattooed Vegetable**
The Beat
The Cinders
M
New Wave Rock
Opera

26 **Ral Pheno &**
the Twitchers
Avalon Boulevard
Streamliner
The Super Heros
Phatt

27 **The Bandaloons**
The Eaters
The Charmers

28 **The Noise**
The Hyway
Surface Music
New Wave Rock
Opera

29 **Pearl Harbor & the**
Explosions
No Sisters
The Humans
Mr. Obnoxo's Variety
Hour

30 **Jim Carroll**
The Mutants
Eye Protection
Bay Area Outra-
geous Beauty
Pageant

JULY 1979

1 **The Sleepers**
The Quitters
The Roomates

2 **Pressure**
Secret Service
1984
New Wave Rock
Opera

3 **The Next**
The Noise
Eye Protection
The Exploding
Pintos

4 **Dead Kennedys**
VS.
The Units

5 **The Humans**
The Beat
The Rebels
New Wave Rock
Opera

6 **No Sisters**
The Push Ups
The Touchtones

7 **Pearl Harbor &**
the Explosions
VIPs
Big Deal

8 **Richi Ray**
The Beans
SSI

9 **The Cinders**
X.Y.Z.
Surface Music

10 **Eye Protection**
The Tools
SSI
The Alter Boys
Snuky Tate

11 **The Tom Landry**
Band
Streamliner

Poster by Bruce Slisinger

Poster by Trident   Photos by Katherine Murray

97

Poster by Roger Reyes

Poster by Roger Reyes

12 **Pink Section**
   The Units
   JJ 180

13 **Crime**
   The VIPs
   The Blow Dryers

14 **Jim Carroll**
   The Mondellos
   The Mummers &
   Poppers

15 **Tuxedo Moon**
   The Humans
   Mertz

16 **The Plugz**
   The Antibodies
   VS.
   New Wave Rock
   Opera

17 **The Touchtones**
   The Plugz
   Tattooed Veg-
   etable

18 **VKTMS**
   The Mondellos
   Menace
   The Insults

19 **The Flyboys**
   The Mummers &
   Poppers
   New Wave Rock
   Opera

20 **Dead Kennedys**
   The Pointed
   Sticks
   6 O'Clock News

21 **Roy Loney &**
   the Phantom
   Movers
   The Pointed
   Sticks
   Times 5
   Bay Area Outra-
   geous Beauty
   Pageant

22 **The Pointed**
   Sticks
   The Rotters
   Mertz
   The Fleshapoids

23 **Leland**
   Tattooed Veg-
   etable
   Lurid Tails
   Monday Night
   Opera

24 **Dead Kennedys**
   VIPs
   The Rotters
   The Punts

KSAN Heretic Hour
Anniversary Party

25 **Pink Section**
   BPeople
   Voice Farm

26 **Psychotic Pinapple**
   The Charmers

27 **Yesterday and**
   Today
   The Angry Samoans
   Trixx

28 **SVT**
   The K-Tels
   Robert Fripp

29 **Stoneground**
   The Superheroes
   The Angry Samoans

30 **The Blow Dryers**
   Impatient Youth
   Menace
   The Alter Boys

Here is my contribution to Dirk's book
(he better not have left before it was finished!)

My night at THE MAB, eh? Truthfully my nights at THE MAB have all blurred together because I hold the record of performing the most in the historic dive, doing the early show between 1978 and 1981…first an over-the-edge comedy and then the popular cult show known as The Outrageous Beauty Revue (except in Dirk's diseased mind which turned it into

The Outrageous Beauty Pageant) every Saturday, and often on other nights as well! I was the guy in the wheelchair with all of those babes! Anyway, the first night I ventured into that den of punk insanity, the singer smashed his beer bottle onto the black brick wall behind the stage, glass shards ricocheted into the audience and right into the arm of one of the women who were with me. Now I have always thought Dirk gave me THE

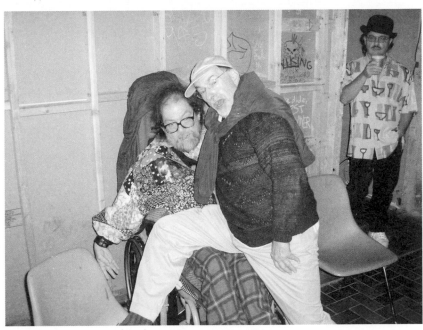
Dirk Dirksen on lap of Frnk Moore.

MAB as a creative theatrical lab because he was an artistic visionary. But it might just have been his way of avoiding being sued! Never know with Dirk! I never figured out his book-keeping method. A lot of bands thought he ripped them off. True, when there was a large audience, we got almost nothing. But when there was nobody in the audience, Dirk gave us fistfuls of cash. But you have to realize that Dirk had a strange mental condition. He thought that I was his brother for whom he has always harbored a painful jealousy because Mom obviously loved me more! He was always threatening to roll me in my wheelchair onto the freeway. But as I said, my MAB nights have all melted together. Like I remember a night when we only had a very small audience … only Frank Zappa, Robert Fripp, a reporter from Readers' Digest, a pregnant woman, a television crew from That's Incredible!, a European film company, and a teenaged punk eating spaghetti tripping on acid. After an act in which Al Goldstein, the publisher of Screw Magazine, admitted he was a virgin, it was time for the finale … our "meat act" … nude dancing girls in cellophane and glitter … dry ice, strobe lights, me in horrific make-up singing sympathy for the devil … a vixen barely dressed in black with two bloody naked monsters lurching threatening in the audience attacking the pregnant woman, carrying her screaming onto the stage, ripping her guts and the unborn fetus out and eating them. This was when the television guy shut off his camera in disgust … and when the brain of the teenaged punk got expanded terminally. He would grow up to be Flea of The Red Hot Chili Peppers. Just another night of cultural subversion at The Mab!

Frank Moore - 11/22/2006

11 years ago, I actually got Dirk to come over to the house for the following interview. It was supposed be Part One. But he died before Part Two. He is that kind of guy.

Frank Moore
11/24/2006

Interview with Dirk, Pt. 1

(In the late 70s, Dirk Dirksen "produced"/booked the shows at the North Beach new wave club, The Mabuhay Gardens.

During the rehearsals of Glamour, when the strip joint got unbearably boring after hours upon hours, I took a walk along Broadway, into what then was the West Coast hardcore punk center, the Mabuhay Gardens or the "Fab Mab". Since I did not have anything else to do, I asked the gruff manager if I could do my next production at his club. To my surprise, Dirk Dirksen was a visionary who, instead of seeing a crip asking for a hand-out, saw me somehow as a misfit artist perfect for his new wave cabaret. Dirk gave me a sheltered theatre for six years, with complete artistic freedom and moral support. The first production was a raping of a high-brow comedy, Meb, which I turned into a multi-media farce, full of camp, nudity, sex, violence and rock n'roll. The straight playwright walked out in horror, the club owner wanted us out, and only a handful of people came. But Dirk wanted to extend the run. He loved it.)

9/6/95 Curtis St. 1:19

Dirk: ... made unless five of my attorneys have approved it, as well as my deceased mother.
Frank: And I don't have any m -
Dirk: Ha, he's gonna say "money". (laughs) See, I can read you like a book, Frank! Except it's much shorter than your WORDY BOOKS! (everyone laughs) Cut to the chase, baby! (F wails) Or I'm pushing you on the freeway. Remember folks, if you're seeing this, it's unauthorized! If you're reading it, it's a different thing.
Frank: And you are ...
Linda: ... watching it? (F - yes, laughing)
Dirk: Allright Frank, let's get to the interview here! (F screams)
Linda: Allright, so I'll be -
Dirk: OH, this is just me and Frank. If, by the way, you know, if anything happens to Frank, I didn't do it!
Linda: I'll be back with some [trails off] ...
Dirk: O.k., now we're alone.
Frank: How did you get started?
Dirk: Harassing you? First time I saw you, it set my wheels in motion. Remember folks, (cracking up) this is unauthorized if you're seeing this. Only the written word. Ah, when did I get started? Ah, well, I believe it's when the doctor spanked me as I was coming out of

my mom. (F screams!) Yes, indeed, that's when it started. I immediately began scheming on how to produce the world's biggest show, which up to this point was the Outrageous Beauty Pageant, for Frank Moore. Ahh, how did I get started. Well, of course, the usual making a circus with the kids on the block, followed by using a 35 millimeter box camera to make black and white pictures for my social studies classes in the 4th grade. That didn't particularly work. Then trying … I conned the nuns into letting me rent films from the public library in the 5th grade and run it on an old projector, 16 millimeter projector. That gave me a thrill of seeing people respond to stuff that I was presenting.

Frank Moore with cast member. Photo courstey Frank Moore Archives.

Frank: The nuns may have warped you.

Dirk: I may have warped, I know I warped them more than they warped me. Ummm, the Sister Superior, name of Sister Boniface used to walk around the recess, the playground at recess with a bat hitting the guys on the knees for laughing dirty, which to this day (chuckles, Frank laughs), that has wonderful connotations for me. Uh, did they warp me? I don't think so. I think even at an early age I had a good dose of … I don't want to use the word sarcasm, because, or cynicism, because that has a negative connotation. I think "questioning" … questioning kind of mind. So, in school, I can distinctly remember taking my eraser and sticking like toothpicks in it with little strike posters, creating little placards with messages like, "On Strike". Because some of the concepts that they were pushing, in a sense, or presenting, that I took exception to, in terms of when I asked questions and I wouldn't get satisfactory answers. So, I got a shock a couple of weeks ago, I was going through some of my personal papers and I ran across some of my grade school report cards. And it was interesting seeing the reality of the grades that they had given me. The few A's, some B's, predominantly C's and an occasional D, which now I can see must have terribly distressed my father and mother. My father was a PhD in physics and math, so a very brilliant guy, and I can see that that must have been frustrating to them, because like I always thought of myself as quite intelligent and possessing a relatively high IQ. I was terribly bored in grammar school, and even worse so in high school. So did they warp me? Well, I think I wouldn't give them credit because I think we have to take responsibility for ourselves. So I've had to fight certain personality, let's call them minuses, or defects. I wouldn't wanna really call them defects, but things that I have tried to turn into positives, that …

Outrageous Beauty Pagent
The Spectator Jan. 10-16, 1980
by spencer Ramsey photo by Dave
Patrick

Outrageous beauty pagent by Ivan Sharpe
SF Examiner oct 9, 1978

'It was dynamite'

Punk: a stinking success

Mon., Oct. 9, 1978 ☆ S.F. EXAMINER—Page 3

By Ivan Sharpe

The music was atrocious. The costumes were sick. And the behavior of the performers was obscene and disgusting. The whole show, in fact, was such a tasteless, tedious travesty you had to wonder about the mentalities of those who staged it.

But the audience loved every minute of it, in spite of being spat upon and showered with everything from scanty underwear to smelly liquids.

"It was dynamite," enthused artist Mark Redlay, 33, as the stage mess was being cleaned up. "Total madness, absurd and perverted," theatrical agent Harold Adler agreed happily.

The place was Broadway's Mabuhay Gardens, cacophonous home of punk rock. And the occasion Saturday night was the first annual Outrageous Beauty Contest.

Organizer was Berkeley's Theatre of Human Melting. "We wanted to have some fun so we decided to do a spoof of beauty contests," said Diane Hall, one of the emcees.

"We were planning something quiet and low key, but it turned out to be much more outrageous than we expected.

"It's just been a wild, crazy night," she gasped after contestant Steve Hoffman wrestled her to the floor and tore off her blonde hairpiece, forcing her to wear a brown paper bag for the rest of the evening.

Mariah Ureel, 23, a petite construction worker, entered the contest because "it was a chance to go right over the edge on stage."

She dripped fake blood from a gruesome head mask, ripped open her T-shirt, writhed erotically on stage and amused the audience with a comedy routine that can only be described as outrageously obscene.

"Why humiliate yourself on stage?" contestant Nancy Kustron, in a weird cavewoman's costume, was asked. "Why? Because it's fun," she replied brightly. Later she had more fun by pushing a cream pie into organizer Frank Moore's face.

Jackie Strebin, almost nude under a layer of silver paint, confided. "My worst fear is that people will find out what I'm really like."

Mariah Urell was outrageously obscene
Examiner/Greg Robinson

"A—————s!" she screamed at the judges, when she failed to make the list of finalists.

Runnerup Helen Phillips, a student from London, said she entered from boredom. "I needed something to excite me," she shrugged.

"Let's give her a cheer for sincerity," yelled one of the emcees when she replied to a question about whether she would marry a midget: "I would if he loved me."

Fashion designer Brian Fedorow, 24, cried when he and his partner were declared the winners. "I've never been happier in my life," he gushed. Highlight of their performance was a disgustingly orgasmic parody of the action in a hair salon.

Just how outrageous was the show? Well, the winner by audience acclaim of the most outlandishly dressed spectator contest was a sweet little blonde named Diva.

She wore a perfectly ordinary dress and is just 5 years old.

Outrageous Beauty Pagent Articles from
San Francisco Examiner and The Spectator

102

Frank: Like?

Dirk: Umm, getting depressed. I feel that probably the only thing that I would say, like is a philosophical absolute, is: Never allow yourself to despair. Therefore, to get anything, to get negative, or upset, or paranoid, those are the kinds of things that I try to get rid of, o.k., you're pointing to "or" ... "b", the letter "b" ...

Frank: ... bitter.

Dirk: Bitter is horrible. Horrible. You got to totally stay away from being bitter. Umm, you're saying yes. I, that's ... yeah. I think, I would say the greatest gift that my mother passed on to me was that she was called the eternal optimist by all that knew her. My father, because of the fact that, as I said, that he was a physicist and a mathematician, was more questioning. He had a good sense of humor that was very sort of based in satire and irony. So in, that sort of presents the picture of someone who is a little bit sarcastic and cynical. And I think that cynicism is sort of a tangent of a little bit of negativity. And though I find it stimulating to have a, like a

Dirk Dirksen at work. Photo by Chester Simpson

smart remark readily available in my quiver of things to shoot at people, that it's better to be a nice, to have nice things to say about people.

Frank: That is irony.

Dirk: Yeah, irony. Yeah, no he was very, everything was irony. He saw life in ironic terms. I do that too, and it's, that I believe is self-depreciating humor.

Frank: Me too.

Dirk: Me too. Yes, yeah, yeah, yeah. I agree. No that was why when you proposed your play, some of the things, the concepts, that you presented, and I think that's where our affinity comes from. So, yep. Anyway, so where did I get started? I'm saying that I don't separate, of saying, "I started with this particular event in my career." When people say, "Well, what do you do?" I don't say, "Well, I'm a producer." I say, "I live." Producing or writing or directing or promoting, it's just a part of my life. I try to enjoy this adventure that is life. O.k.. Does that explain where I got started? Satisfactory answer?

Frank: But in show ...

Dirk: Show business? Uhh, well, the kid's circus in my backyard, when I was five, which would have been Germany in the last years of the second world war. My professional things, what were some of the first things to get paid for?

Frank: Me too.

Dirk: Yes.

Frank: I was in G-e-r

Dirk: Grammar? No. Ger - ma - ny. When?

Frank: '63.

Dirk: How old were you at that point?

Frank: 13.

Dirk: 13? You visited Germany when you were 13?

Frank: For 3 years.

Dirk: Hm, interesting. Did you have any problem with the language?

Frank: We were on base.

Dirk: Oh, military base. Good, good. Makes sense. Was that with your family?

Frank: Yes.

Dirk: How many brothers and sisters were there with you?

Frank: One ...

Dirk: Brother, sister?

Frank: ... brother.

Dirk: Hm, didn't know that about you.

Frank: Why were you in ...

Dirk: Born. My family is from Germany. Been there for many many many many many hundreds of years. Came over here after the war, my father as a mathematician and physicist, was one of the rocket scientists, one of the German scientists. That brought it up, that's what brought us over here. I came in 1947. Didn't know that, did you? (Frank wails) O.k. folks, remember, this is an unauthorized tape, if Frank is merchandising this thing to you, cause he had NO authority, NO license, nnnilch, zilch. O.k., what's next?

Frank: N-a-z-

Dirk: No. He asked if I was a Nazi. (Frank screams) My attitude? Come on. Un-compatible. Besides, I was just a little kid. (Frank laughing) Uh, family? My father was part of a pan-Europe movement before Hitler came to power, so wasn't exactly popular in that clique of people, because the very word "Nazi" is derived from nationalistic, and pan-Europe would have been [a] very international movement, so they were the antithesis of that. Like much of my family were in other parts of the world. My aunt was the wife of the ambassador, I think from Belgium to Finland. My godfather was the English Air Minister, so it would have been like the Secretary of the Air Force. So, just didn't fit the role of a German nationalistic person.

Frank: Your uncle was a ...

Dirk: ... Senator. Great-great-grand uncle, Everett Dirksen, yes. Also a show business [can't hear]. Yes. Too conservative for my tastes, in some ways. Wrong side of the aisle as far as political parties. But an interesting man, and very bright, both politically and a frustrated actor. That's what he, he had wanted to be an actor. He made a number of recordings, albums, that were, that used his ability as an orator, because he was considered one of the best orators that [the] Senate has seen, and ... the interesting thing with Dirksen was that he probably gave the only legislative victory that President Kennedy had, and that was the atom bomb test ban treaty. And he was very criticized at the time because he was a leader of the Republicans, and he got Kennedy the votes that were needed to pass that piece of legislation. And when he was confronted on having flip-flopped, so to speak, from the conservative view of that day, and the more militaristic view, to one of banning the bomb, at least testing of it, he said, "Well, there are only two kind of people that can't change their minds. They are either in insane asylums or in the cemetery. And I'm not in the one yet, and I don't think I'll end up in the other." Something to that effect. So, he said it makes sense, and that's why ... and that was pretty much near the end of his career, so that's the uncle story.

Frank: I remember that.

Dirk: Oh, oh, yeah, yeah, yeah, yeah. I mean, that was a big big moment in history, of the atomic era. And, I mean, here we are, a replay, with France doing it in the Pacific. I'm involved right now in a, what is called a Rolling Petition, which is employing the modern technology of the web pages and the FAX too and it's in support of what Greenpeace is doing. A gentleman by the name of Robert Manning has proposed this petition. He had a great success during the Persian Gulf War. Before the war started, when they were making, rattling sabers, Robert in three days collected over 55,000 signatures against America entering into a war against Iran, to resolve it peaceful. He stopped the moment that the actual invasion took place because he said, "Well, I am an American and it would be seditious for me to, once that first shot is fired, to give aid and comfort to the enemy. And he stopped the petition. And it was using an 800 number and Faxes. And now he is acting as a consultant to Greenpeace, in an effort to stop testing in the Pacific, because we, all of us concerned with this issue feel that boycotting the French in terms of the products that French citizens are manufacturing ... well, some of those citizens, the polls that have been taken would indicate that 60% of the French population is against the tests. So if we are, if we would boycott their products, we would probably hurt the very people, that the majority of those people are against these tests. It's quite often that it's not the individual. Like when you were sort of half-kiddingly pecking out the word "Nazi". A lot of people in every country, whether it's Japan and Pearl Harbor, whether it's Germany and the concentration camps, whether it's America and racism, or, you name it. There isn't a country that is without its flaws or its sins. But the individual citizen, in many cases, isn't the guilty party. It's the power structure. And it is ignorance on their part. It is fear. It is despair on their parts. It is greed. And most of the vices of man, whether it's greed, anger, lust, whatever, whatever the vices are. They're really all based in ignorance. Because if you are well-educated and hopefully secure in your knowledge, then you're not going to freak out, and you will take the attitude, "O.k., I'm going to try to figure out how to solve whatever problem I'm on." Sometimes I'm amazed that people will spend literally fortunes to go on trips to Africa, to go on Safari, where you have mosquitoes, where you have snakes, where you got insects, scorpions and whatever. Heat, humidity. And they'll go and bust their butts climbing up mountains, facing avalanches, sandstorms. But what is it in search of? Adventure! And yet, if you look at, hey, riding the BART can be an adventure! I mean look at it, couple of days ago somebody tried pushing a woman under the thing. I mean, that's pretty hairy. Of course, I mean urban life is pretty much an adventure to survive in. I think you've made an adventure out of the lot that was handed to you. In terms of the physical problems that your body gave you. It imprisoned you. But you've made an adventure of them. And you've become an inspiration to people. You're definitely an inspiration to me, in terms of whenever I feel badly, I've been lately going to visit an outfit called Recreation Center for the Handicapped, have been working for them for about four years, out in San Francisco, by the zoo. It was founded some forty years ago by a woman who felt that people with disabilities should have the ability to participate in recreation, and to experience the nice things, of seeing the parks instead of being locked up. And Janice founded this place, and to me it has become like a happy drug. I go out there, where a lot of people say, oh it's depressing to be around people that are, that have to be lifted by pallets, or that are in wheelchairs, or that are drooling, or they can't communicate. But boy when you see a human that's trapped in that prison, that is refusing to give up — that becomes an inspiration. And I think the same thing is, last year we did a satellite link-up from Golden Gate Park, an interactive video link-up, with Sarajevo. And to see ... there were four or five people in a theater that were performers and artists that we had communications with. The U.N. peace-keepers had brought them there because of the snipers were acting up very actively at that point. So they had to be brought in by armored personnel carriers. And we were communicating with them. And they were talking about the ingenuity that it took by the doctors who were working without electricity in the operating rooms, and very little medicine. And they were talking about the performers that had to overcome the lack of electricity, but they were still doing theater. So they make it an adventure.

Frank: That is where I get the best.

Dirk: Oh, absolutely. Yeah. In adversity, by taking on adversity as an adventure ...

Frank: And not seeing it as a p-r-i-s-

Dirk: Prison. Yes. Yes. Yeah, yeah, yeah, yeah, definitely. The, I think in the book "From Here To Eternity," one of the characters who is incarcerated, Pruitt I think is the character's name, he gains his strengths from going into his, into himself, into his own brain or mind, and shutting everything out. Because he was caught in the physical cage, he couldn't. I ... and that's the way that he survives. To a degree, that is like people who, in the face of adversity will fantasize. I try to remain realistic to a degree because if, in my position of trying to put on a play or, like we did, or to run a club or a theater, or to write a book, you have to have deadlines, you have to have discipline, and sometimes you just can't do all of that in your head. You have to physically get around. But the thing is, in your, as I've observed you, you've created relationships with people. You've contributed to them in inspiration, and thereby gotten them, like myself, to support your endeavors. And it becomes a mutually beneficial adventure. And therefore you're using leverage as ... I thoroughly believe in that. That, for instance, with the recreation center out there. We do their videos. We do it pro bono, meaning that all we charge is for the cost of the tape, or the money it takes to drive out there for the gas or whatever. And we've created I think three full-length documentaries that they use in fund raising and securing jobs for people in their supportive employment. I've acted as a consultant, saying, "Boy, how about going to ... this person has a real good idea ..." And the specific thing is, I suggested some couple years back to, since they have a lot of land, to grow vegetables for use in their kitchen, as well as maybe selling it to gourmet restaurants. And, lo and behold, I made the suggestion, and about six months later, Ruth Brinker [sp.], the founder of Open Hand, who's now doing a gardening project for homeless people, was doing the same, was proposing the same thing for use in the city. So, it's those kinds of ideas that I enjoy exploring, of taking the energy of one person and giving it to another. That just because you may not be capable of growing the groceries, if you have the land, somebody else may have the hands to plant and till and pull the weeds, water and all of that. But that person may not have the capabilities, like the speech, if a person has the disability of not being able to speak for, effectively for selling something. But somebody else who may have had their limbs crushed or whatever and is now in a wheelchair, may still have the total capabilities of communicating verbally. But because of the fact that they're confined to a wheelchair, society sort of goes, "Well, we don't think we want to hire this guy." But if those three people ... it's not the blind leading the blind. But if you have a blind man, and one that can see, somebody else that may not be able to speak, but they all get together, and pretty soon you do have a whole human being. And I think the same holds true in the arts. Somebody may be a marvelous painter, but an absolute disaster when it comes to being a business person. They may be a great painter, but not have the vision of how to merchandise it. Or they may be a great painter, and not have sufficient self-esteem to be able to put a value on what their doing. And so if people of good-will come together, and of talent, and of creativity — and you're certainly an example, with everything that you see in Frank's environment, you have been able to turn around, and it may not be that you did all of it, but you attracted the people, that love you and that have come to respect you, that you inter-act with. And I think that's a wonderful lesson. That someone who, after all is confined to a wheelchair, like yourself, has been able to give to people. And that is why when you came, those many moons ago ... boy it must be almost twenty years, '95, 18 or 19, how many? Do you remember?

Here I'm interviewing this guy ... and remember folks, if you're seeing this tape, Frank has no license to do it. He's stolen it again and ripped me off again. My good naive intentions coming out here.

Frank: '76.

Dirk: So 19 years. Yeah. Yeah. Boy, you certainly survived. Did you ever think you were gonna be this old?

Frank: No. I did not want to get, when I was 25.

Dirk: 25, yeah, yeah, yeah. Well, you learn. And you gotta keep surviving to be in the game, so that's the main thing.

Frank: One time I was talking to Bill Graham. I said I was doing a show at the M-a

Dirk: Mabuhay? What did he say?

Frank: He said, "Shit." (Dirk laughs.)

Dirk: Well, he had colorful language. Command of the language.

Frank: And I said, "Well, it is the only place that would book me."

Dirk: Yeah, book me. Yeah.

Frank: "Will you?" (screams)

Dirk: Did it shut him up?

Frank: (screams)

Dirk: Well, in many ways he was a great guy. And in some ways he was myopic in his view. He once told me that you either expanded or you contracted. And if you contracted, you eventually ... this was in response to saying, "Why do you keep, you know, why do you have to keep going bigger and bigger?" And he said, "Well if you don't expand, you con-tract and then you die." This was in a discussion that we had about ... I felt that at a certain point, that if you made a venue too large, it defeated the purpose of setting up the show in the first place.

Frank: I have worked hard not to get big.

Dirk: Well, everything except your head. You've always had a big head, right? Yeah. No, no. You've done good shows, and you can't do what you do if there isn't the personal contact. 'Cause that's what it's all about, in your kind of theater. The only thing that, in my comment to ... and maybe this is where I'm touchy when people say, "Well, you were the only guy that would book us." Well, good for me. It wasn't just that I was desperate to book anything, because I turned down a certain ... I mean, I turned down some acts. So what was my criteria? Well, my criteria was that you had to have something that was basically original. I wasn't interested at, per se, cover bands. And ours was obviously, a heavy percentage of the theater that we presented was based in music. A lot of the rock 'n roll theater, let's call it that, or humor, was based in music.

Frank: But you had things like The J-a-p-

Dirk: Japanese dancer. Yes. Have you followed Koichi Tamano ? I just did a show with him at the Anthropology Museum up here at UC two weeks ago for Hiroshima day. He's still going strong, and as a matter of fact I'm gonna go and do some video with him. And remember folks, if Frank is selling you this video, it's an unauthorized version! He SAID he was only going to use it for the audio for this article he's writing on me. I don't think I'll ever see this article in writing, but anyway ...

Frank: And maybe is on TV.

Dirk: This tape? (Frank screams) No way, Frankie! No way. No, no. No, no. You haven't got a release. Folks, if you see this tape in public, he's breaking his word. And Frank never breaks his word. So I got him.

Frank: I did not ...

Dirk: Nope, silence is consent. Silence is consent.

Frank: When (laughing) have I ever s-i-l-

Dirk: Boy, you got me. Try it again. Start fresh.

Frank: S-i-l- ...

Dirk: Try another word. That one I don't get.

Frank: I am always noisy.

Dirk: Nosy or noisy? (laughs)

Frank: And I did not give you my word.

Dirk: Heh, heh. Well, Frank, I won't give you any more words! So we're at an impasse. This is an interview, folks. If he uses this video, this guy, Frank Moore, is conniving me. Anyway, keep going.

Frank: How did you get the idea for the ...

Dirk: ... Mabuhay? That was the ...

Linda: Wait, hold that thought.

Side 2

Dirk: That was a concept to give me the ability to document emerging performers, to document them at the time that the seminal moment occurs, when somebody is first trying their act, or their piece. And I wanted to document it. I had had this concept of documenting it through the use of Super-8 film. And I had sold that concept, or had pitched that concept to CBS, and it just didn't work in terms of ... I had thought that because people were using Super-8, that they would have used the medium to record some interesting things. But it was really all poor quality, the stuff that I got after asking for submissions. The formula now, of course, is very successful with video of, you know, funniest home video. The material that we got, and this was like mid-60s, was just really, people couldn't relate to it. And the structure of television sort of requires thirteen weeks, or ninety days of programming times four, so that you got a whole year of programming. And after about a year, all that I could come up with was less than for two hours, or two and a quarter. So that would have been less than five episodes, instead of thirteen. And all of that was, much of that seemed inferior, so I went back to the proverbial drawing board to try figuring out how could I get that? And I figured, well, if I had a theater in which I could set up the mechanisms or the systems of documenting, either through audio recordings, film ... this was pre- the small video cams. They were black and white, and they were very poor quality. So we really didn't think that video would be the right documentation medium. But that film would be. And that's why, and I felt that I needed a theater to do it in. And so we went looking for theaters ...

Frank: Who we?

Dirk: Who we, who we ... oh when you say we? I use the word "we" interchangeable with "I" or "me". I guess it's the imperative "we" or "he". Because of the fact that I always had people that worked with me. The same way you have Linda and your friends that helped you with the Outrageous Beauty Pageant. Some of these friends have been with me for literally twenty years, twenty-five years. And some, a great number of my friends are deceased because of either as a result of murder, plane crashes, AIDS, drug-overdosing, car accidents. Unfortunately like in the last probably six years or seven years, I think that I've buried some 67 or 68 people that at one time or another were involved with me or employed. So the thing is the "we" has always been sort of a loosely knit group of people that have worked with me ... some of whom have held positions of being called partners in business arrangements, and who still are.

Frank: How did that get started?

Dirk: I moved up here from Los Angeles where I was working as a TV producer and writer and producer of concerts and things, and said, "Well, I like San Francisco because it's a very tolerant city. I like San Francisco because it's beautifully, geographically beautiful. Because in Los Angeles at that time, the smog was at its worst in years. And it was just depressing getting up and seeing brown sky.

So I basically finished what business relationship I had in L.A., came up here and sort of, not bummed around, but slept on floors of friends of mine for about a year. Got the layout. I had come up here, the first time that I came up, I mean when I started to come up, I had gotten myself a booking for a friend of mine at the Playboy club. And that brought me to the North Beach area. Because I wanted to get, I wanted to have a project that would lead me into the various media contacts and such. And I booked him at the Playboy club. And when that first day, while he was doing the show at the Playboy club, went up and had dinner up on Broadway, and ran into the Mabuhay. Had checked out, I had primarily gone to check out the On-Broadway, which was the second floor, above the Mabuhay, but had found out from the guys up there that they had just signed a renewal of their lease, and that they had a play in there, so it wouldn't be available. And they said, "Well, why don't you go downstairs and check out the Mab. They look like they may need a hand," in terms of that they had just started, weren't doing too well. So that's when I met Ness. And after a few months, found out that his Monday nights were, Monday and Tuesday nights he was closed, and talked him into giving me the Monday nights, and that we would, or that I would guarantee him a hundred and I think seventy-five a day at the bar. And in very short order, we put in a group of, a female comedy troupe, feminist comedy troupe called Le Nicolettes, which were sort of a guerrilla comedy troupe. And they did the Monday nights and Tuesday nights. We'd schlep in the stage Sunday night. And they would perform, and we'd schlep in the backdrops and the whole thing and then schlep it out Tuesday night, store it next door in a warehouse behind an art gallery on the other side of the alley. And that went on for about a year and a half. Or a year. And in that time, we would have bigger successes on Monday and Tuesday night than Ness would for the weekend nights, the Fridays and Saturdays, in his ... what he was running was a Filipino piano bar and supper club, using acts from the Phillipines. One of them was an Elvis impersonator, [can't hear name], and another was a very popular performer in the Phillipines a few years before, who had, I think, left the Phillipines because of disagreements with the Marcos government, and was living in San Francisco. And she was a very talented singer. And her husband had asked if I'd be interested in doing a television show because she had a Filipino sort of community show on channel 20, which was "Kimo [sp.] TV". So I created a show for her which employed a lot of comedy, slapstick sort of blackouts and a few songs. And I said, the couple of requirements before I would undertake the show, 1) would be she should lose 20 lbs.. The other was that she shouldn't sing every song in the show because I felt that that would take away from her being the headliner. And that I would choose, that I would have the say-so on what dresses she would wear, in terms of the wardrobe. She would submit the wardrobe and I would select what she would wear for the songs. And that I had, in essence, artistic control on the program. We did 27 episodes, and some of those were run 20 and 30 times on that station, with great results. And in the interim, the things at the Mabuhay, the Filipino audience kept getting sparser and sparser, and my sort of avant-garde rock theater became more and more the in-thing. And because of the policy that we had sort of set up, which was - you send us a cassette with at least three of your songs. They all have to be original. A picture, an 8 X 10 black and white. And the name and ages of your band or your group. The reason for that was so that if we wrote a press release that we could say, "... and so and so is the bassist, and she or he is 26 years old, or they're" ... whatever. It wasn't a question of trying to control any particular age bracket. But because of the fact that there was a liquor license there, they had to be over 21, and that's what we were trying to find out. So that if the person said, we had to believe them, if they said they were over 21. So that there would be no prior restraint, that we would know what kind of music, so that the genre ... because people sometimes would mis-explain what their genre was, but if you hear it, you have a rough idea. And that would give us the idea of the sound problem because we had a theater above us. And the theater was in, they would perform up until 10:45, 11 o' clock, so we couldn't start before 11:00. So that was the reason we gave you the early time slot, because you didn't have any really live music. Yours was mainly recorded music or very acoustic music. Every once in a while when you guys would turn your amps up too much, the people from the theater would come down because we would trespass on their sound space. So it was the early after-hours show in essence, because we started when most places were closing down. Around 11:30, 12 o' clock, most performance places in those days were closed.

The other unique thing that we did is we did three acts, three full bands, in a matter of three hours, from eleven to two. And that required a really adroit, high energy stage crew that would get them in and out, because there weren't any big gaps in between. So by this compression of cramming three bands, sometimes a couple of comedians or other acts, fire-eaters, you name it, jugglers, in between, it was a constant non-stop of entertainment. So, in a sense we delivered a three-ring circus between these hours of 11:00 and 1:45, when we'd have to collect all the drinks, and start getting them out. This lead to a number of sort of things where I became the host, or the ring-master. And the only way to deal with the age bracket of the audience, the audience of this age-bracket, was ... you couldn't say, [goofy voice] "Now, ladies and gentlemen, it's time to go!" So I began insulting them and berating them, used a police whistle, a little plastic bat and an assortment of everything with helmets with lights flashing on ...

Frank: Remind me of wrestling.

Dirk: Yes, yes. Oh yeah. I mean, it was absolutely, we tried to push the envelope in terms of physical, slap-stick, music, you name it, it was all sort of ... Everything from industrial ...

Frank: And c-a-r-

Dirk: Crazy, crazy. No ...

Frank: ... carnival.

Dirk: Carnival type of thing? Carny? Yeah, yeah, yeah. Yes. Yeah, absolutely. Yeah, no that's why your Outrageous Beauty Pageant fit well into that. There's an interesting ... you know who Flea is, of the group ... you know?

Frank: Yes.

Dirk: Well, Flea, one day was telling me ... I'm trying to remember the name of his group. Chili Peppers! Red Chili Peppers, Red Hot Chili Peppers. Flea first saw your act when he was in a group called Lee Ving Fear, Lee Ving's Fear group. He was the bass player in Lee's, in Fear. And he had come up here, I think ... he was like fourteen years old. The bass was bigger than he. And he came in early in the evening, did his, or the afternoon, did his sound check, and then you guys came in and set up. And in those days, the Filipino restaurant was still there, the Filipino kitchen was still available. So we used to feed all of the performers that were either too poor or didn't have money or wanted, we'd give 'em either a spaghetti dinner or some of the Filipino dishes. And there was chicken assad- whatever. And so he got, he was sitting there, and you guys came on and you did the Sympathy for the Devil routine where, for those of you that didn't see Frank's show, Frank would come out, or would

be wheeled out painted up as the devil in his wheelchair. And the music would come on, and he would lip-synch the music, and sing it also, right?

Outrageous Beauty Revue on stage ot the Mabuhay. Photo by Micheal LaBash

And they had a couple of pregnant women in the chorus, is that correct? Yes. And ... no, no, the pregnant women were, I'm sorry, all of these people were in semi-nude stage, with all sorts of trippy costumes and Frank singing away, with dry-ice on the floor, fog, dry-ice fog and strobe lights, you name it, very good theatrical effects. And the people would come in and, this was the early-dinner show ... so there would be these tourists with some Filipinos ... (Frank screams) ... in between, and me running up and down the stairs saying, Oh yes, I'm sorry, theater owners. We'll keep the noise down. And we'd be turning down Frank's amps. And the music would be getting into it, The Rolling Stones Sympathy for the Devil. And, all of a sudden, two of the women that were dressed sort of like banshees from hell, would run into the audience, kidnap these two pregnant tourists, who of course were shills, some of Frank's crew. And these women would be protesting, saying, "No, no, no. I don't wanna sing. No, I don't wanna get involved." And instead, the cast members would kill them and tear out two baby plastic dolls out of their stomach wrapped in various cow entrails and others, as if these poor women were being slaughtered for their fetuses. Which, at that point, many of the audience who had come to get the dinner, would be throwing up and running out. Well, Flea just loved it. He said it inspired him to become (FRANK SCREAMS) the performer that he is today, Hot Chili Peppers. So anyway, there you are. Now ...

Frank: My cast gave me s-h- ...

Dirk: Ahh, some poo-poo. Yes, they well should have, Frank. You were just a disgusting pervert. You always have been. And the only way, the only reason you get away with it is because you're in the wheelchair and then you claim that people are discriminating ...

Frank: They thought it was too v-i- ...

Dirk: ... o-l-e-n-t. Violent? Well, it was more disgusting than violent. It was just pure shock theater.

Frank: It was like Dawn ...

Dirk: ... of the Dead. See, I can just finish your thoughts for you, you don't even need your Ouija board. Yeah, it was. Yeah. It was terrible. Yeah. But it was definitely cutting edge, and it gave you the ability to pursue your ... your demons. (laughs) And you did a great job.

Frank: My cast saw the Mab as a d- ...

Dirk: Dive. I think that was short-sighted of people. Because it had a great amount of free-dom. And sometimes the chaos ...

Frank: Yes.

Dirk: Yeah, yeah, yeah ...

Frank: Most a-r-t ...

Dirk: ... art is ...

Frank: ... -i- ...

Dirk: ... is?

Frank: ... t ...

Dirk: ... his. No. Start again.

Frank: Most artists ...

Dirk: Most artists! O.k., most artists ...

Frank: ... would kill ...

Dirk: Yeah, yeah, yeah. Absolutely.

Frank: ... to have a theater for three years.

Dirk: Like you did. Yeah, absolutely. (Frank screams) Yeah.

Frank: To do anything ...

Dirk: Yeah. ... they wanted to pursue. Yeah, yeah, yeah. Agreed, agreed.

Frank: But they would not listen.

Dirk: Yeah, yeah, yeah ... No, I agree. That was a unique situation. I don't take credit as the sole influencing ... I mean, as the ... I put a certain energy into it, created the peripher-ies, which was the concept of giving artists, create the peripheries, act as the steward of the door, which brought in the money for the advertising, and the pit-tance of the bands getting, sometimes at the most, five bucks or ten bucks. And on some weekends, some acts would get eight, nine hundred. Probably, the most that an act probably ever made up there was like 3000 bucks for a single performance. So it was a system of where 65% of the door came to the show from, and 35% went back to the club for the expenses ... 65 went to the acts, was split up amongst the acts. And 35 was for the advertising, the door security, and the equipment, the lighting and sound staffing. O.k., now, you were gonna say something here.

Frank: But even when Zappa came and loved it, they did not believe him.

Dirk: Believed him, uh huh.

Frank: They did not b-e-l-i ...

Dirk: Believed or beloved by ...

Frank: ... e-v-e that he really liked it.

Dirk: Oh

Saran dancers with Frank Moore at the Mabuhay. Photo by Micheal LaBash.

yeah, it was tough. People, because they got too hung up in the fact that the place didn't have plush seats, it wasn't a traditional theater. But in order to take the opportunity of spontaneity, you know, pursuing, exploring, it couldn't be set up like a traditional theater. Somebody, a filmmaker, once did an interview — let me just share this thought and then I'll go back to your question there. A filmmaker was saying it was interesting for him to see that people would get up, move the chairs, the table, wherever they wanted them to be, or they'd put 'em up on stage, all of a sudden interact by sitting on stage. And even in your Outrageous Beauty Pageant you sort of promoted that kind of attitude for the people in the audience to get involved in the Outrageous Beauty Pageant.

Frank: To break the stage ...

Dirk: Yeah, yeah, yeah ... Absolutely. It was a constant challenge of seeing somebody get, start what looked like that they were destroying something. And, you know, did you ...? We'd have to make the judgment, or I'd have to make the judgment. This individual is gonna do some damage ... or they're just, you know, pursuing an idea. But it was definitely a very interesting thing to see because it was pandemonium, it was crazy, it was anarchy.

Frank: It is on the edge.

Dirk: Yes, it was on the edge. Absolutely. I agree. Ahh, Frank, it is now 7:30. How much longer do you want to go tonight on this? I can give you another time, because I sort of gotta be back by 8:00, 'cause I got an appointment. I know I'm running late. You tell me what you wanna do.

Frank: We can do it again.

Dirk: Next week?

Frank: Yes.

Dirk: O.k., so I'm gonna call ... or I'll work it out with your schedule with Linda, and then we'll do another session like this. Do you figure that that'll do it for you, for the article, that you got enough material?

Frank: Yes.

Dirk: Good going. Did we, did the interview go the way you wanted it? O.k.?

Frank: Yes.

Dirk: Good. All right. Should we holler for …? (goes to the door) I QUIT! I'M NOT GOING TO DO ANYMORE! BECAUSE HE'S JUST NOT BEING NICE!

Frank: (screams)

Dirk: Ah, the reason I, I was pointing to Frank that I sort of gotta be back by eight, 'cause I had figured I would be here earlier.

Linda: Yeah.

Dirk: So, he would like to do it again. He says we did all right. So …

Linda: (laughs) I heard a lot of screaming.

Dirk: Well it's getting too dark. My picture won't turn out.

Frank: Flea …

Dirk: Oh, Flea story. Is that what you want me to tell? (Frank - yes)

Linda: Yeah, yeah.

Dirk: Oh, it's Flea of Chili Peppers, Hot Chili Peppers, one time told me of the impact that, when he came when he was fourteen, he was in the group Fear with Lee Ving. And they had sound check, and then you guys came in and we were feeding him dinner. And that's when you guys did the Sympathy to the Devil number, you know, with the girls, I mean the pregnant women being dragged out of the audience. And he just thought that was the greatest theater because, I think he said, "Oh, I was on acid, and I just thought it was wild … this Filipino piano bar and supper club …" Because, you know, if you walk through it, of, you do a sound-check, there's a stage, there's the rattan furniture and all of that, you see piano bar, Filipino supper club … the guy says, "Oh, let me feed you dinner." He's eating dinner, he sees some tourists around him. You guys come on … (Frank and Linda laughing) … the dry-ice fog, they rip the women up. He said that made such an impact on him that that's why that theater, the influence of why he put so much theater … so …

Linda: Whoa! (laughs) (Frank wails)

Dirk: This was like, ten years ago, or when he was, when it wasn't Chili Peppers yet, when it was still Lee Ving. He was up in the dressing room telling me the impact this thing had had … the Outrageous Beauty Pageant. So there you are! (Frank screams) So, this is a publication that a friend of mine runs up in Mendocino. Just sort of get acquainted with it because I think we might be able to explore something up there. O.k.? A show, or something. Because they do a lot of interesting art … o.k.? All right! Well, I'm gonna …

Linda: So are we setting up another time?

Dirk: Yes, I had said … I think I ought to do it when I have my book, at the house. O.k.?

Linda: O.k., so we'll call you.

Dirk: Yeah. We'll do a, again another evening, just like this. O.k.? A little bit earlier. All right? Yes.

Linda: Yeah. Yeah.

Dirk: Good. O.k. One cookie up here. O.k. You be good. All right. O.k.? (hugs) Okey doke.

Poster by Anomymous

31 Dred Scott
Streamliner
Shiek Vaselino &
the Zealots

AUGUST 1979

1 Dred Scott
Contraband
Pressure
Video Beam The-
ater

2 Richie Ray
Times 5
The Outfits
Thursday Opera

3 Shakin' Street
Dread Scott
The Mummers &
Poppers
Video Vaudeville
Hour

4 No Sisters
The Mondellos

Mummers &
Poppers
Bay Area Outra-
geous Beauty
Pageant

5 Leland
The Impostors
The Corvairs

6 Surface Music
Vambo
Luxx Paramour
Monday Night
Opera

7 The Superheroes
Shiek Vaselino &
the Zealots

8 VS.
No Alternative
VKTMS
Impatient Youth

9 Psychotic Pine-
apple

The Blitz

10 The Mutants
The Fleshapoids
Video Vaudeville

11 Crime
The Units

12 Tuxedo Moon
Sleepers

13 Eye Protection
Times 5
The Toons
The Symptoms
No Alternative

14 The Mumbles
The Suspects
The Twinkyz

15 Pink Section
Human Hands
Nervous Gender

16 The Simpletones
The Crowd

17 Jim Carroll
The Crowd
6 O'Clock News
Video Vaudeville

18 Yesterday and
Today
Mr. Clean
Outrageous
Beauty Pageant

19 The Simpletones
Stoneground
Streamliner

20 Tuxedo Moon
The Symptoms
Psychotic Pine-
apple

Pheno & the
Twitchers
Seizure

21 Surface Music
The Reactors
The Delusions
The Aggravators

22 Eye Protection
Joseph Stewart
The Bandaloons

23 The Next
The Reactors
The Penatrators

24 Dead Kennedys
The Go Go's
The Penatrators
Video Vaudeville

25 Rox
The Go Go's

26 The Symptoms
The Punts
The Alter Boys
Electronic Aviary

27 The Senders
Pressure
The Magnetoes
Back-a-Live
The X-Isles Rock
Opera

28 The Senders
The Originals
The Noise
Mertz
The Tools

29 Eye Protection
The Mondellos
The Blitz

Poster by Anomymous

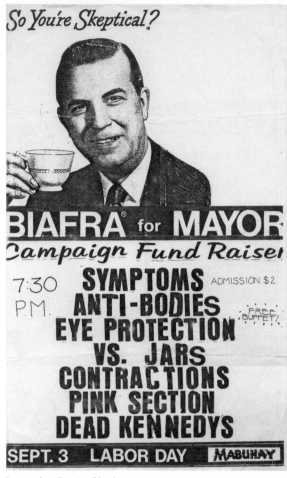

Poster by Bruce Slesinger

30 **Noh Mercy**
    Los Microwaves
    The Urge

31 **Shakin' Street**
    VIPs
    Video Vaudeville

SEPTEMBER 1979

1   **Jim Carroll**
    The Corvairs
    Ankoko-Buto

2   **Shakin' Street**
    No Sisters
    6 O'clock News

3   **Benefit for Biafra**
    Mayoral Campaign
    Dead Kennedys
    Eye Protection
    The Symptoms
    VS.
    The Contractions
    Anti-Bodies

    The Jars

4   **X-Ray Ted**
    Nervous Gender
    The Now
    Impatient Youth

5   **The Eaters**
    Seizure
    The Tools

6   **Contraband**
    The Fillmore
    Struts
    The Amputees
    Target Video
    New Wave Films

7   **The Plugz**
    The Mutants
    Mertz
    Video Vaudeville

8   **Dead Kennedys**
    The Silencers
    Ankoko-Buto

    Bay Area Outra-
    geous Beauty
    Pageant

9   **The Plugz**
    The Imposters
    The Sneakers

10 **No Sisters**
    Psychotic Pine-
    apple
    Times 5
    Sudden Fun
    The Corvairs
    Child's Portion

11 **No Alternative**
    The Contractions
    Impatient Youth
    The Anti-Bodies

12 **Stoneground**
    The Tom Landry
    Band
    Rockin' Horse

13 **The Push-Ups**
    The Corvairs
    The Young Adults

14 **The Nervebreakers**
    The Offs
    Fast Floyd

15 **Tuxedo Moon**
    The Piccadillos
    Winston Tong
    Bay Area Outra-
    geous Beauty Pag-
    eant

16 The Noise
   Lightspan
   Foxx
   Blair Miller's Delusion

17 The Next
   Times 5
   Pressure
   The Eaters
   The Tools

18 Streamliner
   The Charmers
   Avalon Boulevard

19 D.O.A.
   VKTMS
   Times 5
   The Tools
   SSI

20 D.O.A.
   VS.
   The Brainiacs

21 Jim Carroll
   The Imposters
   The Fillmore Strutz
   Video Vaudeville

22 Roy Loney & the
   Phantom Movers
   The Mondellos
   The Eaters

23 Free Party: 8 Groups

24 Jim Carroll Band
   The Jars
   XYZ
   The Outfits
   The Anti-Bodies

25 The Aggravators
   Tattooed Vegetables

   The Magnetoes
   The Voids

26 Eye Protection
   Rubber City Rebels
   The Blitz

27 The Symptoms
   Psychotic Pineapple
   Surface Music
   Secret Service

28 No Sisters
   The Mondellos
   Times 5

29 SVT
   Rubber City Rebels
   Eye Protection
   Bay Area Outrageous Beauty
   Pageant

30 The Imposters
   The Corvairs
   Glide

OCTOBER 1979

1 SF Rent Control
   Benefit

2 Red Asphalt
   The Nomads
   The CIA

3 The Noise
   The Jars
   Eye Protection

4 VS.
   Los Microwaves
   The Contractions

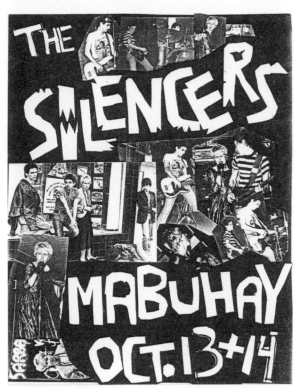

Poster by Anomymous

Poster by Roger Reyes

117

The Night they raided Mabuhay by Michael Goldberg

Not everybody loves punk rock. Last Friday night San Francisco's finest joined in the critical disapproval of punk by busting the Mabuhay Gardens, San Francisco's punk Mecca. And the bust has sparked speculation .about police pay-offs, and political intrigue.

San Francisco police arrested 17 persons, closed the club down for the rest of the evening and charged Mabuhay owner Ness Aquino with "maintaining a premise where narcotics are sold and used" and "contributing to the delinquency of a minor."

"They treated Dan White better than they treated the people in the Mabuhay who did not commit any major crimes," said an angry Aquino the day after the bust. Aquino spent five hours in jail Saturday morning before he was released on bail. "The police showed up at the club just before midnight and announced, 'We're going to shut this place down.' They just came in," said Aquino, "started grabbing people and hauled them out to their paddy wagon."

Most of the arrests were for "being under the influence of drugs in a public place." The drugs referred to would appear to be marijuana; in the police report, the only "drugs" mentioned are "thin rolled cigarette (s)."

Dirk Dirksen, whose production company, Dirksen-Miller Productions, books all acts into the Mabuhay and produces all the performances there, believes the police would like to shut the Mabuhay down. "They're using the liquor thing as an excuse to harass us because they don't agree with our avant-garde theater."

According to Dirksen, "They (the police) started to pull the doorman off the front door. My doorman says, 'Hey, I got my cash drawer to watch.' They asked him where the cash drawer was and as he started to point to it, the sergeant in charge of the operation took his night stick and hit him with it saying, 'Don't point at me you son of a bitch!' "

The raid comes on the heels of harassment by some police of Mabuhay patrons approaching the club or leaving along Broadway, over the past few months. New West contributing photographer Chester Simpson was grabbed by a policeman while standing outside the pinball hall next door to the Mabuhay earlier this year.

"This policeman came up to me, "said Simpson, "and said, 'I'm arresting you for being drunk.' I hadn't even had one drink. I said, 'Look. I'm not drunk.' And he said, 'Your word against mine'"

Simpson was hauled off and "detained" overnight on the drunk tank. According to Simpson, police refused to give him a sobriety test. "They do not conduct themselves like officers of the law," said Simpson. "They conduct themselves like hoodlums. Before they arrested me, they were arresting this guy who is in a punk rock band. They came up to him and said, 'Let's see some fucking ID, asshole. 'Those are the exact words."

According to Dirksen, on several occasions he has called the police and asked them to

DMPO/ON BROADWAY THEATRE

HOUSE OPERATIONS

SUBJECT: SPECIAL ACTIVITY REPORT

	DATE(S) & TIME(S) OF OCCURRENCE
	_ 6/25/83 12:45 am

NAME OF PERSON GIVING STATEMENT	DOB OR AGE	RESIDENCE PHONE	BUSINESS PHONE
Marshall Greer	23		
RESIDENCE ADDRESS	BUSINESS ADDRESS		

DATE OF STATEMENT	TIME STARTED	LOCATION WHERE STATEMENT TAKEN ☐ AT SCENE ☐ OTHER (BE SPECIFIC)
6/25/83	TIME COMPLETED	
STATEMENT TAKEN BY		IN PRESENCE OF (NAMES & ADDRESSES)
Self		

About 12:40 a.m. on June 25, 1983, the subject came to the door of the On Broadway Theater, which was open to the public for a show, and where I was at the time working as doorman-security guard. The man claimed that he had been in the club earlier in the evening, thereby indicating that he had already paid an admission. I asked to see the admission-identification stamp on his hand. He refused to show his hand saying that Fredda Kaplan, who was working with me as cahsier at the door, "knew him'. The subject then passed us and rushed up the stairs into the club. I asked fredda if she did know him, she said, "no, he crashed the door," so I followed him. At the top of the stairs I joined the subject and again asked to see his hand "stamp". He refused. I asked him to return to the door with me, and repeated my request at least once more. Each time I asked him to return to the door, he refused, and became more agitated. He tried to rush past me; I blocked his way; he tried to puch me several times and I defended myself. After no more than 10 seconds of scuffling with him, James Kennedy, a DMPO volunteer who was working as a "roving" security guard, came to my aid. Kennedy restrained the subject, carrying him to the bottom of the stairs, where he released the subject and asked himto leave. After a verbal outburst, the subject again tried to atta and again was restrained by Kennedy. At this time police who were passing t=he club too the subject into their custody. The police officers took statements from the subject and me, declared the incident a "mutual combat," and released the subject. The officer took my statement was #120.

About 10 minutes after the subject was released by the police, the subject returned and tried to reenter the club. He was restrained at the door while I remained inside the club. The subject left for the final time after screaming for about 10 minutes at the door staff.

PAGE	OF	SIGNATURE OF PERSON GIVING STATEMENT
		Marshall Greer

Police Report concerning the On Broadway theather.

119

come down and clear drunks and other "undesirable" characters off the sidewalk in front of the club. Dirksen cites Simpson's "detainment" as one of several instances in which the police "show up, mention complaints which I had made to them, and arrest the wrong people. They put us in the position of being the bad guy, of not maintaining peace in the neighborhood.

Every effort has been made, according to Dirksen, to prevent minors from drinking and to have violent and/or intoxicated individuals arrested. "I have made over ten citizen's arrests in the past year and a half," said Dirksen. "I've personally been beaten up, had my nose broken four different times and had six

pairs of glasses broken attempting to maintain order in the club. I think as an individual connected with the Mabuhay, but without proprietary interests, I have shown a high degree of respect for the regulations that we operate under."

It appears that some police would rather find violations within the club, than deal with the criminal and lowlife types who hang out in North Beach and occasionally enter and disrupt the Mabuhay. On Saturday Nov. 18, for example, a group of ten came into the club.

"These animals beat up a number of people in the club," said Dirksen. "They broke my doorman's nose. They broke my nose. Now I ended up with photos of the ten thugs that a photographer, who was in the club during the incidents,- took. We have the pictures of the people who invaded us, but the police have not made any attempt to contact us. There's no follow-up. Yet there's this eagerness to nail us on alleged offenses."

Dirksen believes that the media image of punk. helped along by heavily publicized incidents like the murder of Sid Vicious' girlfriend, have predisposed some police against the club. Dirksen said, "They see it as a punk scene. But punk is just a part of what we do here- We are presenting avant-garde theater. We've had great jazz performers like Sun Ra and George Shearing. And people do not understand the satire of punk. Our people are in costume, they are not thugs. And the few real thugs that participate in illegal activities are not admitted.

"I'm not some bizarre rebel or revolutionary who wants to *86' the police department or tear at society's fiber. We're off the side of law and order. We don't want thugs or drunks in the club."

Several sources familiar with the night club scene on Broadway have suggested that some police are on the take from certain club owners there. According to these sources, the Mabuhay was busted because neither Dirksen nor Aquino kicked in.

"We've never paid off," said Dirksen, "I'm totally against the concept of a citizen rubbing the back of agencies that take. "I have no knowledge of that happening,' he said.

There had also been some speculation that the raid was connected, in a roundabout way, to the assassinations of Mayor George Moscone and Supervisor Harvey Milk. On KSJO radio last Sunday evening, journalist Howie Klein said that Moscone and Milk had been sympathetic to the Mabuhay and that the police had to give the club a fair deal because they knew that any "questionable" harassment would be brought to Milk's attention and that Milk would have it investigated.

With Milk and Moscone dead so the speculation goes, the Mabuhay's future is uncertain. If the police were to make a regular practice of busting rock concerts for use of "drugs" in a public place, every music hall in the city would be swarming with men in blue, and the SFPD is well aware of this. This hypocrisy is underscored by the recent passage in the City of Prop. "W," which mandated a relaxed approach to the enforcement of marijuana laws.

Michael Goldberg

5	The Offs	Rude Norton
	Times 5	Impatient Youth
	Geza X	The Dinnettes
	The Mommy Men	The Anti-Bodies

6	The Dis hrags	10	Dead Kennedys
	The Humans		The Feederz
	The Flyboyz		Black Flag
	Catholic Disci-		The Insults
	pline		
	Ankoko-Buto	11	The Pointed
			Sticks
7	The Bags		VS.
	The Dishrags		The Punts
	The Flyboyz		The Wounds
	The Stingers		
	The Dinnettes	12	The Weirdos
			The Pointed
8	Noh Mercy		Sticks
	Geza X		Eye Protection
	The Mommy Men		The Contractions
	Catholic Disci-		
	pline	13	The Weirdos
	Female Hands		The Feederz
			391
9	Female Hands		The Silencers

Poster by Anomymous

Poster by Anomymous

14	Daily Planet	19	The Offs
	The Noise		The Feederz
	The Silencers		The Strutz
	The Jars		Video Vaudeville

15	Times 5	20	No Sisters
	The Push-Ups		The Beat
	The Mumbles		Bob
	The Corvairs		Outrageous
	Los Microwaves		Beauty Pageant
	Knuke the Knack		

16	The Now	21	The Sex Dogs
	The Quitters		The Bucks
	The Nomads		Avalon Boulevard
			The Highway

17	Stoneground	22	Dennis Peron
	The Fillmore		Benefit
	Struts		
	The Corvairs	23	6 O'Clock News
			The Aliens
18	Pearl Harbor &		The Invaders
	the Explosions		
	The Beat	24	The Mondellos
	Das Blox		The Crawdaddies
			Men In Black

Poster by Wasserman

MABUHAY
GARDENS 443 BRDWY

the OFFs

SATURDAY DEC. 15th

Poster by Anomymous

20 Stoneground
Praerie Fire
Johnny Rock and
the Rockers

21 Contraband
The Jars
The Contractions

22 391
The Silver Chalice
The Touch Tones
The Penetrators

23 No Sisters
Eye Protection
The Impostors

24 The Offs
VS.
The Silver Chalice
Times 5
Louder Faster
Shorter
Bay Area Outra-
geous Beauty
Pageant

25 X-Ray Ted
The Penetrators
The Blow Dryers
The Beauty Kill-
ers

26 No Data

27 Damage Maga-
zine Private Party

28 The Dishrags
The Symptoms
The Blitz
The Witnesses

29 The Bags
The Spoilers

30 Dead Kennedys
Madness
The Dishrags

DECEMBER 1979

1 The Mutants
The Dishrags

The Angry Samo-
ans
Louder Faster
Shorter
Madness

2 The Angry Samo
ans
The Contractions
The Jars

3 Gale Force
The Honey Davis
Band
The Outfits
Sapphire
Oquisha
Paradise

4 The Touch Tones
VKTMS
Men in Black

5 Psychotic Pine-
apple
Sudden Fun
The Nu-Models

6 No Alternative
VIPs
The Next
The Corvairs
Fast Floyd

7 The Mutants
The Fall
The Donuts

8 The Readymades
The Contractions
The Donuts
Bay Area Outra-
geous Beauty Pag-
eant

9 Sharp
The Bucks
Rich-Strange
The False Idols

10 Minimal Man
No Alternative
The Castration
Squad
Bob
Flipper

11 The Push-Ups
The News
The Next

12 The B-People
The Punts
Bob
The Sleepers

13 The Mondellos
The Blow Dryers
Eye Protection
The Blitz
The Roomates

14 SVT
Dyan Diamond
The Soul Rebels

ONE HUMP OR TWO?

I was fucking this girl one night and she fell asleep, so I decided to go up to the Mabu-hay. I was putting on my pants when my cousin called me on the telephone.

'Hey Mohammed,' he said, 'What's happening?'

'Well,' I said, 'I was fucking this girl but she fell asleep, so I was going to go to the Mabu-hay. You wanna come?'

My cousin got real excited when he heard about the girl. He said, 'Hey, Mohammed, why don't you let me fuck her, man? It's dark; she'll never know…'

Heh heh heh. My cousin never gets any chicks.

I said, 'Yeah, but you've got a beard, man. If she woke up, she could tell.'

'Just a minute,' said my cousin. 'I'll call you right back.'

A minute later he called again. 'Okay,' he said, 'I shaved off my beard.'

'Aw, too bad,' I said. 'She just woke up. So, you wanna go to the Mabuhay?'"

Mohammed Obeid, "as recollected by Peter Claudius"

■■■■■■■■■■■■■■■■■■■■■■■■■■■■■■■■■

Many of the first punk bands to play the Mab seemed to be former art students trying out a new medium and many of the Mab's patrons were former art students trying to be artists. Between the two, there was about no money. Dirksen had many promotional nights at the club. Looking at the paper one week, I saw the Mab was having a show-up-in-military-garb-

Mabuhay Audience Photo by James Stark

and get-in-free night and that did it for me. Like a lot of Goodwill shoppers, fatigues were a staple in my closet and lacking a full-length mirror, I thought they looked pretty sharp. I called a friend about the great deal and we agreed to go.

I go meet Carol and was momentarily stunned. Then I asked her: What army are you supposed to be in? This question stumped her. Wearing a little red blazer, tan pants and tiny witch boots, she looked as much like a balloon animal as a soldier. My next question was more to the point: How are we going to get in free? It was money for beer or the door but not both. We strategize for a while and figured our best bet was since I was taller and would easily pass the military thing, she would stick close behind me, we'd go in with a cluster of people and she would somehow blend. It was the best we could come up with. So I watched the club for a bit. Dirksen was at the door and didn't seem to be paying attention; good for us. Soon there were a few people at the door and we took our chance and stalked in fast. Or rather, I stalked in fast. Carol got collared, literally Dirk grabbed her by the collar.

"Not you" he said, still not looking up much, "3 dollars." Now inspiration hits her: "You mean I look like a fool and I still can't get in free?" she gasped. "Yeah" he said, "you do look like a fool." And that was good enough, he let her in. That was the way Dirk ran his club. Even if you missed your mark or the band sounded like they had found their instruments in an ally and had never played before, you could find a place at the Mabuhay on force of will.

I always thought it was generous of Dirk to provide free popcorn at the Mab. All the pictures of the club I've seen always show the band on stage with a crush of people on the floor but just behind that crush; little tables with bowls of popcorn. The first band was usually terrible, (sometimes all the bands were terrible) enough to turn any advocate into a critic and the popcorn would go flying. Dirksen would come out between the acts to glare at us, announce the next act, insult the audience and usually the bands too. A little bit bookish and a little bit walrus-y, Dirksen was not an intimidating looking guy. He knew it too, just like the scrawny guys who spiked their hair with egg white weren't dangerous. His ringmaster snarl and the rain of popcorn made the Mab very festive. Eventually the popcorn would go away, along with the other throwables, but it was fun while it lasted.

An Rafferty

■ ■

I'll give you a rough version of the story.

In the Spring of 77 I was frequenting The Mab and trying to form a band. My vision was almost identical to what later became "Psychotic Pineapple".

At the Mab one night I met a guy who claimed to be forming a band with Sylvain Sylvain of the broken up new York Dolls. The guy wanted me to join his band. We got along great, and he kept saying aloud how wonderful our future would be together. I was pretty ecstatic too.

After about an hour of this, another man approached me. He grimly stated: "Look, I'm the manager of this band. We're all queers. Unless you're queer too, we don't want you."

A few days later, I went over to Dirk's house which was about a block away from Van Ness with a very sophisticated friend from Berkeley named Mario Del Campo.

I repeated the story to Dirk and a few others. They immediately grimaced and fled the room. Mario turned to me and admonished: "Everyone is queer here. You can't say stuff like that." I replied that I had told a tale of disappointment, not condemnation. Mario was silent, and I went out the door and took BART home.

DOA Dan

15 The Offs
VS.
Bob

16 The Roomates
Von Trigger
The Stairs
The Whippetts

17 Dead Kennedys
The Contractions
Times 5
The Push-Ups
The Roomates

18 The Jars
The Fleshapoids
SSI

19 The Mondellos
The Contractions
The Cowboys

20 The Touch Tones
Steve A Dore
The Wasp Women
The Hul-a-ball-u-
ers

21 The Push-Ups
391
The Enemy
The Nu Models
Video Vaudeville

22 No Sisters
Times 5
The Contractions
Bay Area Outra-
geous Beauty Pag-
eant

23 Neasden Knights
Stoneground
Huey Lewis'
Amercan Express

24 Christmas Eve
Party

25 The Tools
The False Idols

26 The Mondellos
The Jars
The Soul Rebels

27 The Aliens
The Units
Los Microwaves

28 SVT
Jo Allen & the
Shapes
Das Blox

29 Nervous Gender
Times 5
Bay Area Out-
rageous Beauty
Pageant

31 Mabuhay Legal
Defense Fund
Benefit
The Readymades
No Sisters
Voice Farm
Touch Tones
Little Tommy
(Clone Butt)
Zimmerman &
the Rolling Blun-
der Review
The Jars
The Wasp Wom=
en

JANUARY 1980

1 No Data
2 No Data
3 No Data

Poster by Roger Reyes

4 Times 5
The Aliens
The Cowboys

5 Roy Loney & the
Phantom Movers
The Humans
The Soul Rebels
Bay Area Out-
rageous Beauty
Pageant

6 The Witnesses
Little Death
No Visitors

7 The Mutants
The Soul Rebels
Bob

8 No Alternative
The Tools
The Rockers

9 The Imposters
VIPs
The Jars

10 VKTMS
VS.
Garbage Mouth
The Fleshapoids

11 Rubber City Rebels
The Contractions
Los Microwaves
Doorways
New Wave Ballet

12 The Mutants

Rubber City Rebels
The Soul Rebels
Bay Area Outrageous Beauty Pageant

13 The Tots
    The Undersongs
    The Invasions

14 The Mondellos
    Sudden Fun
    The Urge
    The Whippets
    Stero

15 ROX
    The Magnetoes
    Pierre of Pressure

16 The Punts
    Surface Music
    84 Rooms

17 Psychotic Pineapple
    The Imposters
    The Blitz

18 The Mondellos
    The Lloyds
    The Symptoms

19 Roy Loney & the
    Phantom Movers
    No Alternative
    The Soul Rebels
    Contraband
    Bay Area Outrageous Beauty
    Pageant

20 San Francisco
    The Aggravators
    The Wrong Brothers
    The Suspects

21 The Jars
    Justice League of
    America
    Bare Risk

22 The Blow Dryers
    The Soul Rebels
    VS.
    No Alternative

23 No Alternative
    Little Death
    Secret Service

24 X-Ray Ted
    The Cowboys
    Sharp
    Harvey

25 SVT
    The Push-Ups
    The Contractions
    New Wave Ballet:
    Doorways

26 SVT
    Bates Motel
    The Soul Rebels

27 The Push-Ups
    The Jars
    Rave
    The Outfits
    X-Ray Ted
    The Confessions

28 Los Microwaves
    The Blitz
    Justice League of
    America

29 VKTMS
    The Tools
    The Undersongs
    The False Idols

30 Impatient Youth
    No Alternative

Poster by Anomymous

Men in Black
Little Death

31 The Punts
    The Dickheads

FEBRUARY 1980

1 SVT
   The Young Canadians
   Daily Planet

2 Times 5
   The Young Canadians
   Zev
   Johanna Went
   Bay Area Outrageous Beauty
   Pageant

3 The Suspects
   The Magnetics
   Surface Music
   New Critics

4 The Wrong Brothers
   The Invasions
   Rich and Strange
   Pretension

5 The Super Heroes
   San Francisco
   The Confessions
   Barry Beam

6 Von Trigger
   Jet Stereo
   The Invasions

7 8 Eyed Spy featuring Lydia Lunch
   The Offs

8 The Mutants
   8 Eyed Spy
   Johanna Went

9 Dead Kennedys
   8 Eyed Spy
   Zev
   Outrageous Beauty
   Pageant

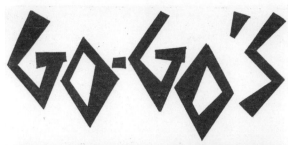

MABUHAY
FEB. 16-17

Poster by Anomymous

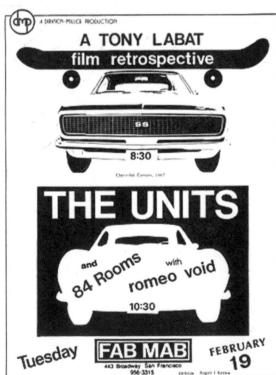

Poster by Roger Reyes

10 Social Unrest
The Young Canadians
Nikie Limo
The Delusions

11 SVT
The Fast
The Cowboys

12 The Mutants
Romeo Void
The Facts
Plus

13 Voice Farm
Tommy Zimmerman & the Gnashville Pins
The Inflatable Boy

14 The Touch Tones
The Wasp Women
Bay of Pigs

15 Crime
391

16 The Go Gos
The Alleycats
The Offs
Bay Area Outrageous Beauty Pageant

17 The Go Gos
The Alleycats
Daily Planet
The Balls

18 The Automatic Human Jukebox
The False Idols
The Tri-Matrix
The Regime

19 The Units
84 Rooms
Romeo Void

20 Harvey
The Motive
The Tots
Little Death

21 The Soul Rebels
The Contractions
The Motive
The Witnesses

22 Lene Lovich
Bruce Wooley &
the Camera Club
391

23 Lene Lovich
Bruce Wooley &
the Camera Club
391
Outrageous Beauty
Pageant

24 Budy
Surface Music
The Tri-Matrix
The Dispensers

25 Day-Glo Outfit
The Soul Rebels
No Alternative
The Satellites
The Regime
Social Unrest

26 The False Idols
No Alternative
The Wounds
Justice League of America

27 391
UXA
The Lewd
The Insults

Daddy Dirk and the Trial by Fire

There are some firsts you never forget—your first acid trip—first fuck, and if you ever played in a band—your first gig at the Mabuhay Gardens.

For me, it was 1980.

I'd formed a band, The Rabble (guitar, bass, drums and me, Tiz Gurto—lead singer).

I'd been trying to catch Dirk's ear for months—sent the obligatory demo tape, a photo of the band and followed up with a series of phone calls, which when answered, were nothing short of an exercise in humiliation. Dirksen wasn't the nurturing type.

Dirk never remembered who you were, and once you re-introduced yourself for the five hundredth time, he'd let you know your music was pedestrian and then insult your family, your penis and your lack of intelligence.

If Dirk ever got around to actually engaging you in dialogue, he'd more often than not cut you off in mid-response and restart his litany of insults. It was fairly well hopeless—but you'd always come back for more—you had to. You either played the Mab or you were nothing.

I remember one evening brainstorming with my wife (I'd even put her up to calling the "Pope of Punk," fronting as our manager—she was no luckier with Dirk than she was with me—we were divorced after a few short months). Anyways, on that particular night I'd rushed out to the nearest newsstand and bought a Playboy magazine. I cut out strategic body parts from the host of hotties that graced the glossy and pasted them over the equivalent sections of the band's bodies on our 8 x 10 promo photo.

My guitarist wound up with tanned, taut boobies, the drummer a freshly shaved snatch—for the rest of us—tits and a fine ass—maybe even a pretty face. Once I completed my collage, I added the text, "How 'bout a date? We deliver!"

Within days Dirk called me! He not only gave us our very first booking but we were slated to appear on a Friday night, on the same bill as Black Flag, and we weren't even the opening act (we went on second). Score!

Needless to say, we were ecstatic and the band threw itself into daily rehearsals. We figured this was our big break. Dirksen must have really seen something in us. Little did we know that the "Master of Mayhem" was setting us up for the ultimate trial by fire.

The Rabble was something of a grunge band, which would have been fine if it had been the mid-nineties, but this was 1980. I had a shock of curly, red hair—something akin to Roger Daltry—while the rest of the band had suburban bobs. We were definitely not hip—Dirksen must have been cackling in his sleep.

Now to Dirk's credit, the Fab Mab was the epicenter of the punk movement. But it was also the only venue where a band, of any ilk, could get a gig. Usually, however, he'd book by musical styles—in our case, he'd thrown us into a hard-core crowd, sandwiching us between serious punk acts—with 90% of the audience there to hear and see L.A.'s top Punk phenom—Black Flag.

Of course we were just stupid thrilled. Again, we were the second act on a Friday night and this our first gig! We really thought Dirk had us pegged for up and comers.

When we got to the club the evening of the gig the joint was packed—skin heads, Mohawks, pierced skin, tattoos, black leather and a Cheshire grinning Dirksen.

I remember going up the stairs behind the stage where Black Flag was holed up, greeting them all and getting blank stares and curled lipped scowls in return.

Dirk's introduction of our band was less than flattering, but of course, that was Dirk—we thought nothing of it. As soon as we struck the first cord to the first song, however, the spit, the insults and the catcalls began.

As we jammed through such mid-tempo numbers as, "You Can Groove In The Modern World," the intensity of intolerance heated up—people actually made their way to the front of the stage so their loogies might hit the mark.

They hated us. And for good reason—we were completely inappropriate, but of course, Dirk knew that. The funny thing was, the whole tension filled experience invigorated me—I reveled in the combative atmosphere—but the rest of the band was shell-shocked. We ambled through our set, skulked off stage and the drummer and guitar player promptly quit (I don't think either ever played in a band again!)

As we passed Dirk, standing in the wings, he seemed pleased and plenty amused—his arms folded, a shit-eating grin—his beady eyes never breaking contact with my own.

What was interesting was from that day on Dirk took my calls, knew who I was and even invited me up to his California Street office.

When I formed another band, with a new name and new songs, he booked us—again and again. I always felt that I'd earned Dirk's respect on that Friday night in 1980.

My band ultimately claimed the distinction of being the only one, "Banned for Life" at the Fab Mab. Of course, by that time, Dirk had moved his operations upstairs to the On Broadway Theater and so the ban never really amounted to anything more than a choice reputation. But then, that was Dirksen—doling out the tough love behind his P.T. Barnum façade long before the psycho babblers put the concept on the books.

By Kent Wallace aka Tiz Gurto

Sunset Thomas & Sol y Mar Productions

■■■■■■■■■■■■■■■■■■■■■■■■■■■■■■■■■■■■

Offs outro November 7, 1980.

(Audience applause.) OK! The Offs will be back again tomorrow night. They really don't want to expend there energy unless you really want them-—so you either makes lots of noise or you don't get any more noise. Your doing a poor imitation of a tourist audience—the level of applause would suggest that your tour buses are now loading. The Offs have remained unimpressed with your appreciation of them so far—it would appear that the Offs have actually learned not to be so insecure as to run out immediately at the first clap, so there going to perform again tomorrow night and that's it—you're far to flakey of an audience to deserve a encore. Audience Boos. It's very sad but that all the rote. Tomorrow evening another thrilling night at the almost legendary Mabuhay Gardens but that's it for tonight. Alright animals, drink up, put away the empties and get rid of the biggest empties of them all—yourselves. How ever resist the temptation of putting your self in our trash cans because they are over flowing already. Alright, you have approximately another 446 seconds in which to enjoy the Phillippino Supper Club piano bar atmosphere of the Mubuhay. We're now going to play you some tape to soothe you animals before releasing you back on the public.

Dirks comments from The Offs, Live at the Mabuhay Gardens Nov. 7 1980
Courtesy Terry Hammer, Vampir Records, www.angelfire.com/liveperformances/livetapes.html

Ad for Rotten Record Chart by R. Flip. Photos by Erich Muller

131

RECORD REVUE

D. E. V. O. --*Duty Now For The Future (Warner Brothers):* They continue to pull their collective spud. Spudboy Dance Party .... Spud Finds Andy Hardy...Here's Spud In Your Eye! If you Still liked them, "post-Saturday Night Live", you'll love this. The clean-machine sound of industry-in-the-faking. Come to grips with Video Age and its myriad compulsions, sex at work and play, and science gone too far. GO DEVO.

FABULOUS POODLES --*Mirror Stars (Epic):* In need of house -breaking....or just plain breaking.

PERE UBU -- *Dub Housing (Chrysalis):* More than the return of Croaking Behemoth. Funnier than Samuel Beckett. Uglier than the Alien. Like an attack of stomach flu at the 2001 Disco. Highly Recommended.

RAMONES --*Rock'n' Roll High School (Sire):* My biggest regret is that the only part of co-starlet P. J. Soles in this package is her voice on the non-Morones take of the title song. Otherwise, pretty tasty for an anthology-type soundtrack. A poster or an inflatable reproduction of the nubile Ms. Soles would make it a best seller.

AQUARIUS RECORDS 595 Castro St. 94114
phone (415) 863-6467

1. HARMONY IN MY HEAD - THE BUZZCOCKS
* 2. DRIVIN' - PEARL HARBOR & THE EXPLOSIONS
* 3. TOUR OF CHINA - PINK SECTION
* 4. CALIFORNIA UBER ALLES - DEAD KENNEDYS
5. ESSENTIAL LOGIC ep - IAN DURY
6. DO IT YOURSELF - THE MUTANTS
* 7. INSECT LOUNGE ep - THE UNITS
* 8. COWBOY - THE UNITS
9. PICTURES ON MY WALL - ECHO & THE BUNNYMEN
10. BABYLON'S BURNING - THE RUTS

san francisco california

TOWER RECORDS Columbus at Bay 94113
phone (415) 885-0500

1. HARMONY IN MY HEAD - THE BUZZCOCKS
2. IN THE DARK/ELECTRICITY - THE ORCHESTRAL MANUEVERS
3. I SLEPT IN AN ARCADE - BLACK RANDY
4. FOLLOWER - PRAG VEC
* 5. INSECT LOUNGE ep - THE MUTANTS
* 6. CALIFORNIA UBER ALLES - DEAD KENNEDYS
* 7. DRIVIN' - PEARL HARBOR & THE EXPLOSIONS
* 8. TOUR OF CHINA - PINK SECTION
* 9. UNITS ep
10. XEROX - ADAM & THE ANTS

RATHER RIPPED RECORDS 1848 Euclid Ave. 94709
phone (415) 848-6495

1. HARMONY IN MY HEAD - THE BUZZCOCKS
2. THE FOLLOWER - PRAG VEC
3. TWIST A ST. TROPEZ - TELEX
4. MY RELATIONSHIP - STATIC
* 5. NON ep
* 6. TOUR OF CHINA - PINK SECTION
* 7. COWBOY - THE UNITS
* 8. SICK OF YOU - MR. CLEAN
9. ELECTRICITY - THE ORCHESTRAL MANUEVERS
10. BIG HITS OF MID-AMERICA VOL. III

berkeley california

TOWER RECORDS 2510 Durant Ave. 94704
phone (415) 841-0101

1. FEAR OF MUSIC - THE TALKING HEADS
2. XEROX - ADAM & THE ANTS
3. I SLEPT IN AN ARCADE - BLACK RANDY
4. HARMONY IN MY HEAD - THE BUZZCOCKS
5. TRY ME - BOBBY BERKOWITZ
6. ELECTRICITY - THE ORCHESTRAL MOVERS
7. ALL-NIGHT PARTY - CERTAIN RATIO
* 8. TOUR OF CHINA - PINK SECTION
* 9. COWBOY - THE UNITS
10. THE B52s

ROTTEN RECORD TOP TEN THURSDAY KSAN

FM 88 9

● 89.7fm KFJC "WHITE NOISE" M

KFJC NEW ADDS
1. IDENTITY PARADE
2. NINA HAGEN
3. CULTURE SHOCK/GLASS HOUSE - SHA
4. THE EP - WAZMO NARIZ
5. YOU - THE IDOLS
6. ALL NIGHT PARTY - CERTAIN RATI
7. NEW MUSIC - THE SMIRKS
8. ZEROX - ADAM & THE ANTS
9. WORLD WAR/ROCKERS - U.K. SUBS
10. IS CHESTY DEAD? - MOLLS call i

● 90.1fm KZSU "OUTCASTES III"

1. CHELSEA
2. BEACH BLVD. (SIMPLETONES cuts)
3. I SLEPT IN AN ARCADE - BLACK
4. THE B52s
5. HIJACK THE RADIO - THE NERVEB
6. FEAR OF MUSIC - THE TALKING H
* 7. CALIFORNIA UBER ALLES - DEAD
8. HARMONY IN MY HEAD - THE BUZZ
* 9. INSECT LOUNGE ep - THE MUTANT
10. GANGSTER - THE SPECIALS
call i

● 90.7fm KALX "NEW WAVE HOUR"

1. THE CLASH
2. CHAINS - THE WAD
3. Both NERVEBREAKERS records
* 4. CALIFORNIA UBER ALLES - DEAD KENN
5. SAVE THE WAIL - LEW LEWIS
6. NINA HAGEN
7. AIN'T THAT A SHAME - BRIAN JAM
8. TATOOED LOVE BOYS - THE PRETEN
9. FALLEN - PHILLIP RAMBOW
10. TOWN & COUNTRY - BARRY ANDERS
call i

● 92.3fm KSJO "MODERN HUMANS"

1. ROKY ERICKSON (new album tape
2. AT HOME HE'S A TOURIST - GANG
3. HARMONY IN MY HEAD - THE BUZZ
4. BABYLON'S BURNING - THE RUTS
5. THE INTERNATIONAL COWBOYS
6. YOU - THE IDOLS
* 7. INSECT LOUNGE ep - THE MUTANT
* 8. CALIFORNIA UBER ALLES - DEAD
* 9. TOUR OF CHINA - PINK SECTION
10. BARRY ANDREWS call i

INTERZONE T. BARRIGER

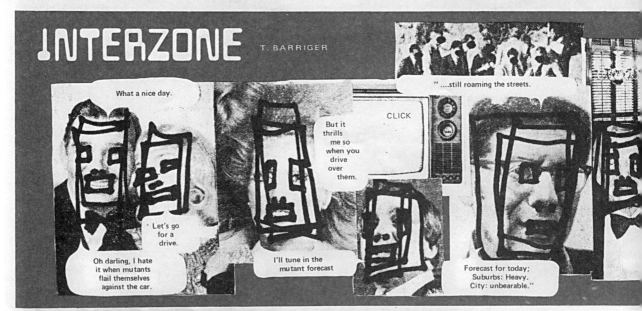

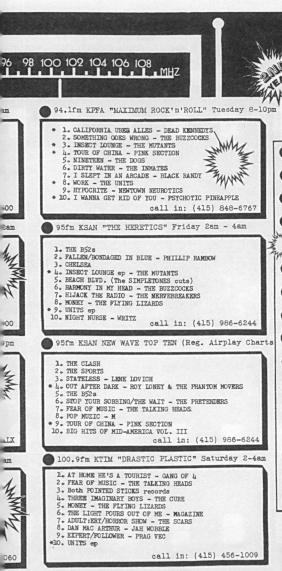

96 98 100 102 104 106 108 MHZ

● 94.1fm KPFA "MAXIMUM ROCK'n'ROLL" Tuesday 8-10pm

* 1. CALIFORNIA UBER ALLES - DEAD KENNEDYS
  2. SOMETHING GOES WRONG - THE BUZZCOCKS
* 3. INSECT LOUNGE - THE MUTANTS
* 4. TOUR OF CHINA - PINK SECTION
  5. NINETEEN - THE DOGS
  6. DIRTY WATER - THE INMATES
  7. I SLEPT IN AN ARCADE - BLACK RANDY
* 8. WORK - THE UNITS
  9. HYPOCRITE - NEWTOWN NEUROTICS
* 10. I WANNA GET RID OF YOU - PSYCHOTIC PINEAPPLE

                    call in: (415) 848-6767

● 95fm KSAN "THE HERETICS" Friday 2am - 4am

  1. THE B52s
  2. FALLEN/BONDAGED IN BLUE - PHILLIP RAMBOW
  3. CHELSEA
* 4. INSECT LOUNGE ep - THE MUTANTS
  5. BEACH BLVD. (The SIMPLETONES cuts)
  6. HARMONY IN MY HEAD - THE BUZZCOCKS
  7. HIJACK THE RADIO - THE NERVEBREAKERS
  8. MONEY - THE FLYING LIZARDS
* 9. UNITS ep
  10. NIGHT NURSE - WRITZ

                    call in: (415) 986-6244

● 95fm KSAN NEW WAVE TOP TEN (Reg. Airplay Charts)

  1. THE CLASH
  2. THE SPORTS
  3. STATELESS - LENE LOVICH
* 4. OUT AFTER DARK - ROY LONEY & THE PHANTOM MOVERS
  5. THE B52s
  6. STOP YOUR SOBBING/THE WAIT - THE PRETENDERS
  7. FEAR OF MUSIC - THE TALKING HEADS
  8. POP MUZIC - M
* 9. TOUR OF CHINA - PINK SECTION
  10. BIG HITS OF MID-AMERICA VOL. III

                    call in: (415) 986-6244

● 100.9fm KTIM "DRASTIC PLASTIC" Saturday 2-4am

  1. AT HOME HE'S A TOURIST - GANG OF 4
  2. FEAR OF MUSIC - THE TALKING HEADS
  3. Both POINTED STICKS records
  4. THREE IMAGINARY BOYS - THE CURE
  5. MONEY - THE FLYING LIZARDS
  6. THE LIGHT POURS OUT OF ME - MAGAZINE
  7. ADULT:ERY/HORROR SHOW - THE SCARS
  8. DAN MAC ARTHUR - JAH WOBBLE
  9. EXPERT/FOLLOWER - PRAG VEC
* 10. UNITS ep

                    call in: (415) 456-1009

DIRKSEN-MILLER PRODUCTIONS

NEW WAVE ROTTEN RECORD CHART NO: 54

2nd YEAR

● ROTTEN RECORD TOP TEN WEEK OF AUGUST 24, 1979

LAST WEEK / THIS WEEK

(-) 1. HARMONY IN MY HEAD
         THE BUZZCOCKS
         (UA import)

* (1) 2. CALIFORNIA UBER ALLES
          DEAD KENNEDYS
          (ALTERNATIVE TENTACLES)

* (5) 3. INSECT LOUNGE ep
          THE MUTANTS
          (415 RECORDS)

* (3) 4. TOUR OF CHINA
          PINK SECTION
          (PINK SECTION)

(4) 5. FEAR OF MUSIC
         THE TALKING HEADS
         (SIRE)

(-) 6. I SLEPT IN AN ARCADE
         BLACK RANDY
         (DANGERHOUSE)

(6) 7. THE CLASH
         THE CLASH
         (EPIC)

(-) 8. AT HOME HE'S A TOURIST
         GANG OF 4
         (EMI)

(-) 9. CHELSEA
         CHELSEA
         (STEP FORWARD)

(-) 10. HIJACK THE RADIO
          THE NERVEBREAKERS
          (WILD CHILD)

NUMBER ONE A YEAR AGO:
CAN'T STAND THE REZILLOS -
THE REZILLOS (SIRE)

SYMBOL / CODE

* Local Bay Area Group
☼ In Concert at Mabuhay this week.

A DIRKSEN-MILLER PRODUCTION
CHARTICIAN: RAL PHENO
DESIGN / ARTIST: ROGER I REYES
PRODUCER: DIRK B. G. DIRKSEN
COPYRIGHT (C) 1979 DIRKSEN-MILLER PRODUCTIONS

RECORD REVUE

LOU REED -- *The Bells (Arista)*: Quasimodo swings again.

SIOUXSIE & THE BANSHEES -- *The Scream (Polydor)*: "Genius is pain!" quoth Lennon. "OW!" agrees Siouxsie Sioux, formerly a swastika-clad go-go girl for the Sex Pistols. Fronting every groupie's dream, her very own rock band, Sixouxsie indulges her violent, sorid fantasies. Original songs like "Carcass" and "Nicotine Stain" vie for one's digust with a dolorous cover of the Beatles' "Helter Skelter". A Squeaky Fromme pick-to-click. ("Hong Kong Gardens", a suprisingly sprightly left-field hit in England, is included to sweeten the bitter pill. Buy the single.)

PATTI SMITH GROUP -- *Wave (Arista)*: The Ballad of Todd Rundgren - Verse XVIII (with a bullet). Punk Madonna or professional amateur....Todd does it all for you! He'll fix your voice, edit your material, whip up the surefire hit and bring the ship into port under budget. So you wanna be a rock 'n' roll star? So does our heroine, Rimbaud ramifications aside: "Just get an electric guitar and take some time and learn how to play....." Practice what you preach, Patti.

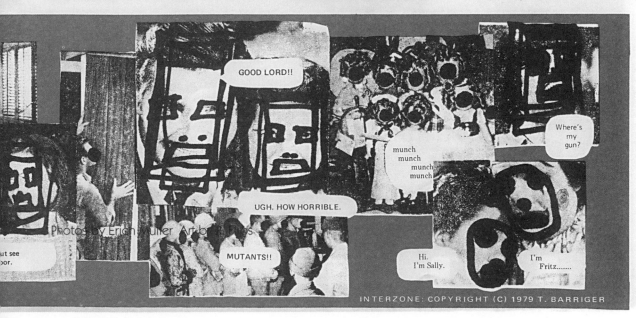

GOOD LORD!!

Where's my gun?

munch munch munch munch

UGH. HOW HORRIBLE.

MUTANTS!!

Hi. I'm Sally.

I'm Fritz.......

Photos by Erich Muller Art by R. Flus

INTERZONE: COPYRIGHT (C) 1979 T. BARRIGER

A very suspect character at best me thinks. He used to annoy everyone by referring to everything that happened on stage(and off) at the Mab as 'the theatre of illusion'...this to his credit I suppose. I generally tried to avoid the man thinking of him as a slimy old queen, which apparently he was but really no matter. Dirk was basically a business man and became infamous inadvertently through his role as the MC at the Mabuhay. He was the guy you loved to hate. Harmless really and I'm quite sure he had his charming sides as well but I really couldn't tell you what those were. He would more often than not stand in the wings stage left and stare at the delicious young male drummers pounding and sweating away at their kits. I myself took this as an off-beat compliment of sorts and all there is to add is God bless his perverted little soul. RIP Dirk.

Danny Furious after a hot and sweaty set. Photo by James Stark

Danny Furious, Avengers

■■■■■■■■■■■■■■■■■■■■■■■■■■■■■■■■■■■

As a promoter Dirk was in his own right quite brilliant, as a human being he was an obnoxious ass with very little respect for anyone . He saw an opportunity with the Punk scene to make some money, he really could not care less about the music, it was his chance to be the ringmaster in his own circus and he made a very good one.

Killerwatt were the first band to spray paint their name on the back wall of the stage. First time I asked Dirk if it was OK to do so. His reply was I don't give a fuck!

Ken Cameron, Lead singer Killerwatt

■■■■■■■■■■■■■■■■■■■■■■■■■■■■■■■■■■

My name is Terrell Winn and I put together the Jim Carroll Band with my writing buddy Brian Linsley, if you remember the band. Weren't many Black Punk Rockers in the 'scene outside of Bad Brains and me of course. One beautiful thing about Dirk was that he never, never related to me any different than the other idiots hanging around Sundays waiting to get on that weeks line-up. Black White, Asian, Hispanic, it did not matter to Dirk as long as you had a band and showed for the gig. He once booked JCB after we got an impressive fan base with the Go-Go's opening for us. Bunch of nice girls and quite innocent at the time. Not after they met Jim and the band. Let's say they graduated from R n R high school after we spent time together. Belinda took a real shine to Jim; Charisma carries a lot of weight I guess. This may note be an amusing anecdote but as they say:" If you remember the '60's you weren't there." Ditto for the '80's.

Thanks, 'Terrell Winn, Jim Carroll Band

PUSHUPS:LOS MICROWAVES VOICE FARM FAB MAB FEB 28

Poster by Anomymous

28 **The Push-Ups**
Los Microwaves
Voice Farm

29 **No Sisters**
The Symptoms
The Blitz

MARCH 1980

1 **The Offs**
The Rockats
Romeo Void
**Bay Area Outra-
geous Beauty
Pageant**

2 **Sharp**
Mindsweeper
The Magnetoes
The Insta-poids

3 **Benefit for Stu
dents Against
Nuclear Energy**
The Punts
VKTMS
No Alternative
Beisen Babez

4 **Rox**
Harvey

The Audios

5 **The Limit**
The Beans
The Spikes
The Drivers

6 **Black Flag**
The Enemy
The Boxes
The Invasions

7 **SVT**
Soul Rebels
Black Flag

8 **Soul Rebels**
The Pushups
The Enemy
The Limit

9 **VS**
No Alternative
The Witnesses
The Neutrinoz
C'Est La Guerre

10 **Haight Ashbury
Free Clinic Ben-
efit**
The Symptoms
The Jars

The Fleshapoids
07080
Phone Bill

11 **The Tools**
Social Unrest
45
The Breakouts

12 **Von Trigger**
The Bucks
Shiek Vaselino
The Zealots
The Schematics

13 **Jo Allen &
the Shapes**
Das Blox
**The New Mum-
mers**
UNS

14 **The Lloyds**
Cha Cha Billy
The Invasions
The Clones
**Doorways New
Wave Ballet**

15 **Legionnaire's
Disease**
The Clones

**Bay Area Outra-
geous Beauty
Pageant**

16 **Legionnaire's
Disease**
Fast Uns
Ire

17 **Nasty Habits**
The Instamoids
The Tots
The Verbs

18 **Benefit for False
Idols**
False Idols
**Justice League of
America**
The Roomates

19 **No Alternative**
False Idols
Social Unrest

20 **Cornel Hurd**
Nasty Habits
The Jars

21 **No Sisters**
Ultra Sheen
The Silencers

22 **Eye Protection**
No Sisters
The Suburbs
The Fabians

23 **The Silencers**
The Fabians
The Imposters
The Confessions

24 **James Dunbar for
School Board Ben-
efit**
The Neutrinoz
The Insults

Poster by Anomymous

Poster by Napoleon Balero

APRIL 1980

Justice League of
America
Red Asphalt

25 The Lewd
The Roommates
The Wrong Broth-
ers

26 The Punts
Das Blox
Romeo Void
The Witnesses

27 Bates Motel
Sharp
Barry Beam
The Blitz

28 Jim Carroll

The Soul Rebels
Bob

29 Geza X
Johanna Went
`Zev
The Non
Outrageous Beauty
Pageant

30 Geza X
The Mommy Men
VS.
Zev

31 The Instamoids
Life By Mail
Mindspeer
The Boxes
The People

1 Los Microwaves
The Schematics

2 No Alternative
Oquisha Paradox
The Abnormals
Jane Dornacker

3 The Contractions
Bob
The Witnesses
The Appliances

4 Dead Kennedys
No Alternative
Social Unrest

5 Dead Kennedys
Soul Rebels
VKTMS
Bay Area Outra-
geous Beauty
Pageant

6 Red Asphalt
The Enemy
The Nocturnals
USA

7 James Dunbar
Campaign Benefit
SVT
Eye Protection
The Pushups
6 O'Clock News

8 The X-Isles
Whispering Wil-
lows
Rich and Strange
The Delusions

9 Legionnaire's Dis
ease
VS
The Witnesses

Damage Magazine interview with Dirk Dirksen

Damage Magazine: You may be the most controversial concert promoter who ever lived. Lots of people hate you, some people love your everyone seems to have something to say about you. How come?

Dirk: I might be controversial in other people's minds. I'm certainly not contro-versial in my own mind. I'm just a char-ming, delightful individual.

Damage: Then what's their problem?

Dirk: Primarily lacking a sense of humor. Secondly, they're devoid of any sense of reality as to the operation of a theatre. Most of the complaints seem to stem from the fact that I've insisted on a tight door. Our formula of compressing the schedule to be able to present 3 groups between 11:00 and 2:00 requires constant pressure on all concerned to get the act up and off the stage in time. While this constant change on stage gives off an aura of high energy, it also creates tension. While this concept gives more artists the opportunity to present their work to an audience, it also shortens their time. This latter fact is a distinct advantage for the audience in most cases because it forces the artist to put forward their best.

However, it seems to smart some egos. And, in addition to these things, we still have to get the audience out by 2:00 in order to remain in compliance with the state laws governing the Mabuhay.

I view my role as that of an administrator representing the-artist with the ownership of the "four walls" of the Mabuhay, to being a mediator between the artist involved in each show…to provide the day-to-day continuity

Collecting money has never ranked high in making anyone popular. I think it's-very selfish, particularly of American audi-ences, to think they should be on a perpetual guest list. To me, that's totally Wrong. The artist has the same needs as the members of the audience, plus the expenses of the performance itself. What the hell is the artist supposed to live on? Indifferent applause? We live in a rip-off society and the ones' screaming "free music! Stop the rip-off" strike me as being blind to their own rip-off.

Damage: But there are plenty of rip-offs…

Dirk: Yes, there are plenty of incidents in which audiences are not given equitable return for their money and time. When what is paid for performance and production values is siphoned off to buy off someone's ego with three Rolls Royces'. Where it seems more is spent on hype than production values. However, on the other hand, many people ignore that art - music- experimenting with theatrical concepts is expensive. On top of that, you never know whether the damn thing is going to work or not. This leads the money-oriented individuals to seek the safety of endless repetition of successful formulas. From my perspective, that's where the greatest danger of rip-off exists, ie, the revivals that clutter up legitimate theatre on Broadway, the movies, the Bee'Gees, Disco...all stagnant.

Rock and roll, for me, is contempor-ary theatre. Speaking of rip-offs, recently we had an interesting situation. I" was approached by the wife of an artist well-known for his innovative approach to music and theatre. She indicated she was "going out on her own to explore" and would I book her band, I innediately scheduled a date, feeling here's a person walking in the shadows of someone hailed and lionized by the media and the audience, wanting herself more the "mentor" than a participant in the group. The act did not come off the way we had repre-sented it in our ads. After the show and the furor had subsided, I reviewed my files to see if I had been misled and in turn, misled the audience, I asked myself "What had we expected her to perform for us? Had we ever seen her perform? What was her her "art form?" Maybe her "art form" was to create the group's facade or front...yes, to act as a front for someone else... '

Damage: Sort of like Andy Warhol?

Dirk: Right, perhaps it was really a "great art experience" that most of us missed and maybe those individuals who received a refund really didn't get into the spirit of the performance that evening. I think what you've got here is another example of the interesting struggle between the perceiver and what the media leads you to expect.

Damage: Dirk, part of the controversy seems to center around the idea that, in lots of people's minds, you're the epitome of the capitalist, exploiter, on one hand, you say you're the protec-tor of the artist's interests, but on the other, you're making a living out of putting on shows at the Mabuhay...

Dirk: I make a living, where?

Damage: I assume from the Mabuhay?

Dirk: I don't make a cent out of it. Last year, I invested $8,600 of my own television earnings to pay production costs of printing, advertising, staff, etc… at the Mabuhay.

Damage: So why are you doing it?

Dirk: It's a long range plan or idea, a dream or whatever you want to call it. It's my goal as an artist - my art for is that of producer/director, my medium is film, television and theatre. 9 years ago I wrote a show as a proposed summer replacement for the Red Skeleton show on CBS called "Whatever." The idea was to weave together the creative, visual expressions of filmmakers, video artists, dancers, sculptors, etc. These independently arrived at pieces could be different time lengths. One of my objec-tions to TV is its identical time structure, 30, 60, 90 minutes; 6, 12, 18 commercial in-terruptions, spaced at set intervals of...

Obviously extremely limiting. There are thought patterns which take three minutes to explore and after that are a bore and, on the other hand, there are ideas which require a longer time to properly express. And no amount of editing or creative re-arrangement will do then justice. My format proposal requested an hour in prime time for a potpourri of expressions - visual pieces that could not merit a full program on their own, but when presented together with other works would fill out the established time patterns of TV. These works would make their appearance almost like a guest on a talk show. The host would shift the audience's atten-tion from one to the next. Where the "rating appeal" of the individual piece would not be the criteria for present-ing it, but where the combined energy of the contributed pieces would provide the audience appeal. The network people though the idea had merit, but rejected it because they felt it was impossible to collect enough material. Over the last 20 years, working as a television director and producer on a great number of remotes, "live location telecasts," I've encountered the challenge of having to compromising the quality of the telecast for the live performance or visa-versa. A very frustrating experience for all concerned. So I began exploring the idea of creating a space in which I could produce a concert, a drama, any kind of show or theatre and be able to record the event without compromising the quality of the performance either for the live audience or the hoe viewers. It occurred to me to set up my own studio facility which would serve as or be a theatre in which artists would present their works. This would allow me to spend By time and creative energies overcoming the chal-lenges of inherent in "live versus home viewers."

In setting up this video facility', I explored L.A., N.Y. and S.F. I chose the City because of its readily available pool of creative people, its history of tolerance, its relatively snail geographic spread and the weather which, for me, is more stimulating than L.A. or New York City. The prob-lem was how could I bring all these elements together and get the program I envisioned.

Damage: So you discovered the Mab, a Filipino "family style* restaurant and piano bar?

Dirk: Yes, a live theatre of great diver-sity: dance, drama, comedy, music, circus... I wanted it all. And that's exactly what we've had at the Mabuhay for almost five years. The "in-media" only discovered it when the first punk groups came to it, at that time there was a kind of punk aware-ness. But we'd been doing theatre way be-fore that, for two and a half years. The Mabu-hay, in terms of major media coverage, has existed three years, but prior to that I had staged Les Nickelettes, a feminist guerilla comedy group, we had done the Straight Theatre which staged a couple of plays by colleagues of Andy Warhol, we put on George Shearing, benefits for a ballet, all sorts of things. Then the Nuns and Mary Monday came alone, it was a continuation of the idea of cross-pollinating,, of making it a hangout for journalists, filmmakers, people doing things...

Damage: Hot very controversial...

Dirk: Some works were highly controversial and also the controversial entered because a number of people saw the Club out of his-torical perspective. It was "who's this s.o.b. up there collecting?" If you analyze the collecting, the Mabuhay is not owned by me. It's owned by Ness Aquino and his family, a family that had suffered great financial setbacks at the time that I came along. I offered to renegotiate with his creditors and with the tax people if he'd give me access to the building seven nights a week. The thing was to use the Mabuhay, which is located on a main enter-tainment thoroughfare, as a place in which artists like, let's say, Bruce Connor or Mindaugis, Target Video and all the other people that are writing, photographing, filming and taping can come in and capture their perspective of an act and we would then, at a later time, present it as a variety format on television. We'd take, for example, a film clip from artist A, from artist B, from artist C, maybe of the same act, so you'd see it from three perspectives. I felt that would be an in-teresting, stimulating and informative way of presenting per-formances. It would be real television.

Damage: What kind of stuff have you done on TV?

Dirk: I came into television at age 17,. I started producing live TV in L.A. from twelve midnight Saturday to twelve noon Sunday morning, It was a remote show in which we used 120 amateurs a night doing whatever they wanted to do. It was live from the showroom of an Oldsmobile dealer. A whole number of major stars did their trips, pulled their punk humor. People like Lenny Bruce, who came on dressed as a zoot-suiter with Jack Sheldon who's now the orchestra leader for Merv Griffin, blowing the trumpet for a different song than Lenny was singing. The mistress of ceremonies was the sister-in-law of the car dealer. This was live television's golden age. I've been an executive producer on national television. I did "Never Too Young," a soap opera on ABC which featured three "rock" groups a week. I've done sports shows, concerts with groups like Chicago, the Supremes, Ray Charles. But my interest has always been in getting the greatest number of people involved and, if you look at the Mabuhay, we've done just that.

Damage: How many performers play the Mab a month?

Dirk: Almost a thousand a month present their wares, *so to speak, to the public. There isn't anyone in San Francisco, there isn't anyone in L.A. who has that kind of track record...consistently, seven nights a week. OK, if I'm an exploiter, why the hell am I there seven nights a week for two years without a break? The only time I wasn't there was when I went to the Whiskey to present the Nuns down in L.A. In fact, we sent the Nuns, Crime, The Offs, The Readymades and a number of acts all over the west and never charged a percentage or anything else. We ran up bills of about $1500., mostly on telephone calls, attempting to get other people to accept new wave. The groups may not have made any great money, but I hope that our efforts helped them to get more exposure. Now that had really nothing to do with making money for the Mabuhay. Nothing. It has to do with my desire to see the artists involved succeed. My long range plan is and has been to do a TV show. I've spent five years- patiently working at eliminating the usual roadblocks and getting to that point. All five years at the Mab unpaid, just to be in a position to fulfill

my project. I probably live on less money than the majority of people that frequent the Mab. I don't think I've brought a new pair of shows or pants in three years.

Damage: OK, if you not making money, is the club making money? If it's not going into your pocket, whose pocket is it going into?

Dirk: Add it up yourself. After subtracting rent, taxes, material costs, help, maintenance, electrical hills which run hundreds a month. It's very expensive. The Aquino family who own the Mabuhay Gardens

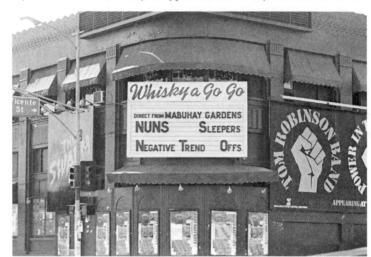

Photo Courstey of Dirksen Archives

have run into a sizable debt. Ness and his wife and family have the same problem of putting shoes on their kids, of paying the rent as everyone else does. Ness drives around in a 4 or 5 year old Ford. He's paying off his debts, but he's definitely not making a fortune.

Damage: Still a lot of people are uptight about $4.00 or $4.50 you charge to get in...

Dirk: We charge $3.00 or less for 85% of our shows. Some of those same shows are presented in San Francisco for $7.50 and $8.50 with most of the performers getting less. We charge $4.00 or $4.50 on weekends, which is the only time we can make more than it costs us. That's a simple fact of life. We charge a reasonable rate for those acts.. The acts get 65% of the total. The remaining 35% is budgeted for technical crews, telephone, .

Damage: A lot of people resent the way you act on the stage...

Dirk: The point has been that I'm nasty on stage. If anyone cares to take a look, they'll see that I have never blown smoke up anyone's behind on stage. I have been equal to all. I enforce the door the same way for all. I have tremendous fights with the restau-rant when they want to let ten people in for free to increase business at the bar. I've said no! If they say, well, they're our friends. I've said no! I've had fights to the point of walking out. Crime can attest to that. I walked out 10 minutes before they went on because four people were let in by the restaurant over what I felt was a fair number, listen, if it's exploitation, where am I making a fortune? If it's that I'm callous, where is my insensitivity?

Damage: What's the Mabuhay's policy on minors?

For one thing, it's misunderstood. The policy as prescribed by the Alcoholic Beverage Control is that when you provide food - which we do - you're-entitled to admit anyone in the company of an adult, if however an under 18-year old wants to remain on the premises after 11:06, that's taboo. Over 18 are always admitted provided they have the I.D. in their possession. They won't be able to drink, but they can get in. How many of the audience that comes to Broadway is under 18? Very few. For those few to jeopardize the platform for almost a 1000 artists a month is illogical. If a rock group feels that it needs to show itself to 7, 4, 5 or 3 year-olds, hey, there's the Saturday matinees at one-thirty.

Damage: What's the admission?

Dirk: I think a buck. Again, it's another case when people say we're unresponsive, I say "fie, fie, you're ignorant, you didn't check your facts." Unresponsive? The groups that work with us have complete access to our books in terms of the grosses and expenses. If a performer wants to come in and look at our books, they've always been open. I don't know for a fact, but I don't think any other organization does that in terns of financial statements and things of that sort.

Damage: Talk about the changes that have taken place in the kinds of people that come to space...

Dirk: It changes everyday.

Damage: Hasn't it really become pretty preppy? Lots of people from the suburbs?

Dirk: No. I think we're too antagonizing to ever become preppy. I certainly hope so. If we ever get to the stage where the instamatics take over, well, there's a conscious effort on part not to let it get too preppy. As annoying as our "burger eating morons" are, I certainly prefer their company.

Damage: What did you think about the boycott against Bill Graham's Screamers' concert last month?

Dirk: I think the Graham Organization is making an error on that particular booking. I know they want to do something for new wave. They're coming from the perspective of wanting to bring new wave to the main-stream concert audiences. I think being presented by the Graham Organization is a great career plus for any artist. The price they asked reflected legitimate costs of that location and let's not overlook the group's hefty fee demands. They want to translate or transport a performance which works on an intimate level to a larger venue. More in this case is definitely not better. It is insensitive of the current audience rebelling against the large impersonal hall which only super stars can fill. I don't question their integrity, just their perspective. I hope their concept works, despite my reservations, because otherwise every critic of new wave will use their failure to say "See, stick to disco!"

Damage: There are plenty of people in the scene who boycott the Mabuhay, how do you feel about that?

Dirk: If people want to nail us in terms of boycotting, I think they really should understand the value of what it is they're boycotting. You may have disagreements with me on certain points, Christ, why not? But it's not grounds for boycotting because the effect is only negative on the scene. It doesn't solve anything. I certainly can't be accused of being inaccessible.   , -

Damage: Do you like the people who come to the Mab?

Dirk: Of course. For all the shit I put up with, I'd have to. Is it a need to be loved? God, I would be out there kissing ass if I wanted to be loved. If it were publicity, I don't need it. Even though I've had six pair of glasses broken, two ribs kicked" in, my nose broken five times there, I'm still there every night. I'm not a masochist. I don't have any leather in my apartment, to the best of my knowledge. For me, it's simply a desire to have a platform for people to express themselves, including myself.

Damage: Someone asked me to ask you if it's true you hate punks?

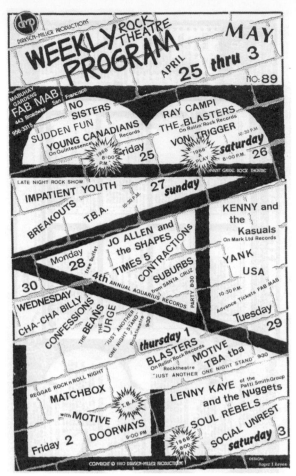

Poster by Roger Reyes

10 Sudden Fun
Social Unrest
Secret Service
The Titans

11 Soul Rebels
The Lewd
Ultra Sheen
Doorways New
Wave Ballet

12 SVT
Soul Rebels
Barry Beam
Bay Area Outra-
geous Beauty
Pageant

13 Punts
Surface Music
Dickheads

Black Flag

14 No Alternative
Black Flag
Tools
False Idols

15 Jet
X-Isles
Tatooed Veg-
etables

16 Jim Carroll

17 SVT
Symptoms
Social Unrest

18 The Mutants
The Plastics
The Scientists

Single Bullet
Theory
Doorways Dance
Revue

19 Pointed Sticks
The Plastics
The Modernettes
Single Bullet
Theory
Bay Area Outra-
geous Beauty
Pageant

20 The Tots
The Bucks
The Lozers
The Dispensers

21 Horizon Unlim-
ited Benefit
Cha Cha Billy
The Rockers
The Confessions
The Sponges

22 Harvey
The Titans
Life By Mail
Super Hero

23 The Schematics
The Prisoners
Surf Pistols
Ped X-ing
"Just Another
One Night Stand"
Preview

24 Pointed Sticks
Bob
The Saints
False Idols
"Just Another
One Night Stand"
Premiere

25 No Sisters
Sudden Fun
Young Canadians
"1968" A Play

26 Ray Campi
The Blasters
Von Trigger
"1968" A Play

27 Impatient Youth
The Breakouts

28 Jo Allen & the
Shapes
Times 5
The Contractions
The Suburbs

29 Kenny & the
Kasuals
Yank
USA

30 Cha Cha Billy
The Confessions
The Beans
The Urge

MAY 1980

1 The Blasters
Motive

2 Matchbox
Soul Rebels
Harvey
Doorways Dance
Theater

3 Matchbox
King Snakes
Lenny Kaye &
the Nuggets
Soul Rebels
Social Unrest

4 Lenny Kaye &
   the Nuggets
   The Invasions
   See Spot

5 Stoneground
   The Impostors
   The Titans
   Impatient Youth

6 False Idols
   Social Unrest
   The Witnesses
   The Looserz

7 Young Canadians
   The Verbs
   The Bucks

8 Jim Carroll
   Lenny Kaye &
   The Nuggets
   Social Unrest

9 The Young Cana-
   dians
   Jayne Door & the
   Knockers
   Cha-Cha Billy

10 SVT
   The Young Canadi-
   ans
   The Tools
   "1968" a play

11 The Soul Rebels
   The Plugz
   Impatient Youth
   The False Idols

12 07080
   The Witnesses
   The Bi-Products
   Boys Life

13 Eye Protection

VKTMS
The Lewd
The New Critics

14 The Enemy
   Mindsweep
   The Saints
   The Undersongs

15 Bob
   Eye Protection
   Social Unrest
   The False Idols

16 SVT
   Barry Beam
   The Scientists
   Doorways New
   Wave Ballet

17 The Contractions
   Eye Protection
   Social Unrest

18 Secret Service
   The Cowboys
   Ram
   The Appliances

19 The Appliances
   Zamora
   The Crooks

20 SVT
   Soul Rebels

21 New Critics
   The Hostages
   The Bucks
   Neasden Knights
   Ibbilly Bibbilly

22 Psychotic Pine-
   apple
   Sudden Fun
   The Titans
   Wild Remains

Poster by Anomymous

23 The Offs
   The Payolas
   Snake Pit
   The Skids

24 The Offs
   Soul Rebels
   Romeo Void
   Bay Area Outra-
   geous
   Beauty Pageant

25 The Confessions
   Payola
   The X-Isles
   The Whippetts

26 City Arts Benefit

27 Second Annual
   Musical Dog
   Awards
   SVT
   Stoneground
   Eye Protection

Black Flag
Social Unrest
The Enemy

28 Harvey
   Wild Remains
   Funktionaries
   The Prisoners
   Improv Alterna-
   tive

29 No Data

30 Eye Protection
   Times 5
   The Witnesses
   Doorways New
   Wave Ballet

31 No Sisters
   Soul Rebels
   The Dickheads
   Bay Area Outra-
   geous Beauty
   Pageant

About the Dummies

The Dummies were the opposite of glad handing – it was a chance to insult everybody possible, acknowledging what they were especially bad at. Worst male vocal, Don Vinyl – a tough hustling out of the closet gay who jumped into the mix fearlessly, really a visionary now that a large chunk of other Americans are exiting puking. Deborah Iyall as worst lyricist was a joke within a joke, as she wrote the iconic "I might like you better if we slept together", really the only song by any of us jokers that 's still in national play. The categories themselves shine above the tippy toe wall of niceness that chokes all current public discourse: Sleaziest Manager, Most Posturing Band, Ugliest Band, and finally Most offensive band: The Tattooed Vegetables – I think I get them mixed up with Psychotic Pineapple in the recesses of my club memory, which is like the mcs for the night, Jane Dornaker and Biafra. One half died in a helicopter crash, one half still on fire.

Photo by Erich Mueller

Jennifer Blowdryer

■■■■■■■■■■■■■■■■■■■■■■■■■■■■■■■■■■■■

Dummy was a Cockapoo

She got her name when I went to visit the Joey Bishop Show. The crew he had to tape that show was a crew I had used on a soap opera. So I came to visit those guys and had the dog with me and let her walk around. Just before the start of the show and Bishop was standing there getting his lights ran over to him and sat come here , come here he goes, "Ha! Ha! Ha! even get his own dog And then she takes off down, she had just says, "O you Dummy". name. So Dummy was a

When she came to the dog just loved the asleep in back of the

Photo courtesy Dirk Dirksen Archives

and cues down, Dummy on his shoes, I'm going, and nothing happens. So Look at that, that jerk can't to come to him Ha! Ha!." and runs over and he looks pissed on him. Then he That's how she got her show business dog. the Mab, it was amazing, noise. She would fall speakers. She had a thing

she would do. If I put my heel down she would jump up on my leg and just dry hump like mad. So when I would go and introduce an act I would put my foot down and raise the heel up and she would just jump on and like on command dry hump like mad and when I put it down she would quit and walk off. The audience would be grossed out.

Dirk Dirksen

DUMMIES PHOTOGRAPHS BY ERICH MUELLER

andy prieboy
EYEPROTECTION

PRIEBOY ANDY

david javelosa
LOS MICRO~WAVES

JAVELOSA, DAVID
LOS MICROWAVES

billy sharp
SHARP

BILLY SHARP
WORST MALE VOCALIST

danny christy
CONTRABAND

DANNY CHRISTY
WORST VOCALIST
CONTRABAND

gloria balsam

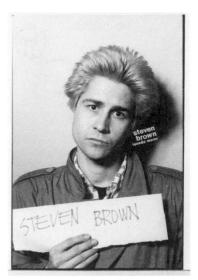

steven brown
tuxedo moon

STEVEN BROWN

johnny silvers
SILVERTONE

JOHNNY SILVERS WORST

FRED MABUHAY
GOLDEN DRAGON

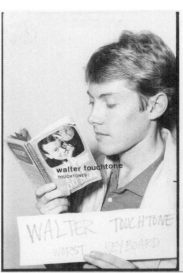

walter touchtone
TOUCHTONES

WALTER TOUCHTONE
WORST KEYBOARD

heidi
familiar
V.S.

HEIDI FAMILIAR

will shatter

WILL SHATTER
WORST BASSIST

GINGER COYOTE
JOURNALIST

michael snyder
JOURNALIST

Michael Snyder
Journalist

olga de volga
V.S.

OLGA de Volga

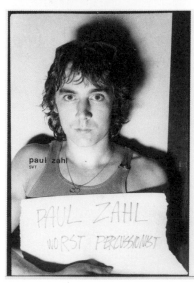

paul zahl
SVT

PAUL ZAHL
WORST PERCUSSIONIST

MARIAH UREEL
PERCUSSIONIST
SUPERHEROS

mikal
waters
SOUL REBELS

MIKAL WATERS
WORST VOCALIST
SOUL REBELS

nyna vktm
VKTMS

NYNA VKTM
WORST FEMALE VOCALIST

B PEOPLE

JULY 10 & 11

MABUHAY GARDENS

443 BROADWAY

Poster by Anomymous

THE VERBS

FAB MAB

with: THE NOISE

TUESDAY JULY 22

Poster by Anomymous

JUNE 1980

1 The Witnesses
Baby Murphy
Tri-Matrix

2 Social Unrest
The Silvertones
The Lewd
C'est La Guerre

3 Boys Life
Elements of Style
Good Samaritans
Paradox
Tri-Matrix

4 Noise
Press
Rockers
The Unnatural
Act

5 Secret Service
Press
X-Isles
The Dots

6 The Soul Rebels
Bob
The Dots
Ultra Sheen

7 SVT
Jane Dornacker
Cha-Cha Billy
Bay Area Outra-
geous Beauty
Pageant

8 07080
The Hostages
The Tots

9 The Silvertones
The Saints
Two Tones

10 The Invasions
The New Critics
The Prisoners

11 The Verbs
The Appliances
The Bucks
Lost Angeles

12 The Bent (formerly
the Deadbeats)
Social Unrest
The Subhumans

13 Dead Kennedys
The Subhumans
Black Flag
Doorway New
Wave Ballet

14 Dead Kennedys
The Bent
The Subhumans
See Spot
Bay Area Outra-
geous Beauty
Pageant

15 Impatient Youth
Noize Boyz
Der Lifer

16 VKTMS
The Lewd
Social Unrest
The Witnesses
The Spectators

17 The Titans
X-Ray Ted
The Neutrinoz
The Memos

18 Silvertone
VS.
The Middle Class
Ultra Sheen
Larry Talbot

19 Eddie & the Sub-
    titles
    Ultra Sheen
    Larry Talbot

20 The Mutants
    The Diodes
    The Electrody-
    namics
    Jeorgia A's
    Girl's Life

21 The Mutants
    The Offs
    Social Unrest
    Bay Area Outra-
    geous Beauty
    Pageant

22 The Bachelors
    The Even
    The Electrody-
    namics

23 Silvertone
    The Zeros
    VS.
    C'est La Guerre
    Nuevos Robuts

24 The Verbs
    The Breakouts
    The Whoremones
    Little Death

25 Bob
    The Dickheads
    Jet
    Improv. Alterna-
    tive

26 Harvey
    The Whippetts
    Rox
    The Prisoners

27 Roy Loney &
    the Phantom

Poster by Anomymous

Movers
Silvertone
    The King Snakes

28 Crime
    The Contractions
    The Memos

29 The Lewd
    Golden Gate
    Jumpers
    Sheik Vaselino
    Ibbilly Bibbilly

30 Benefit for Bay
    Area Network
    to Resist Mili-
    tary Conscription
    VKTMS
    Social Unrest
    Regime

JULY 1980

1   The Prisoners
    Whispering Wil-
    lows
    Neasden Knights

    Silhouette
2   Jayne County
    (formerly
    Wayne County)
    VKTMS
    Social Unrest

3   Mary Monday
    Fast
    VS
    See Spot

4   No Sisters
    Bob
    Silvertone

5   The Offs
    The Fast
    Ultra Sheen
    Bay Area Outra-
    geous Beauty
    Pageant

6   VKTMS
    The False Idols
    The Breakouts

7   Eye Protection

    The Readymades
    Bob
    No Sisters

8   The Paradox
    The Tots
    Tri-Matrix
    The Gyrations

9   Silvertone Party
    The Plugz
    Impatient Youth

10 The B People
    Human Hands
    Barry Beam

11 SVT
    The B People
    Indoor Life
    New Wave Ballet

12 SVT
    Human Hands
    The Verbs
    Bay Area Outra-
    geous Beauty
    Pageant

150

APPLIANCES

PLAY Liberace

AT THE MAB

JULY 22

The helpful young publicity man said to Libby. "Whatever you want, I'm your man." But he didn't realize just what Fatso had in mind.

Poster by Anomymous

13 The Wasp Women VS.
The Cosmetics

14 VKTMS
Social Unrest
The Witnesses
Kathleen

15 The Paper Tears
X-Ray Ted
The People Who Knew Brian
Da Crooks

16 The X-Isles
The Good Samaritans
Jet
The Memos

17 The Enemy
Dred Scott
The New Critics

18 Jim Carroll
Dred Scott
Ultra Sheen
Doorways New Wave Ballet

19 Jim Carroll
The Enemy
The Angry Samoans
Bay Area Outrageous Beauty Pageant

20 The Angry Sa moans
The Hostages
Boys Life
The News

21 Church of Rock'n'Roll Benefit
The Cowboys
The Neutrinoz
The Byproducts

The Cookie Monsters
16 Fingers

22 The Verbs
The Noise
The Appliances
The Elements of Style

23 VKTMS
Social Unrest
The Witnesses
The Tenants

24 Silvertone
The Neutrinoz
Ultra Sheen

25 The Mutants
Zilch
Social Unrest
Doorways New Wave Ballet

26 Shakin' Street
Silvertone
Zilch
Bay Area Outrageous Beauty Pageant

27 Damage Magazine Party

28 The Regular Joes
The Whoremones
Neasden Knights

29 Chaser
The Cowboys
The UnNatural Act
The People Question

30 The Imposters

The Jars
The Saints

31 Bob
Eye Protection
Cabaret Mathode

AUGUST 1980

1 The Contractions
The Young Canadians
UXA

2 Roy Loney & the Phantom Movers
The Readymades
Bay Area Outrageous Beauty Pageant

3 No Data

4 Punk Globe Party
Dead Kennedys
VKTMS
The Verbs
Ultra Sheen
The Spectators

5 New Critics
The Hostages
Fresh Points
The Citizens

6 The Darts
Silvertone
King Snakes
The Saints

7 The Darts
Ultra Sheen
Dick Heads
Frisco White

8 No Sisters
Peter Bilt & the Expressions

84 Rooms
Doorways New
Wave Ballet

9 Dead Kennedys
Flipper
Circle Jerks
Bay Area Outra-
geous Beauty
Pageant

10 Noise
Lost Angeles
Wrong Brothers
Sponges

11 The Offs
Eye Protection
Social Unrest

12 Confessions
The Spectators
Bi-Products
Eddie Paris

13 Peterbilt & the
Expressions
Das Blox
Romeo Void
Elements of Style

14 Readymades
New Critics
The Symptoms
Boxes

15 SVT
VKTMS
The Cowboys

16 SVT
Eye Protection
Doorways New
Wave Ballet

17 Mary Monday
The Neutrinoz

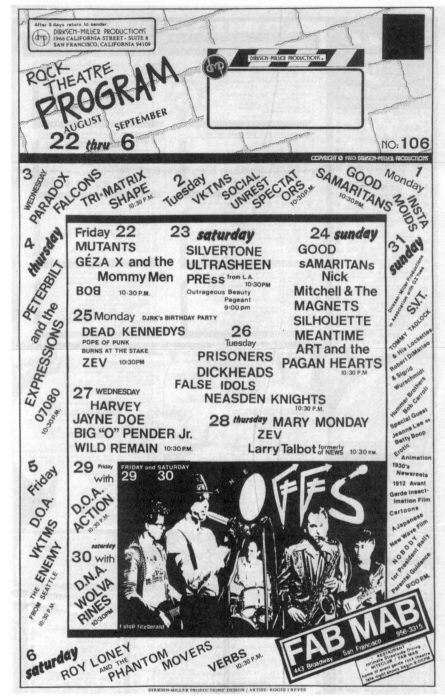

Poster by Roger Reyes

Bay Area Outra-
geous Beauty
Pageant

18 Harvey
Golden Gate
Jumpers
A-T's

19 The Whippetts
Ms. Justice
Golden Gate
Jumpers
The Balls

20 Beluga Whale
Press
Detroit Blues
Band
Delton Ace

21 Geza X & the
Mommy Men
Eye Protection
Barry Beam

22 The Mutants
Geza X & the
Mommy Men
Bob

To understand the impact, influence and importance of the Mabuhay in its heyday, it helps to recall what the world was like at that time.

The nineteen-seventies was, for the most part, a dismal and forgettable era in the history of American popular music. As the decade began, the tremendous flood of musical creativity which had characterized the 'sixties seemed to dry up and disappear overnight, to be replaced at first with a lot of silly, sing-songy, soft rock, and then, as the decade wore on, with the soulless, heartless, mindless madness called Disco. It supplanted live rock music in nightclubs, bars and public venues everywhere, while nobody raised a word of protest. Maybe music had been in the toilet for so long by then that a whole generation just didn't know any better.

Some said that the old farts who owned and controlled the music and recording industries were hoping rock'n'roll could just be ignored into non-existence, that its time would pass like a bad dream, and that new technology (in the form of drum machines, talking guitars and various electronic gizmos) would soon render live music, and even live musicians, obsolete. If that was their plan, it seemed to be working. The canned music clubs were attracting a paying audience which didn't appear to know or care that DISCO SUCKS' Popular music had lost its way, and even its sense of direction. Indie labels, the Internet, and affordable computers were still years away. Current music offered no relief or inspiration, and by 1975 the 'seventies was shaping up like a good decade to stay home and listen to old records, which is what my friends and I mostly did.

Then we started hearing about a new, live punk-rock music scene going on every night inside a Philippine restaurant called the Mabuhay Garden, located near the east end of the Broadway strip in San Francisco's North Beach. Right away 1 was suspicious. The only reason a hippie ever went to North Beach in those days was to pick up his girlfriend after work at one of the strip clubs. For years, Broadway had been the exclusive domain of old greaser businessmen who had to pay to get laid. Nobody under thirty could even afford to live there. The beatniks who made the neighborhood famous had left a long time ago.

And ptink rock, what was that about? I'd heard the term applied to the New York Dolls a few years before, but they had never interested me. What kind of self-respecting individual would call himself a punk?

I finally got around to checking out the Mabuhay in person after my friend Mervyn got a job bartending there. Having a buddy behind the bar can do a lot to make a place interesting......

Peter Claudus

■■■■■■■■■■■■■■■■■■■■■■■■■■■■■■■■■■■■■■■

Showdown on Broadway, Boulevards

The Broadway boom continues unabated. The Fab Mab, The Back D.O.R., and Stone are jammed every weekend with people thirsting for live music. Meanwhile, noted new wave prophet Dirk Dirksen sees the potential for a bust. Money is tight. On the average, weekly attendance is down. "The next six months will tell the tale," broods Dirksen. "The local scene may

To understand the impact, influence and importance of the Mabuhay in its heyday, it helps to recall what the world was like at that time.

The nineteen-seventies was, for the most part, a dismal and forgettable era in the history of American popular music. As the decade began, the tremendous flood of musical creativity which had characterized the 'sixties seemed to dry up and disappear overnight, to be replaced at first with a lot of silly, sing-songy, soft rock, and then, as the decade wore on, with the soulless, heartless, mindless madness called Disco. It supplanted live rock music in nightclubs, bars and public venues everywhere, while nobody raised a word of protest. Maybe music had been in the toilet for so long by then that a whole generation just didn't know any better.

Dirk with VS, Photo courtsey Kathy Peck.

Some said that the old farts who owned and controlled the music and recording industries were hoping rock'n'roll could just be ignored into non-existence, that its time would pass like a bad dream, and that new technology (in the form of drum machines, talking guitars and various electronic gizmos) would soon render live music, and even live musicians, obsolete. If that was their plan, it seemed to be working. The canned music clubs were attracting a paying audience which didn't appear to know or care that DISCO SUCKS' Popular music had lost its way, and even its sense of direction. Indie labels, the Internet, and affordable computers were still years away. Current music offered no reliefer inspiration, and by 1975 the 'seventies was shaping up like a good decade to stay home and listen to old records, which is what my friends and I mostly did.

Then we started hearing about a new, live punk-rock music scene going on every night inside a Philippine restaurant called the Mabuhay Garden, located near the east end of the Broadway strip in San Francisco's North Beach. Right away 1 was suspicious. The only reason a hippie ever went to North Beach in those days was to pick up his girlfriend after work at one of the strip clubs. For years, Broadway had been the exclusive domain of old greaser businessmen who had to pay to get laid. Nobody under thirty could even afford to live there. The beatniks who made the neighborhood famous had left a long time ago.

And punk rock, what was that about? I'd heard the term applied to the New York Dolls a few years before, but they had never interested me. What kind of self-respecting individual would call himself a punk?

I finally got around to checking out the Mabuhay in person after my friend Mervyn got a job bartending there. Having a buddy behind the bar can do a lot to make a place interesting......

Peter Claudus

Poster by Roger Reyes

Poster by Roger Reyes

23 Silvertone
Ultra Sheen
Press
Bay Area Outra-
geous Beauty
Pageant

24 Good Samaritans
Nick Mitchell
& the Magnets
Meantime
Art & the Pagan
Hearts

25 Dirk's Birthday
Party
Dead Kennedys
Zev

26 The Prisoners
The Dickheads
False Idols
Neasden Knights

27 Harvey
Jayne Doe
Big "O" Pender Jr.
Wild Remains

28 Mary Monday
Zev
Larry Talbot

29 D.O.A.
Action

30 DNA
The Wolverines

31 SVT
Tommy Tadlock
& his Lockettes
Robert DiMatteo
& Sigrid Wur-
schmidt
Hummer Brothers
Bob Carroll

1 Good Samaritans
The Instamoids
Zolar X
Balls
Eddie Paris

2 VKTMS
Social Unrest
The Spectators

3 Paradox
The Falcons
Tri-Matrix
Shape

4 Peterbilt & the
Expressions
07080
The Enemy

5 D.O.A.
VKTMS
The Enemy

6 Roy Loney & the
Phantom Movers
The Enemy
84 Rooms

7 Black Flag
Fall of Christianity
The Rabble
The Cosmetics

8 The Sponges
Meantime
Wrong Brothers

9 The Tools
Zobop (formerly
X-Ray Ted)
The Neutrinoz
The Memos

Poster by Anomymous

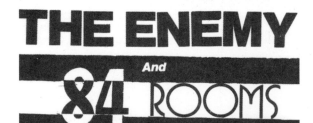

Poster by Anomymous

How I got to play the club....

After experiencing English punk music and the San Francisco scene with seeing the appearance of The Damned in March 1977, a major priority for me as a musician became to play at the Mabuhay Gardens. This opportunity would make itself clear in June. Through a friend, Gene Amenta, a Glam band I was performing called Ginger got an opening slot for the SF band Premier on a Wednesday at the Mabuhay Gardens in June 1977. Originally the opening band was supposed to be Ginger; unfortunately that band broke up a week after accepting the job.

The Next with Mike Tringali at the Mab. Photo by James Stark

Fortunately this was a situation I was not about to let go simply because the band vaporized. It was time to commit one weird sin, with the selfish purpose of getting into this club at any and all costs. I made the decision to not tell Gene or Premier that Ginger was no longer together. I was going to bring in some "ringers" and lie about the identity of Ginger to break into this music scene. The results of this episode would reverberate though the club for several weeks.

The afternoon of the gig the band came to the club to sound check; my car was parked around the corner on Pacific Avenue. Because I failed to read the parking meter when I left for sound check, my car was towed and impounded at the City Yard. I would not discover my plight until I returned to my car after the sound check, I was lucky to get the help of a friend to loan me $75 to get my car out of the impound lot before the evening festivities. This was a portent of an evening to remember.

During the band sound check, Gene and his band came in the room; Gene asked me who the folks on stage were? I simply answered "It's the band" without looking at him directly. I think he knew there was some hoodwinking coming down, but no words were exchanged. I intuitively felt there would be some repercussions for what I had done. But I really didn't care.

To clarify: It wasn't lying about who the band was that caused the trouble. It was the use of a chemical fogger that leaked to the second floor at the beginning of the band's set. At that time "Evolution of the Blues" was in performance in the On Broadway Theater directly above the Mab. When the "smoke" could be seen coming up from the floor, someone pulled a fire alarm. Within five minutes there were three fire trucks blocking Broadway outside the club including a hook & ladder. When the firemen burst in through the alley side entrance, the band had detonated a pair of flash pots. Of course the room was pea-soup consisting of the chemical fogger and the residue left by the flash; no doubt the firemen were initially confused with a room full of people, band and smoke.

157

The firemen entered stage-left, and then caught the attention of our road crew. The officers asked Hal, our roadie what we used and Hal handed over a half-empty bottle of flash powder purchased earlier in the day from StageCraft in Berkeley. The fire department absconded with the flash powder and left the building. The band continued to play and was not interrupted by the false alarm intrusion.

Because I was on the opposite side of the stage from the firemen and due to the zero visibility, I never saw the fire department and had no knowledge of what had just happened.

At the end of the evening I went to Premier's manager, Bill Masselli about getting paid. Bill turned beet-red and proceeded to yell at me about the use of a fog machine and flashpots and the false alarm it created. Maybe being oblivious to the situation kept me from reacting to this man. After handling his tirade, I received $10 for the effort. I must admit I was not impressed with the take from the door, but I admitted total success to accomplishing what I had set out to achieve; get into this club and create a scene.

The next day after sleeping on everything that happened, I wrote a song about this experience called "You Can't Go Home". The first verse summarizes the story:

It's really too bad that you can't go home
They took my car away and towed it to Nome
I can't get it out, I don't have no money
My baby found out and I lost my honey
But you can rock and roll…..

The following week Dirk Dirksen had a mandatory band meeting to explain to everyone if theatrical effects are to be used to let the club know to prevent another false alarm episode. The lead guitarist from Premier, Angie was in the room for the meeting, everyone was laughing at Angie about the blame placed on Premier when actually it was the devils from Fremont responsible for the havoc.

Mike Tringali

■ ■

A frequent patron of the fabulous Mab was Ed Langdon, a.k.a. Brother Ed, a genuine San Francisco hippie survivor from the 'sixties, when his psychedelic liquid light show, "The Brotherhood of Light," illuminated Bill Graham's music shows at Winterland, the Fillmore Auditorium and the Fillmore West. Although he was somewhat put off at first by name "punk rock," Ed soon became a Mabuhay fixture and numbered the VKTMs, Kathy Peck, Jennifer Blowdryer, Ginger Coyote and dozens of other Mab regulars among his large circle of friends.

Ed was diagnosed with cirrhosis of the liver in 1984 and died in 1992. He was remembered for the true Renaissance man that he was—a poet, an artist, a gourmet chef, a drug smuggler, a drunkard, a dope-dealing whoremaster, a patron of the arts and a wonderful human being— at a widely attended memorial celebration of his life which was held at the Kennel Club and hosted by…who else? … Dirk Dirksen.

BROTHER ED, a Mab regular

TATTOO YO MAMA

It was a dark and stormy night,...

The telephone lines were starting to warm up as punk rockers around the City were starting to call each other and inquire about the latest rumor.

It was 1981. The Rolling Stones were on tour and coming to San Francisco's Candlestick Park to promote their latest album, "Tattoo You".

The immediate cause of the telephoning was an item in the San Francisco Chronicle. In his column, Herb Caen, mentioned that on the tour, the Stones had been playing smaller clubs, unannounced, for the diehard fans and as a lark. I think they had played at the small clubs in Toronto and Worcester, Mass earlier in the tour.

Mr. Caen stated that the Rolling Stones were going to do the same in SF, and there was a 95% probability that it would be at the Mabuhay Garden on Broadway.

The instigators of this rather benign hoax were George Epileptic, a radio DJ at local college/underground music station KUSF and punk musician/impresario Mike Reid. George and Mike worked at the Electric Theater in SF and they both had the natural punk attitude of disruption and humor. They playfully started a rumor that the Stones were playing unannounced at the Mabuhay and the rumor eventually got around to Herb Caen, apparently, and he cemented the tale by putting it in his column.

Now, the Mabuhay Gardens was a Filipino restaurant by day and punk rock hellhole by night. The prediction by Herb Caen was news to club owner Dirk Dirksen. The Rolling Stones and the bands that played at the "Fab Mab" could well be from parallel universes and I would say most of the Mab habitués would look down their noses at the Stones and their fans. Maybe decades before the Rolling Stones were cutting edge and envelope-pushing, but by the '80s they were the epitome of mainstream arena "Rock". Or so the punkers believed.

As the punk rockers started calling each other, the phones at the Mab started heating up as well. The more Dirk denied even the remotest possibility that the "Greatest Rock and Roll Band in the World" was coming to his club, the more the faithful believed it to be true.

Epileptic approached Dirk with the idea to assemble a band of misfit punkers to do Stones covers. Dirksen, never one to miss an opportunity to create mass chaos and fun, jumped on it and gave them a date. To cap it off, when the listing for the night's entertainment was run in the Chronicle, it featured a mysterious band no one on the scene had heard of named, "Tattoo."

My friend, Susan Miller, guitarist for the Tanks got a call from George to play. I was drafted as well for a couple of songs. The only other face I remember was Brendan Earley from the Mutants. Both he and I knew Stones from our checquered cover-band past. (Don't tell any of my friends!)

The afternoon of the show, I meandered down to the Mab to maybe squeeze in a sound check or, shudder a practice. At 5 PM there were hundreds of people lined up on the sidewalk for a 8PM door opening.

Dirksen spent hours walking up and down the sidewalk with a bullhorn, announcing, "The Rolling Stones are not playing here tonight! Go back to the suburbs!.

And so on,...

When the doors opened the throng paid at the front, moved in, and sat on the floor in front of the stage. The occupancy level was exceeded quickly, and there was a line outside.

Several regular Mab bands opened before "Tattoo", the only one I remember was Sid Terror and the Undead. An old-school first-wave punk band. The Stones fans looked on as Sid harangued and confronted them. He had an intense stage presence and the songs were about, well, the undead. The Stones fans bobbed their heads and tapped their feet, and were generally amused, but between sets chanted for the Rolling Stones.

Yeah, well, Tattoo hit the stage with an epic drunken avalanche of chaos that sounded just like the Rolling Stones at their second or third rehearsal. It was actually kind of cool.

To be honest, the crowd eventually seemed to get that the joke was on them and they played along and got with the rock and roll spirit of the whole night.

Dirksen at his finest.

Bruno DeSmartass, 2019

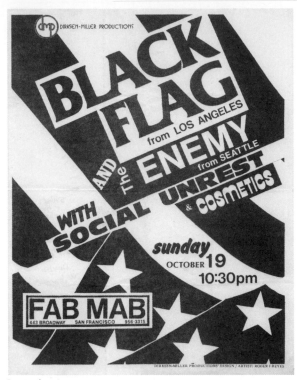

Poster by Anomymous

Poster by Anomymous

28 The Spectators
Chrome Dinette
Krayons
The Conservatives
The Negatives

29 Silhouette
Chaser
Little Death
Yank
Alternate Living

30 Harvey
Question
The Breakouts
Species

OCTOBER 1980

1 The Symptoms
The Memos
Push
Young Adults

2 415 Records Party
The Units

Baby Buddha
Naked City

3 Black Flag
The Rabble
The Lewd
The Verbs

4 Eye Protection
Paradox
Doorways

5 Video Rouge
The Cowboys
The Rabble
Portables

6 Punk Globe Libra
Party
VKTMS
No Alternative
Kathleen
The Breakouts
Alienation

7 The Hostages

Phil Phillips
07080
The Fleshapoids

8 Zobop
The Breakouts
Chrome Dinette
Algo

9 Rik L. Rik
Witnesses

10 Rik L. Rik
Witnesses

11 SVT
Jim Carroll
Doorways

12 SVT
The Question
Boy's Life
Strap D'Etro
X-Men

13 Rock Against the
Draft Benefit:
Witnesses
Social Unrest
Brain Damage
Too Bad
No Alternative

14 Titans
Hoovers
Two Tones

15 No Data

16 Harvey
The Dickheads
Golden Gate Jump-
ers
Two Words

17 DOA
The Young Canadi-
ans
Modernettes

Poster by Anomymous

Poster by Anomymous

18 No Sisters
Anemic Boy-
friends
The Spectators

19 Black Flag
The Enemy
Social Unrest
The Cosmetics

20 The Lewd
The Lubricants
De.deTroit

21 The Mutants
The Blackouts
Our Daughter's
Wedding

22 Eye Protection
Young Canadians
Feederz

23 DOA
VKTMS
The Tenants
False Idols

24 DOA
The Feederz
The Blackouts
Layers of Scum
Dance Theater

25 The Units
Los Microwaves
Video Rouge
Doorways New
Wave Ballet

26 Tommy Tadlock
& His Lockettes
The Bandaloons
Moonliters
Ulna & the Femurs
Rocket Man

27 Benefit for
District Elections
Keith Joe Dick
Jane Dornacker
Chas-Cha Billy
Der Lifer

28 Neutrinoz
King Snakes
Phantoms

29 Peterbilt & the
Expressions

30 Paradox
Trixx
Extremes

31 Wall of Voodoo
VKTMS
Keith Joe Dick

NOVEMBER 1980

1 Benefit for West-
ern Front:
The Donuts
The Press
Bay Area Outra-
geous Beauty
Pageant

2 The Humans
VKTMS
Funktionaries

3 Walk for Survival
Benefit
Golden Gate Jump-
ers
The Neutrinoz
Zobop

4 Brittley Black
& the Ripper of
Crime
The Cowboys
The Witnesses
Golden Dragon
Ventures
The Undead

5 Impeachment
Party:
Barry Beam
The Instamoids
The Appliances
Der Lifers
The Flexopumps

6 Eye Protection
The Breeders
Silhouette

7 The Offs
No Alternative
Impatient Youth
Doorways Dance
Theater

8 The Offs
The Witnesses
The Stupeds
The Lewd

u n i t s

& LOS MICROWAVES
& VIDEO ROUGE

FAB MAB
SAT. OCT. 25

Poster by Anomymous

Poster by Anomymous

9 St. Regis
People Who Knew
Brian
The Conservatives
Chaser
Fire

10 X-Mas Eve
The Memos
The Breakouts
False Idols

11 Necromantics
Meantime
Simple Tactics
Nocturnal Emis-
sion

12 The Sirens
The Valkays
Match Heads
The "O"

13 Bob
84 Rooms
Mr. Orange

14 Flamin' Groovies
Aliens
Hika Su
The Appliances
Doorways Dance
Theater

15 The Contractions
Peterbilt & the
Expressions
Harvey

16 The Visitors
The Mercenaries
Blake Quake &
the Tremors
Planet
The Whippetts

17 KUSF Party:
Crime
No Alternative
Sluts A Go Go
The Hoovers
Kathleen
Baby Doodle

18 The Hoovers
The Neutrinoz
Push
The Rakes

19 VKTMS
The Witnesses
Alienation
Under Songs

20 Peterbilt & the
Expressions
Chrome Dinette
P.C. 2000

21 The Wolverines
The Lewd
Doorways Dance
Theater

22 24K (formerly
Killerwatt)
The Units
VKTMS
Bay Area Outra-
geous Beauty
Pageant

23 Neasden Knights
X-Men
The Spectacles
The Saucers
Too Bad

24 Baby Doodle

Fall of Christianity
The Outfits
The Tots
The Sponges

25 Little Death
The Breakouts
Algo

26 Paradox
Farallon
The Trixx
Tri-Matrix

27 The Zeros
The Middle Class
The Wounds

28 The Mutants
Johanna Went
Legal Weapon

Poster by Anomymous

kusf 90.3 fm **party!**

CRIME

NO ALTERNATIVE
SLUTS·A·GO-GO!
HOOVERS
kathleen
monday
NOV. 17 ! 9:30

FAB MAB
443 Broadway
San Francisco
956-3315

Poster by Anomymous

29 The Mutants
Mission to Burma
Legal Weapon
Bay Area Outra-
geous Beauty
Pageant

30 Monicker
The "O"
Krayons
Artichokes

DECEMBER 1980

1 Impatient Youth
Woundz
The Blackouts
Crusifix

2 Athletico
Spizz-80

3 Athletico
Spizz-80

4 The Blasters
Ryth a Rama
Mindsweeper
Super Hero
Outrageous
Beauty Pageant
Revue & Costume
Ball

5 SVT
VKTMS
The Verbs
Doorways New
Wave Ballet

6 SVT
Chrome Dinette
Video Rouge
Ankoku-Buto
Dance Theater

7 Ness' Birthday
Party

8 Creep Magazine
Benefit

9 Mick & the Mag-
nets
Enigma
The Vandals
Good Samaritans

10 The Prisoners
Tenants
The Cosmetics
Two Words

11 Flexopumps
Alienation
Layers of Scum
Ankoku-Buto
Dance Theater

12 Video Rouge
Impatient Youth

13 Peter Bilt & the
Expressions
Ultra Sheen
Chrome Dinette

14 Fire
Match Heads
The Hostages
The Rakes

15 The Hoovers
Algo
Strap D'Etro
The Breakouts

Marli and Two of his nieces, Carla and Cynthia
Ron Jones on Dirk

Hey Dirk! Quite a family you have here. For most of us Dirk Dirksen is the impresario of the cabaret. Kathy Peck told me that ten thousand bands passed through the Mab, that seems like a lot. Every band was his favorite band toy, no matter who you were. He got top billing, actually, according to Denise every band got top billing, each and was allowed to discuss the bill, It was Dirk who gave us a start and loved you for who you are. Wearing a penis nose he taught us it was better to throw popcorn than beer bottles and that everyone has a spot on the stage of life. He said, "You don't have a long time, the stage is small, there are other acts to follow even if they suck.

Audiences are feral junkies, fame eludes them. To Kathy, Dirk was a father she never had. Someone who was always called on just to say how are you, how about breakfast at the Seal Rock Inn. Only Dirk could take care of Kathy's dog, Tutu, aka Satan Assistance, good name for a band. To the various cats on Treat Street Dirk was known as the Dog Lucifer. He kept Tutu in mind with cats purring. Dirk kept care of so many. For a lot of time some what distance in the back of our minds, like a miracle in waiting often wearing a tutu or offering a hand when you need it. A place holder in our chaotic lives, someone that cared for us, someone who really cared for us.

For Marli, Dirk's sister, Dirk will always be her baby brother hearing the bombers over Germany minutes before the sirens would sound. Born into a family of Aeronautical Engineers and Architects who ruled a straight line, laws of physics and button down minds. Dirk preferred to wear a hat with pom poms. In his sisters words, " We had formal gardens, Tulips all in a row, Dirk's yard was all over, Daffodils next to Marigolds, Calla Lilies and fine looking Tomato plants. The Dirk that Marli knows loved classical music and family. He thought like a tyrant yet if one had faith and faith in one's pursuit a person could over come every obstacle. That is faith to be helped along by Damon's loyalty, ah Damon, Dirks loved one, protected one, partner. Dirk and Damon, Dirksen and Malloy corrupted the world with vision of positive spin and cosmos of fairness and humor, he simply prevailed. Dirk provided the dream and Damon turned the knobs and pushed play.

For Carla and Christiania, Dirk was that crazy uncle, everyone needs a crazy uncle, someone to give permission to play and be silly. Not to take things too seriously not try and control everything, It is fun being connected to a yoyo but it even better when Dirk just wants to be with you, spaghetti dinner, watching the Simpson's, without saying a word his way of saying I love you. By the way it was Christiania who provided him with plants for his lost and found garden, you didn't know he was a gardener did you and it told me what made Dirk such a great gardener and human being it was his belief that we define our selves in our moment of weakness. Even those abuse plants would flower in beauty and them seed themselves, reach back and help others, reach to the sky. For Oliver, who keep care of him now so gently. For Oliver sitting there next to his mother Carla and his grandmother Marli, Dirk would be a legend. I suspect that one day all of us will think of him as the real Pope. Dirk will be this mysterious presence that his mother and grandmother will try to explain but you know sometimes life can't be planned or explanted only appreciated.

For the children of the Mission and many of you might not have know this, Dirk was the funny looking chef providing a Food Bank meal of Venezuelan Cashews, lots of olives, Chocolate Bavarian Beef, Fire Pasta, a Banana Carrot Cake, Salami Roll and a gallon of Cow

Girl Whip Cream, it was his receipt. He prepared a Turkey dinner for a holiday meal and some how arranged for a visit from Santa. Who else would bring the SFPD together with the children at Mission Rec. It was Dirk who taught the value of make it yourself meal. Not be afraid of what you can do with a knife in your hands, maybe you should be a little afraid. The importance of improvisial cooking using what ever you can find and eating at a table with friends.

For me, Dirk and Damon were business partners, although I hardly call what we did a business. Never had a contract, never shook hands on a deal, never had a lawyer, We kind of wandered into making story telling videos not talking about full color surround sound lots of home movie images and a Jazzy score. This was about growing up in San Francisco, neighborhood heroes, moments that change our life's, gave meaning to it all. The everyday events at the Recreation Center for the Handicap, a Special Olympics basketball team that never lost a game, providing a Reader Digest version of Swan Lake. Putting on unlimited shows at the Metreon, Borders, Transmission and

Dirk and Damon at work. Photo from Dirkson archives

countless coffee houses. A video about the murder of Jo Jo White that's required reading in Danish schools, you didn't know that, Unity Festival, and a mini documentary about Saint John's third grade girl's basketball team and just last month a video essay, the first poetry reading by mentally disabled artist at Creatively Explored. Thanks to Damon we created a web site to sell these CDs, In five years, this includes international sales, we sold 57 copies, (Laughter and applause) That's about ten copies a year with a discount if you bought more than one. Dirk kept elaborate records of the sales on tiny pieces of paper and tried to figure out if there might be a profit in our adventure. That what it was, it was an adventure, it recorded things that mattered, to be given for free to those that matter. Special Olympics basketball team, Sisters of Perpetual Indulgence, Seniors performing a water ballet interpretation of South Pacific, mentally disabled poets, Creatively Explored, everybody got a free copy to take home and play for their friends. You see, Dirk is a seeker of light. In order to feel good about yourself, be proud of your contribution of being on stage at least once or in a story telling picture, to see themselves, to receive recognition and dream about doing it all again. So Dirk was a lousy accountant but he was also a loving big brother wearing a funny hat, a father to Kathy and of course Asian Children. He was an Impresario, a loved one, a mentor to Damon, crazy uncle, do it yourself chef, Gardner of the lost and found and media mogol, but most of all, Dirk, circle of my friends, I will miss you dear friend O how I will miss you. Your off like a comet in the future, a mischievous jester, you believe in us, a better life, we miss you standing in the shadows of our life, cheering us on, becking us to forever to be true to ourselves. I can hear the bombers, they sound like drummers.

Dirk. Dirk now do me a favor will you? Every now and then a circle will be, repair to the ocean listening to your whispers, feeding the kids across the street, telling stories, honoring the disabled, the elderly, taking care of everything, playing Charades after Thanksgiving dinner and we are eating breakfast at Seal Rock. We are sitting at the Columbarium Dirk it is a strange place. You know what is wonderful, looking at your sun drenched nitch in your Coco Pot container, its got a crack in the back so we turned it the right way. There's an order here at the Columbarium,

Dirk in his Coco Pot. Photo by James Stark

finality or is there. How reality and fantasy blur to us here for the day. Good News! Good News Dirk! Damon is doing great. When Carla's lawyer asked, "How did Dirk get into such a financial bind" He spoke clearly, "Dirk never spent money on a cruise or on himself."

Kathy, she is organizing a cookout at the Great America Music Hall thanks to Dawn and Slam's. Boy, Dawn really came through, everyone came through. Punk bums, punk bands on stage accompany by poets from Creatively Explored your kind of show. Did you know that Chet Helms is just up the stairs. I wonder if I rub your Coco Pot is something unusual would happen. Look over shoulder Dirk, we're here, we're all here, good-bye Dirk.

Look there are bomber overhead, getting closer, Auschwitz, Baghdad, Contractions, Flipper, White Debutants, Mutants, Meet you at Swan Lake.

Look, look, look away, Dirk is gone.

Ron Jones

Poster by Anomymous

Poster by Anomymous

ARSENAL

FAB MAB
Saturday 14th Feb.

Poster by Anomymous

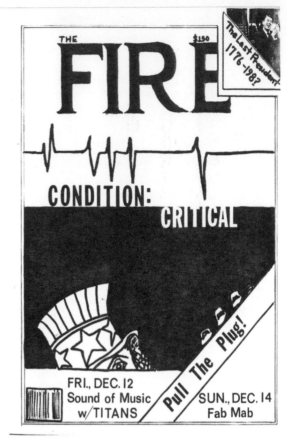

THE FIRE
$1.50

The Last President
1776-1982?

CONDITION: CRITICAL

FRI., DEC. 12
Sound of Music
w/TITANS

Pull The Plug!

SUN., DEC. 14
Fab Mab

Poster by Anomymous

Bad Attitude
Mr. Orange

30 **Hoovers**
The Verbs
The Spectators
Wild Remains

31 **SVT**
Dirk "Cannon-
ball" Dirksen
Barry Beam
The Neutrinoz

JANUARY 1981

1 **The Hoovers**
Cha-Cha Billy
Neasden Knights

2 **Snakefinger**

3 **The Plugz**
VKTMS
The Tanks

4 **Security**

5 **Forget It Maga-**
zine Benefit
Impatient Youth
The Roomates
Social Unrest
Same

6 **Silhouette**
Monicker
07080
The "O"

7 **Mr. Clean**
The Sponges

8 **The Imposters**
Farallon
Tri-Matrix
Mad Hatter

9 **Black Flag**
The Lewd
The Woundz

10 **Black Flag**
No Alternative
Impatient Youth
Outrageous
Beauty Pageant

11 **Arsenal**
Flexopumps
Two Words

12 **Silhouette**
Brain Damage
The Reporters

13 **Hard Attack**
The Sirens
Krayons

14 **Dead Ends**
Instamoids
Parental Guid-
ance
Young Docktors

15 **Ripper Magazine**
Party:
Red Rockers
No Alternative
Social Unrest

16 **Subhumans**
The Middle Class
Red Rockers

17 **The Contractions**
Appliances
Ryth-a-Rama
Bay Area Outra-
geous
Beauty Pageant

18 **Security**
Mr. Orange
The Extremes
Alienation

19 Romeo Void
    Voice Farm
    Robert Mc Mahon
    Jerry Kids
    Translator

20 No Alternative
    Sluts a Go Go
    Wolverines
    M.C. Mickey Nixon

21 King Snakes
    Elements of Style
    Sweet Tommy
    French Kiss

22 Harvey
    Lorelei
    Surface Music
    Algo

23 Second Special
    Giant Jam
    Lorelei

24 Snakefinger
    Readymades
    Prefix
    Bay Area Outra-
    geous Beauty
    Pageant

25 Men in Black
    Jayne Doe
    The Rakes
    Bad Attitude

26 Birthday Party for
    Sandy & Joseph:
    Spys
    New Boob
    Ms. Justice

27 The Neutrinoz
    The Saucers
    Thump Thump
    Thump
    Night Shark

28 P.C. 2000
    The Flexopumps
    07080
    The Visitors

29 The Blok
    The Verbs
    Fire

30 Lloyds
    Viva Beat
    Spectators

31 SVT
    The Wolverines
    Modern Machine
    Bay Area Outra-
    geous Beauty
    Pageant

FEBRUARY 1981

1   Interference
    The Artichokes
    The Sponges
    White Lunch

2   The Visitors
    The Krayons
    Chris Harburger
    & the Captions
    The Colours

3   Silhouette
    Meantime
    Rhyth-a-Rama
    X-Mas Eve

4   Mr. Clean
    Monicker
    07080
    Neasden Knights

5   Paradox
    Third Rail
    Shape

Monday, Jan. 5th at 10 pm
playing a benefit for

FORGET IT! magazine

will be:
(impatient) Youth
Social Unrest
The Roomates
The Same

That's Monday, Jan. 5 at
the Fab Mab (in San Francisco)
Be there!
The magazine is free!

Poster by Anomymous

INTERFERENCE

appearing

February   1st mabuhay
5th Inn of the Beginning   COTATI
7th Ollies w/Subteraneans   OAKLAND
13th Grange w/Contractions   SANTA ROSA

Poster by Anomymous

6   The Adolescents
    Agent Orange
    Crusifix

7   B-People
    The Wolverines

    No Alternative
    Bay Area Outra-
    geous Beauty
    Pageant

8   Indoor Life
    William Talen

The Pope of Punk morphs into Mother Theresa

I never met Dirk in his incarnation as "The Pope of Punk", my first encounter with him was in 1994 when Dirk and Damon documented Unity Foundation's annual Unity Festival at the Bandshell in Golden Gate Park. My first impression of Dirk was that of a hard nosed and abrasive television producer. I never dreamed that we were destined to become friends, associates and even partners in the production of Unity Foundation's "Positive Spin" television program, for which he served as executive producer for the 8 years prior to his passing.

It all began in 1995, when Dirk and Damon moved into a old Victorian house on Treat Avenue in the Mission District of San Francisco. I was working with a coalition of organizations to create special events to commemorate the 50th Anniversary of the Founding of the United Nations in San Francisco. Somewhere along the way the idea of producing a television documentary of the 50th Anniversary Celebrations was proposed. Since Unity Foundation had already worked with Dirksen Molloy Productions we suggested that the coalition hire them to produce the documentary. We were thrilled by the quality of their work, their ability to document the events and almost immediately integrate the footage into the body of the film along with the film footage provided by the United Nations. They also successfully negotiated a deal with an independent television station and secured national satellite time,

Following the UN 50th Anniversary events, Dirk asked me if Unity Foundation would like to have office space in Dirksen Molloy Productions' Treat Avenue facility. I was surprised by the offer, but because we seemed to work well together I accepted. However,

I thought "this is really crazy "The Pope of Punk" and the Hippy producer of concerts in Golden Gate Park are now working together. I thought that Punks and Hippies were suppose to despise each other."

As soon as Unity Foundation moved in, Dirk asked if he could be designated the foundation's Coordinator of Community Projects. I said yes, even tho I wasn't sure what he was planning to do, because he seemed so passionate about making a difference in our local community. And what a difference he made! Dirk immediately began meeting all the neighbors to determine what their needs were. He then set in motion a series of projects which made a dramatic difference in our community. Under the banner of the "Our Block Program" he organized weekly street cleanings, graffiti paint outs, tree plantings, gardening classes, and his favorite - the weekly Children's Cooking Class, where he held court with the young latch key children at the Mission Recreation Center, which was located across the street from our office. He had a real way with the kids and they all loved and respected him. Building on the momentum of these projects Dirk decided it was time to bring the whole community together. This led to the annual Thanksgiving Day Dinner and the annual Children's Christmas Party which brought together hundreds of children and their families. The local police and fire departments even got involved by providing many of the gifts for the Christmas Parties. We all got caught up in the spirit which led to Unity Foundation producing two Community Unity Festivals at the Mission Recreation Center. Continuing to this day is the local Community Food Program which provides bags of groceries to families in need in the neighborhood. So this is Dirk's legacy in his last incarnation as "Mother Theresa".

Billy McCarthy, Unity Foundation

more Ken Cameron. interview

KillerWatt back stage Mabuhay Gardens, Photo Dirksen Archives

I love The Avengers. Continue the story. I love it.

They'd all only played small clubs. I was the only guy with the equipment for playing bigger venues, so the bass players borrowed my bass equipment. I was on stage all night making sure the stuff worked. That's when I met Jonesy. Later on, I played with him for eight years and did a couple albums with him. I met Sid that night, too. He was the first guy I met from the band and he was very nice to me. It kind of shocked me how nice he was. After that gig, the place almost turned into a riot at the end. I ended up grabbing Paul Cook and taking him to my house. He stayed at my place for three or four days after that last Sex Pistols gig.

I want to know about punk rock and how you got into that.

It was weird, because I was a musician and most of the guys who played punk really weren't.

How did that even happen?

I was playing with everyone up in Nor Cal. If you had a band and needed someone for a bass gig, I was there. I even got to play with Charley Musselwhite and Randy Hansen for a few gigs. Anyway, we had this band called Killerwatt for quite a while. We were more of an AC/DC kind of band. At some point, we started messing around with punk rock stuff. We wrote a song called "I Was A Punk Before You Were A Punk". The Tubes ended up doing that song.

Really?

Bill Spooner, the guitar player from the Tubes, used to play with us a lot. He liked the song, so he took it. They were supposed to give us a song in return. We traded for a song that we didn't even like and never did. They ended up doing that song and giving us no credit, but who cares? Anyway, I knew most of the local punk players pretty well. Some of them used to ask me for help. They liked doing the punk thing, but they wanted to know how to play. I'd give them five-minute pointers, so I got to know a lot of them well, like Will from Flipper. It was really sad when he died. A lot of those guys are gone now, mostly from drugs, such a waste really. Later on, a bunch of us put together a band called the Bobby Death band. This was after we'd been doing gigs with Mink DeVille, Devo and the Dead Boys. Rabbit, who was the cook at the Mabuhay, was in the band. It was a fun time.

You need to break it down some more.

The Mabuhay Gardens was the first northern California punk venue. It was one of the biggest punk venues in the country.

It was San Francisco's answer to CBGBs.

Right. The Mab was insane. It was nuts. My band Killerwatt and the band Mary Monday were the first bands ever to play at the Mabuhay. Mary Monday's claim was that she was the first woman to ever sing and dance at the North Pole.

Very interesting.

The Mab was just a Filipino restaurant with a stage. The owner couldn't make any money selling Filipino food, so he started doing rock n' roll shows. Then the punk thing came in. Dirk Dirksen started doing the booking and The Mab and the punk scene just sort of evolved together. The Mab was an amazingly hellacious - and always fantastic - place to be.

You had the Dead Kennedys and the Avengers.

From what the old lead singer from Killerwatt, Ken Cameron says, The Dead Kennedys hadn't had a gig yet at the Mabuhay, and nobody was really into them when they first started. They really wanted to play though. They just kept calling and saying they wanted to play. We were headliners, so we always had someone open up for us. One night, Magister Ludi was supposed to open. We found out four hours before we were supposed to go on that they couldn't make it. The only band that we could get on short notice was the Dead Kennedys. That was the first time the Dead Kennedys ever played the Mabuhay. It's one of those interesting, little known, little cared about facts.

I care. Let me ask you this, though. What about skateboarding, during that time in the mid '70s? You were living in San Francisco, so there were hills. I'm trying to make the connection.

I was actually surfing in San Francisco. I surfed Ocean Beach and Fort Point.

Did you ever get swept away by the current and end up at the little beach north of there?

Ken Cameron
Lead singer Killerwatt

■■

I was a comedienne/ performance artist that Dirk took under his wing - I had my own one woman show at the Mab and then was part of the early comedy shows that opened for the late night acts. one of my 'claims to fame' was that I was performing at the Mabuhay when it was Ness' supper club - I was working at the musician's switchboard at the time and got a gig singing back up with Amapola and was later demoted to lip syncing... actually that story and my humble beginnings are on this website which a record collector for from the uk put together with some help from me.

When I was down and out (1980) — Dirk hired me to work for his production company - he would ply me with pot and cookies and I'd become totally useless at performing any clerical tasks - which really didn't seem to bother him much and it was because of Dirk's generosity - after I put my single out on Richmond Records — he gave me his mailing contact list - which led to fluffy making it's way to Dr. Demento where it was subsequently included on his 'world worst records' compilation album —amazingly 30 plus years later I'm still getting air play! right now I'm negotiating with a kid's radio station out in Portland to include FLUFFY on a compilation record. I like so many other performers got where I did because of Dirk's support.

I loved the Mabuhay...and what it stood for.... I loved being a part of the punk scene even if i was on the periphery... I named myself Gloria after Patti Smith's version of Gloria - I was definitely 'a Telegraph Avenue Child' — I even wrote a song about the Mabuhay using the music from the song Bali Ha'i.

all the best, cynthia frantz (aka gloria)

■■■■■■■■■■■■■■■■■■■■■■■■■■■■■■■■■■

Hi, I'm Eric Lenchner. In 1977 I was known as Ricky Sludge. I played lead guitar for the Readymades, which included Jonathan Postal, original bassist for the Avengers, and Brittley Black, one of Crime's early drummers. My old high school friend and band mate, the late Morey Goldstein, recruited me into the Readymades. He said there's this scene going on in San Francisco – people are picking up guitars, learning 3 chords and going on stage at the

Ricky Sludge Photo by James Stark

Mabuhay Gardens. (Morey had also turned me on to the Ramones the previous year.) Morey told me he had a vision of me as a total live-wire guitar player, going wild, and wearing a headdress made of guitar cords and wires sticking out every which-a-way. Never got the headdress thing going, but we did play a lot of wild music and had a lot of wild times. We played at Mabuhay with Devo, The Dead Boys, Nico, The Cramps, X, and many others.

At one of our many Mabuhay shows I had a new guitar amplifier which was giving me trouble. We were all on stage, with Dirk ready to introduce us, and I was fiddling with the amplifier, trying to get it to work properly. Dirk announced to the audience that "guitar players should learn how to use their equipment BEFORE they get on stage". I was properly humiliated.

Then, many years later (2004), I hired Dirk and his partner Damon Miller to video tape a benefit concert my young guitar students at the Professor Sludge Guitar Academy were having at the Great American Music Hall for H.E.A.R. (Hearing Education and Awareness for Rockers), Kathy Peck's organization. Kathy, as bass player for The Contractions, and myself, as well as many other musicians, left substantial portions of our eardrums on the floor at Mabuhay Gardens over the years - punishingly loud being the usual volume level.

When I went to pick up the DVD's of the concert from Dirk, he looked me in the eye and said "It's really wonderful what you're doing with those kids – it's a beautiful thing." He went on for some length. I could see he was genuinely moved, and I was very touched that he freely shared his emotions with me. I realized then what an artifice his Mabuhay personality had been. That was Dirk's way of acting punk.

Side bar: At the anti Briggs Initiative benefit at Mabuhay in 1978 we were introduced by Harvey Milk, who said "This next band is the greatest thing since Pete Seeger! Please welcome - The Readymades!". Harvey Milk of course had never heard us before, and probably most of the punks on hand had never heard Pete Seeger.

All my sludge, Ricky, Eric Lenchner

Poster by Anomymous

Poster by Anomymous

9   Punk Globe Val-
    entine Party:
    Alienation
    Bad Attitude
    The Undersongs
    The Rimms

10 **The Reporters**
    Barry Beam
    The Artichokes

11 **Tri-Matrix**
    Tyrant
    The Streets

12 **Mindsweeper**
    Jane Dornacker
    Barry Beam
    Alienation

13 **VKTMS**
    Red Rockers
    X-Mas Eve

14 **The Lewd**
    Red Rockers
    Seven Seconds
    The Tanks
    Bay Area Outra-
    geous Beauty
    Pageant

15 **The Sleepers**
    Tommy Tadlock

16 **Impatient Youth**
    Social Unrest
    X-Men
    The Woundz

17 **Bite on Life Party**
    No Alternative
    Parental Guid-
    ance
    Impatient Youth
    The Saucers
    Ambulance

18 **Paradox**
    Farallon
    Tour de Force
    Diamond Ball

19 **Zev**
    Charlie Mc Mahon
    Preservations

20 **Peterbilt & the**
    Expressions
    Visitors
    Alienation
    Neutrinoz
    Musign Mime
    Dance

21 **Beef (formerly**
    Eye Protection)
    Readymades
    The Verbs
    Bay Area Outra-
    geous Beauty
    Pageant

22 **Extremes**
    The Sirens
    Wrong Brothers
    Plastics
    Medium

23 **Political Prisoners**
    Support Group
    Benefit:
    Wolvarines
    No Alternative
    The Woundz
    The Tanks

24 **The Blank**
    Little Death
    Nobody Famous
    Washed Up and
    Shabby

25 **The Conservatives**
    Tri-Matrix

I-Mortals
Blake Quake & the
Tremors

26 Das Blok
Chrome Dinette
Mojo

27 Black Flag
Eddie & the Sub-
titles
The Stains
TSOL

28 Black Flag
The Adolescents
Minute Men
China White
Bay Area Outra-
geous Beauty
Pageant

MARCH 1981

1 Zobop
New Boots
The Krayons
Box
Assassins

2 Species
The Suspex
The Artichokes
Chris Harburger &
the Captions

3 Forget It Magazine
Benefit:
Woundz
F.Holes
Los Olividados

4 Hard Attack
Authorities
Dodge Darts
Child Prostitutes

5 Our Daughter's
Wedding
Lifers
X-Mas Eve
Four Cats

6 Romeo Void
Neutrinoz
X-Isles
Translator

7 No Alternative
Impatient Youth

8 The Blasters
Alienation
Rhyth a Rama

9 Farallon
Paradox
The Artichokes
Management

10 The Spectacles
Art & the Pagan
Hearts
Uptights
Four Cats

11 Mr. Clean
The Verbs
Barry Beam

12 KPOO Party:
No Alternative
Two Tones
Frank Hymng
Der Lifers

13 Hoovers
Box Boys
Visitors

14 No Sisters
Box Boys
The Appliances
Bay Area Outra-

LIFE BITES
BACK
PARTY

TUE
APR 14
Sluts
a go go
ADAPTORS

LEWD
PG

SIDESHOW
FILMS & FILMING

FabMab
443 brdwy

dmp

T-SHIRTS FIRST 30

Poster by Anomymous

geous Beauty
Pageant

15 Naked Lady
Wrestlers
Uptights

16 KTIM Radioactive
Hour Party:
Mr. Orange
Chrome Dinette
Das Blok
Blake Quake &
the Tremors

17 The Neutrinoz
Exposure
Night Shark
Dizoxen

18 Elements of Style
Mojo

Interference

19 Sweet Tommy
The Verbs
The Sirens
T-Mortals

20 Dead Kennedys
The Middle Class
Woundz

21 Brian Brain
Minimal Man
Charlie Mc Mahon
Impatient Youth
Bay Area Outra-
geous Beauty
Pageant

22 Wolvarines
Frank Hymng

I met Dirk Dirksen in late 1976 in The Mabuhay when I was working at Dolby Labs located a few blocks away on Sansome Street. After work I would head up to Broadway and hang out at the Mabuhay or the Stone which was located across the street. In the hopes of getting hired, I would introduce myself to just about every band I could and ask "Do you have a live sound man?"

After seeing me hanging around for a couple of months, Dirk offered me an assistant stage manager job which I gladly accepted. During this time, I met Dana who was the lead singer of Magister Ludi and started to help the band get bookings.

Magister Ludi was not a punk band, but very loud and over the top, especially when they played at The Mabuhay Gardens. They were more old school rock, just the opposite of what The Mabuhay scene was.

Magister Ludi booked a date at the Mabuhay to open for the New York band, The Dictators. Dana decided he really wanted to upstage The Dictators with "handsome Dick Manitoba." Dana's idea was to have him brought into the club inside a coffin. This lead to other ideas, like using dry ice smoke seeping out of the coffin, then we thought how could it lead to the macabre, we both brainstormed and finalized with the idea of getting a somewhat cleaned up cows leg, still on the bone, to become one of his arms. We hired a professional make-up artist to make Dana look ghoulish. We would eventually wrap the cow's leg around Dana's right arm and shoulder with ace bandages with the hoof just past his hand. Another idea was to get a Hearse that we could park outside the club, but we had to scrap that idea because it was too expensive.

Dana and I and some other band friends rehearsed this in Dana's garage. The first thing we learned was that dry ice smoke can not be inhaled (being that it is carbon monoxide), so we cut a hole in the side of the coffin with a tube for Dana to breath. I went to Dirk and proposed these ideas to him, he loved it and said the crazier the better.

Show day comes and we bring the coffin through the front door of the club with dry ice smoke billowing out and then place it on the stage. Dana jumps out of the coffin with his "new growth" and proceeds to prowl and scream through the bands set. After about three songs the ace bandages come loose and the cow leg falls off which Dana now uses as a prop, kicking it around the stage, swinging it around and bouncing it off the back wall. This was all hilarious, pure Dada theatre. I remember after the bands had played and trying to get both bands gear out the side door the atmosphere became a bit strained with some macho posturing and name calling ensuing. But in the end, there were no fights and it was all very funny and quite memorable.

I had a very good working relationship with Dirk Dirksen on and off for about 4 years and have nothing but admiration for him and his promotional concepts which ranged from insulting the audience to dressing up in a gorilla outfit and running down Broadway to get customers to come into his club.

Ronnie Lantz

Dirk was a total jerk when he was in character, but a true gentleman when not in the public light.

I traded a lot of heckling with Dirk over a few years. As the Nuns first soundman, to soundman and then band member of Crime, I saw it unfold from the very first days. In early 1977 we'd ride on busses in SF with our spiked jackets and spiky hair and people would glare at us saying, "What the hell are you???" As Howie Klein said, it was more of a hang-out than a music club, we were just there to be with our freaky friends. Then in mid-77 the news media picked up on "punk rock" and suddenly we were underground art-rock ground zero. That was actually around the time Dirk appeared on the scene, after Ness went through a string of disastrous booking agents. I think Crime was the band Dirk loved to hate the most, but as Crazy Horse seems to be saying, he really did understand and love what was happening. I recall once giving Dirk a ride to Marin County to pick up some cans of film he was desperate to get a hold of, and on the way back he bought me and my girlfriend dinner. He was clever, cool and charming over dinner, a side of him I'd never seen since I only had contact with him in the club, where he was always "in character." Like Howie, I hadn't seen Dirk very often over the last decade or so, except once or twice at various "reunion" events. But no one who was around back in the day will forget him.

Joey D/Kay

■■■■■■■■■■■■■■■■■■■■■■■■■■■■■■■■■

I'm Keiko Shimosato from the San Francisco mime Troupe. I just wanted to say how much we appreciated Dirks' work with us. He and his partner filmed Crawford Gulch for us several summers ago. He was a very sweet and earnest person to work with. I also had the luck to have been in the Fab Mab scene way back when... He terrified me then, but hey I was sixteen. The man I met a few summers ago was a wonderful videographer and I was glad to have met him again. Thank you Dirk Dirksen. The San Francisco Mime Troupe Thanks you from the bottom of our hearts.

Keiko Shimosato Carreiro

■■■■■■■■■■■■■■■■■■■■■■■■■■■■■■■■■

However, I have been assembling a plethora of stories and antidotes for you for the book. Dirk and I had a love/hate relationship that tended more towards the love side of the coin. I would never have become a musician and enjoyed the life I lead if it were not for him. I dare say that even studying organic chemistry, teaching it and now taking on medical school would not be possible if it weren't for Dirk. You see, by Dirk letting me play at the Mabuhay Gardens, I gained the confidence I lacked as a geeky teenager. I think of him every time I overcome something posing a problem. 18 months ago I nearly died from cancer. However, those little life lessons that Dirk taught me proved extremely valuable and helped me win that battle. For those of us that carved out careers, we would not have been given a chance by anyone else. Onward and Upward!

Hugh Thomas Patterson, aka, Johnny Genocide

Poster by Karl Hinz

APRIL 1981

1 April Fool's Party
3rd Annual Musi-
cal Dog Awards:
Red Rockers
Impatient Youth
The Untouch-
ables

2 Jo Allen & the
Shapes
The Squares
Mojo

3 Dead Kennedys
U.K.Decay
Dodge Darts
Fried Abortions

4 Dead Kennedys
U.K.Decay
Red Rockers

5 Punk Globe Party
Red Rockers
Alienation
X-Mas Eve
6 Finger

6 Reporters
Data
Box

7 Shiek Vaselino
Zealots
Bad Attitude
Night Shark
Exposure

8 The Reporters
Saucers
Special Effects
Too Bad

9 Mindsweeper
Harvey

Alienation
M.C. Jane Dor-
nacker

10 SVT
VKTMS
Adaptors

11 Giant Jam #3:
Two Tones
Mojo
Bay Area Outra-
geous Beauty
Pageant

12 King Snake
Mojo
Algo
French Kiss

13 No Alternative
Woundz
The Tanks
B Team
Amputators

14 Parental Guidance
The Lewd
Sluts a Go Go
Adaptors

15 Silhouette
Meantime
Chris Hamburger &
the Captions

16 Dickheads
07080
Neutrinoz
Monicker

17 Mutants
Woundz
Church Police
Vincent

18 Mutants

23 The Defectors
The Whoremones
The Concert Beans

24 Amputators
Dead Ends
Al Million & the
Robots
The Rakes
Box

25 The Adaptors
Delta
The Tenants
Algo

26 KUSF Party:
Jayne Dooracker
and Cha-Cha Billy
Jayne Doe
84 Rooms

27 Barry Beam
07080
The Saucers
Les Nickelettes

28 The Hostages
Der Lifers
Interference
Bay Area Outra-
geous Beauty
Pageant

29 X-Men
The Conserva-
tives
Suspex
Monicker

30 Tri-Matrix
The Agents
Patricia & her
Nasty Band
Tour de Force

31 No Doubt
Silhouette
The Reporters
The Vandal

Poster by Anomymous

Poster by Anomymous

Disposals
Red Cross
Alienation

19 Bad Attitude
Allies
Conservatives

20 Monicker
New Boots
French Kiss
Data

21 Security
Mr. Clean
The Stains
White Lunch

22 The Verbs
Harvey
Ryth-a-Rama

23 Farallon
Trouble Boys
Patricia & her
Nasty Band
Trixx

24 Subhumans
Adolescents
The Tanks

25 No Sisters
Eye Protection

B Team
Bay Area Outra-
geous Beauty
Pageant

26 Church Police
Mr. Orange
The Jokes
Nocturnal Emiss-
sion

27 Spectacles
Lifers
Art & the Pagan
Hearts
Armour Karma

28 Sic Pleasure
Toiling Midgets
Seven Seconds
The Tanks

29 The Streets
Paradox
Tyrant
Immigrants

30 Richi Ray
Silhouette
Voices
Cats Are Clean

MAY 1981

1 VKTMS
Angry Samoans
Sic Pleasure
Fried Abortions

2 Wolvarines
Barry Beam
Frank Hymng
Bay Area Outra-
geous Beauty
Pageant

3 Max Dunn Band
Push
Pedestrians
Night Shark

4 No Data

5 The Visitors
Chris Harburger &
the Captions
Little Death
Defectors

6 Elements of Style
Fall of Christianity
Cats Are Clean
X-Mas Eve

7 Translator
Alienation
Wilma

8 Silvertone
Neutrinoz
Reporters

9 Eye Protection
Das Blok
Mojo

10 The Breathers
Exposure
The Mercenaries
Plastics Medium

11 The Conservatives
Vandals
Black & Blue

My first time at the Mab in 1981, I don't remember which punk bands were playing that night. Hard-core punk bands generally had an aura of toughness and danger, of being some kind of threat, and these bands were no exception. As the guys in the next band were ready to begin their performance, Dirk stood at the microphone and introduced them: "What can I say about the next band, except that their mothers love them very much!"

Their mothers love them very much!?!! That's exactly how any hard-core punk band would not want to be introduced. How embarrassing for them, but still kind of funny.

Later, as the last band was leaving the stage, Dirk stood center stage. "All right, the show's over," he intoned into the microphone, "It's time to go and slither back into your little holes, into your little crevices, back to your miserable existence." That's not an exact quote. It was something like that, but he definitely did use the word "slither."

I said to myself, "I need to play here."

So, the next week, I called Dirk's office, and Dirk told me to send him a tape and a photo of myself.

I told him, "I have a tape, but I don't have a photo."

"I don't wanna hear it," he said.

So I got a professional photographer to take pictures of me at one of my gigs. I sent a cassette of my music along with a photo to Dirk, and he told me to follow up by calling him between 3 and 4pm on Wednesday. He added, "and if you get my machine, don't leave a message saying," (switching to a mock-whiny voice,) " 'You said to call between 3 and 4 on Wednesday, and you're not there, blah blah blah!' Just leave your name and number and I'll call you back."

So I called at the right time, got his machine, and left my name & number.

Did he ever get back to me? Yes! He called back and said, "I would like to book you, but first I have to figure out what to do with you. Call me in a week or two. This does not mean I'm not interested. I just have to figure out what bands to put you on the bill with."

When I called him a week or two later, he told me he wanted to have me come and just play a few songs to try me out. There would be no pay. So I agreed. The night of the show at the Mab, Dim Tim of KUSF introduced me, and I played and sang a few of my tunes onstage at the upright piano, on the bill with Barry Beam, whom I really enjoyed. At the end, Dirk gave me $5, which was five more than I was expecting.

By this time, I had already had dealings with lots of bar/restaurant/nightclub owners/managers/bookers. Most of them would just jerk me around, telling me, for example, "Yeah, call me in 3 weeks and we'll do something." Then I'd call in 3 weeks, and if they were there at all, they'd say, "Oh, yeah! Call me in two months," and on and on until a year later they'd disappear, or tell me that they don't book piano players, or whatever. Dirk was not like that. Once he had your cassette and your picture, he would tell you whether he was going to book you or not. If you were punk, artsy,or quirky, or if he just thought you were of interest, he would book you. If he didn't want to book you, he'd tell you so. To me that was refreshing. Dirk was the type of guy I liked to deal with, and deal with him I did.

One time I was in the On Broadway office with Dirk, and Dirk told me that if he ever found out that I was playing for any other promoter, he'd break my arm. "But Dirk," I said, "If you break my arm I won't be able to play at all."

Dirk replied, "That's o.k. If I can't have you, nobody can." (Fortunately it was an empty threat. I did play at other clubs, and Dirk did not break my arm.)

Over the next couple years, Dirk would book me a number of times. Once on heavy metal night, he had me play the grand piano in the lounge outside the main showroom at the On Broadway. Naturally, I was playing whatever heavy metal cover tunes I could, but Dirk stopped me. He didn't want me playing heavy metal on heavy metal night. He wanted the heavy metal kids to experience hearing me playing punk rock on the piano.

On other nights, when punk bands would be playing in the main room, I played my original and punk cover tunes in the lounge between band performances. Punks would throw ice and beer cans at me, but I didn't see anyone walking away. The crowd watching me just seemed to get bigger.

One time, Dirk booked me to play on a Monday or Tuesday night to headline an evening of solo acoustic punk/alternative/new wave acts. My opening acts would be Ralph Eno and Kim Nomad, two hip singer/guitar players who were fun to listen to.

A couple weeks later I was playing a gig in Hayward. Rissa, the punk-rocker came out to see me, and I told her about my show coming up in a few days at the On Broadway.

"Are you sure, DJ?" she asked, "I saw in the paper that Dead Kennedys are playing there that night, and I'm going to the show."

"Yeah, I'm definitely playing," I said, "Dirk booked me to headline the show with two solo acts opening for me, so I think you got it wrong. Dead Kennedys won't be there. If they're playing, it's probably going to be on a different night."

"You better check and make sure," she replied, "because I'm pretty sure they're playing that night...."

After all the promotion I had done for the show, I sure hoped Dirk didn't cancel me! So the next day I called: "Dirk, did you book Dead Kennedys to play on the same night that you booked me to play?"

Dirk replied, "Yes, I did. You're still going to play, aren't you?"

"Sure!" I said.

Dirk also put a couple other major punk bands on the bill. I forget who. Maybe it was the Circle Jerks, or a couple other bands like that. Anyway, when I called Kim and Ralph to inform them about whom was added to the bill, neither one of them wanted to be on the bill anymore.

"It looks like you're the only one with any guts," Dirk said when I told him that both my opening acts cancelled. So I wound up on the bill with Dead Kennedys.

As a long line formed at the entrance to the On Broadway on the night of the show, I took a pen and changed the flyer that I had posted at the entrance to the club. It had my name in big letters, and at the bottom there was enough room to write in small letters: "Also appearing: Dead Kennedys."

I played in the lounge during each break between bands. Jello Biafra, East Bay Ray, and Klaus Flouride were among the crowd watching as I played Dead Kennedys tunes along with other covers and my own songs. Later, I went up and talked to Ray. We chatted a little, and he said he wanted his royalties for the two DKs songs I performed, so I gave him a dime, and he walked away happy.

In 2000, promoter Alan Parowski of Lift-Off Productions asked me if I'd like to play at the Fab Mab Reunion he was going to hold at Club Cocodrie on May 20th. Alan told me, "I invited Dirk to be the M.C., but he said that he wouldn't do it unless I booked DJ Lebowitz to perform at the event."

So I agreed to play, and we got Steve Heck, formerly of Phoenix Iron Works to supply the piano.

As I sat at the piano for sound check at Cocodrie on the night of the show, Dirk came up behind me and put his hands on my shoulders. "You know," he said, "I told the promoter that if he didn't book you to play tonight, I wouldn't come."

"Wow!" I thought. "Alan wasn't kidding."

So I opened the show, followed by Penelope Houston and her band, then Jumbo Shrimp which included Ray and Klaus of Dead Kennedys.

Dirk was the m.c., but he seemed weaker than in the heyday at the Mab. Instead of being his usual sarcastic self up on stage, he was nice! What happened to him? He was not well.

Still, it was great to see him, but after that, I never saw him again.

I'm DJ Lebowitz, the solo piano player (who is not a disc jockey).

■■■■■■■■■■■■■■■■■■■■■■■■■■■■■■■■■■■■■

Remember "hobbit"

Shortly after I started working in the broadway and moved into the backstage area, "Hobbit" came along. his real name was Sean and he was from Fresno, or so I remember. I thought he was a bit . . . something . . . and dirk asked me what I thought of him. I didn't know what to say and the next thing I knew, Hobbit was moving into the dressiing cube across from me.

Dirk made him the stage manager. Hobbit had a mad passion for drawing and often, dirk would leave us, or leave hobbit, sitting in his room. smoking and drawing feverishly, only to return the next afternoon and come up to find hobbit, barely moved, sweating away, drawings scattered across the floor.

After the shows, with Dirk either upstairs counting cash or lighting up, or both (no wonder we never got paid) or downstairs fighting off ted falconi or some such nonsense, Hobbit and the others would be trolling the aisles, kicking seats??we'd find money but more often drugs, pills . . . I'd hand whatever over to hobbit and it would either go in his pocket or into his mouth . . . he was up and down and lots of fun . . . sadly, I heard that he too moved on a few years back. Probably asking Dirk for a job right now.

Bob the Doorman

Poster by Anomymous

12 Parental Guidance
Johnny 3
Meantime
The Act

13 The Hostasges
Johnny 3
P.C.2000
Neon

14 Nervous
Neasden Knights
The Breakouts

15 Flipper
Woundz
Sic Pleasure

16 Romeo Void
Two Tones
Varve
Bay Area Outra-
geous Beauty
Pageant

17 Bad Religion
The Farmers

Vauxhall
Final Thrust

18 Punk Globe Party
The Lewd
Sic Pleasure
Revenge
Neon

19 Algo
The Dicks
White Silence
Pariah

20 X-Men
Hard Attack
Harvey
Agents

21 The Verbs
Undersongs
Spectacles

22 The VIP's
VKTMS
Translator

23 The VIP's
The Middle Class
7 Seconds

24 Giant Jam 4
MX 80
The Lifers
Funchional Ilito-
rits

25 Four Cats
Mr. Clean
Whippetts
Pedestrians

26 No Doubt
The Adaptors
Box
Instamoids

27 Wilma
Meantime
Cliff Fields

28 The Nuns
Undersongs

29 The Fast
Fried Abortions
Dodge Darts

30 The Fast
The Lewd
Impatient Youth
Bar Wars Ballet

31 Exposure
Counterparts
Nonchalants
Zoo-Z

JUNE 1981

1 Bad Religion
X-Men
The Mercenaries
Los Olividados

2 The Spectacles
The Untouchables
P.C. 2000
Parental Guidance

3 The Uptights
The Tanks
The Ghouls
Black Athletes

**4 Blake Quake & the
Tremors**
Chris Harburger &
the Captions
Golden Gate
Jumpers
Mr. Clean

5 The Contractions
Varve
Wilma

6 VKTMS
Translator
The Adaptors
BTeam

**7 Attack (formerly
The Dogs)**
Capa City
Penis Envy
Snap-On Tools

8 Attack
Capa City
The Pastels
The Job

9 The Act
Matchheads
The Farmers
The Pedestrians

10 Tyrant
Stereo
Manta**

183

11 The Contractions
    The Untouchables
    Penis Envy
    Cheap Date

12 D-Day
    Mojo
    Golden Gate
    Jumpers

13 The Punts
    The Fabulous
    Titans
    Elements of Style

14 X-Mas Eve
    Algo
    Bad Attitude
    Ironics

15 Vauxhall
    The Push
    White Silence
    IMF

16 Neasden Knights
    Counterparts
    P.C.2000
    The Vandals

17 Das Blok
    Translator
    X-Men

18 Halfchurch
    Start
    Quiet Room
    Happy Death

19 No Alternative
    Los Popularos
    Modern Warfare

20 DOA
    Los Popularos
    7 Seconds

Poster by Marc Olmsted

21 Final Thrust
    Beep Fooz
    Minus 1

22 Big Boys
    Parental Guid
    ance
    Exposure
    Pariah

23 Big Boys
    The Sheets
    Night Shark
    Artichokes

24 7 Seconds
    War Zone
    Blistering Agents
    Fried Abortions

25 Benefit for
    Haight Co-Op
    Nursery School:
    No Sisters
    Paul Krassner
    Jane Dornacker

    Outskirts

26 Crime
    The Wolverines
    The Reporters
    Bar Wars Ballet

27 Hymingstein
    Alienation
    The Jars
    Varve
    Bar Wars Ballet

28 Authorities
    Whippets
    Counterparts
    Rangers

29 Algo
    Big Boys
    White Silence
    Daddy X

30 Penis Envy
    Red Asphalt
    Patricia Hurts
    Ironics

JULY 1981

1   Uptights
    Box
    Ghouls
    N.K.G.

2   Dead Kennedys
    Dicks
    Stains

3   VKTMS
    Agent Orange
    B Team
    Brat
    Bar Wars Ballet

4   VKTMS
    T.S.O.L.
    Sic Pleasure
    The Undead
     Bay Area Outra-
    geous Beauty
    Pageant

5   Punk Globe Party:
    Brat
    Translator
    The Spectacles
    The Sheets
    Minus 1

6   The Softies
    Soldiers of Fortune
    Vauxhall
    Armourd Karma

7   The Woundz
    Half Church
    X-Mas Eve

8   T.S.O.L.
    A.L.A.
    A.K.A.
    Belsen- 06

9   7 Seconds

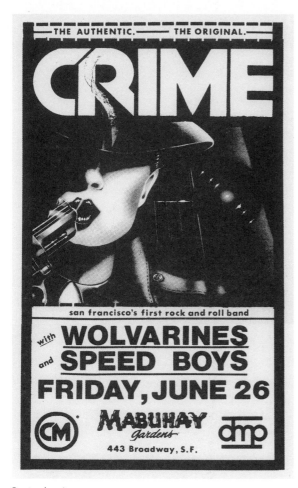

THE AUTHENTIC. THE ORIGINAL.

CRIME

san francisco's first rock and roll band

with WOLVARINES and SPEED BOYS

FRIDAY, JUNE 26

MABUHAY Gardens
443 Broadway, S.F.

CM   dmp

Poster by Anomymous

The Deprogram-
mers
Revenge
Crucifix

The Room
Social Unrest
2 Words
Quiet Room

10 Minimal Man
Audio Letter
Fred Splinter
Bar Wars Ballet

11 The Hoovers
Interference
Varve
The Sheets
Bay Area Outra-
geous Beauty
Pageant

12 Damage Magazine
Party

13 Perv Mag Party
No Alternative
Fried Abortions
War Zone
MikDow

14 The Whippets
Ironics
Parental Guid-
ance
Minus 1

15 Bob & the New
Hearts
Outskirts
Pastels

16 The Middle Class
The Stains
The Dicks

17 Das Blok
Silvertone
Crueltones
Bar Wars Ballet

18 Flipper
The Middle Class
The Stains
The Dicks

19 Zoo-Z
The Act
The Pedestrians
Los Olividados

20 I.M.F.
The Mercenaries
Hit'n'Run
The Push

21 Translator
BTeam
The Quiet Room

22 Impatient Youth
Sic Pleasure
X-Mas Eve
Angst

23 Farallon
Future
PC 2000
The Next

24 The Lewd
Husker Du
7 Seconds
Blistering Agents
Bar Wars Ballet

25 Wolvarines
The Spiders
Cos

26 Thrust
Meantime
The Match Heads
Batteries

27 Secrets
Art & Pagan Hearts
Sing Sing
Nominal State

28 Das Blok
Breakouts
Start
Taxi

29 Ernst Hymng
Varve
The Lifers

30 New Boots
Night Shark
Blake Quake

31 Dead Kennedys
Husker Du
Toxic Reason
Church Police

AUGUST 1981

1 Flipper
Toxic Reason
The Tanks

2 Victims of Street
Violence Benefit:
War Zone
Society Dog
A.L.A.
Nocturnal Emis-
sions

3 Defectors
Whippets
Extra
Box

Inventing (Punk) Rock at the Mabuhay
By Michael Goldberg

"Better watch out for the new world" – from "Sister Little," performed live at the Mabuhay Gardens by The Sleepers, 1978

As if rock never happened. No Chuck Berry, no Elvis, no Beatles, no Stones.

Sometimes it was like that. Other times it was a raised middle finger to all that preceded them, the punks – a fuck you to the past from the present, from the future.

When you least expect it, the world reinvented in some small out-of-the-way place that no one is paying attention to, and in 1976, in San Francisco, because Dirk Dirksen, a former TV show producer who had since run a surfing business in Santa Cruz, convinced Ness Aquino, owner of a tired Filipino nightclub at 433 Broadway, to let him promote occasional shows there in the evenings, that place, located among topless bars and strip clubs, was the Mabuhay Gardens.

What took place at the Mabuhay felt brand new, it was a new society with new values, coming together night after night, participating in a kind of ritual: a series of bands, alienated from the mainstream, on the small stage expressing their emotions in a raw, visceral manner, and an audience of equally alienated music fans there to hear the emotional (and political) news those bands were delivering.

"It was so thrilling and bracing to see these people whose every aesthetic choice was about repudiating everything that the ['60s] counterculture had stood for," novelist Jennifer Egan told me. Egan, who says that as a teenager she went to the Mabuhay weekly during the late '70s, set part of a chapter of her 2011 Pulitzer-winning book, "A Visit from the Goon Squad," at the Mabuhay.

Of course in the mid-'70s this new world I am talking about, this world that acted like nothing that came before it mattered, was seemingly being invented everywhere. There were numerous ports of entry – in New York, in Cleveland, in Seattle, in L.A., in London – but if you lived in San Francisco, yours was the Mabuhay AKA the Fab Mab, or simply, the Mab.

"In terms of San Francisco punk rock, it was a community epicenter," Egan said. "It was so original …The anger, the pace, the energy and the rage were all incredibly compelling to me. As a sort of troubled teen I could not get enough of it."

Low ceilinged and brick-walled, the first maybe three quarters of the club was a terraced hillside of tables descending to a crowded dance floor. Except that amid the people on the dance floor were small round tables and rattan chairs and sometimes Penelope Houston of The Avengers might be sitting in one of those rattan chairs and some nights, such as on January 3, 1978, Negative Trend singer Rozz Rezabek would climb on top of the huge loudspeakers and leap off what artist Bruce Conner called the "shin high" stage, knocking over people and chairs. The stage was small, but there was room for a drum kit up against the brick wall, two or three musicians in front of it, a singer up close to the edge and plenty of drama.

When the Mab was empty in the afternoon or after everyone finally went home, and you could actually see the place, it was worn out, more than worn out. It had been kicked in the stomach and never recovered. But at night, alive with punks and high school kids like Egan, that didn't matter; in fact, anything less fucked up would have been so wrong. The Mab was where survivors of WWIII converged, a kind of post-apocalyptic hideout for conspiring the new.

Howie Klein, at the time a DJ/writer who started 415 Records during the Mabuhay's heyday and released records by The Nuns and Romeo Void, says he hung out at the club "every night for years. Every single night. Seven nights a week. Literally for years.

"Especially in the beginning it [the Mabuhay] was very much dedicated to punk rock and a punk ethos," he recalled. "The idea of rejecting that which was the establishment at the time and starting something completely new on every level, whether it was the way you dress or the way you think or look at politics. And the Mabuhay was the central place for it to be happening."

At first "punk rock" didn't mean bands conforming to a dress code of Mohawks, black leather jackets and dog collars playing loud, fast, short songs. The punk movement of the mid-to-late '70s began in New York in '74 and '75, then spread to London in '75 and '76. In San Francisco in '76 and '77, the city's version of punk ranged from Sex Pistols-style bands like The Aveng-

Mabuhay interior with early version of The Avengers. Photo curiosity Dirksen Archives

ers to indefinable bands like The Mutants. There was little in common musically or visually between The Aveng-ers, Flipper, The Mutants, Crime, The Nuns, The Sleepers and UXA. While Crime sometimes ap-peared wearing police uniforms, The Mutants might show up all wear-ing white, or as characters out of "Alice In Wonderland" complete with huge playing cards attached to their chests. A week after her boyfriend Michael Kowalsky died of an over-dose, De De Troit, singer for UXA, appeared onstage wrapped in white gauze like some femme fatale version of the Mummy, at one point lying on the stage, eyes closed.

In the early years at the Mabuhay, Dirk Dirksen always said he was presenting "avant-garde theatre." After the police raided the club and shut it down one night, Dirksen told me: "They [the police] see it as a punk scene. But punk is just a part of what we do here… We've had great jazz performers like Sun Ra and George Shearing. And people do not understand the satire of punk. Our people are in costume, they are not thugs."

Still, despite what Dirksen said, various versions of "punk rock" were what mostly hap-pened on the Mab stage.

If you wonder what was so different about the club, maybe this will help: "One time The Nuns' bass player got stage fright and vomited and couldn't go on stage," Klein said. "So The Nuns threw his bass at me and said 'You play, just do this and this.' I had never held a bass before. But I went onstage and played and no one knew the difference."

The scene at the Mab was like a secret society, only it was right out in the open, and anyone could join. The price of admission? Simply wanting to be there.

Egan said, "The fact that a Lowell high school student like me and her friends, who, I mean we took drugs but we were basically pretty straight arrows, could go there and enjoy it was part of the magic … it really did help for that moment to penetrate the larger culture, which would be me, a pretty ordinary high school student who was looking for action with her friends."

Frankie and Johnny of Crime with Howie Klein.

Another San Franciscan who visited the club, dug the scene and never left (well, at least for a year), was the famed Bohemian artist Bruce Conner, who had moved to the city in 1957 and become part of the Beat scene, and then in the Sixties participated in another countercultural shift as a member of the rock 'n' roll light show troupe, the North American Ibis Alchemical Company, projecting psychedelic collages of film loops, photographs and colored liquid light paintings onto the walls of the Avalon Ballroom as Big Brother and the Holding Company or Country Joe and the Fish rocked the place.

Beginning in January 1978, Conner found needed inspiration in his frequent nights at the Mab, and proceeded to photograph the bands and the scene there for Search & Destroy, the San Francisco-based punk magazine.

"In its own way, it [the Mabuhay scene] reminded me of the energy of the poets, artists, filmmakers, and dancers who had been characterized as the Beat generation in the 1950's," Conner said during a 2005 interview with journalist/publisher Mike Plante for his Cinemad magazine. "Then in the '60s some of the same people were called the Hippie generation. This creative phenomenon appeared to become publicly conspicuous in San Francisco every ten years….

"I wish we could find more people with that kind of intensity today," Conner continued. "It's worth gravitating towards that type of environment. A kind of activity that compels people, despite the limits of their technological or professional abilities, to produce, perform, and have their say."

I went to the Mab in early 1978 to see the band Crime, who at times appeared onstage wearing police uniforms. Writing for New York Rocker that year, I described what I experienced that night.

"Crime play loud. So loud that the plate glass window at the opposite end of the club shakes, tables tremble and people hang onto their drinks. Loudness may be Crime's only musical raison d'etre. This band is a literal translation of the concept 'minimal.' Drummer Hank Rank thumps out a simple Bo Diddley beat that is only adequate in the context of the rest of the band. Bassist Ron the Ripper coaxes a thick rumble from his amp that reminds one of the thunder of a bulldozer rolling over rugged terrain. And the guitar playing of [Johnny] Strike and Frankie Fix make you feel like you've been forcefully held underwater for the full 25 minutes of the set."

If you saw Crime or The Avengers or Negative Trend at the Mab, you never forgot it. For many who attended in the early years, these weren't "shows" or "concerts," these were life and death important experiences.

"One of the key things about the punk scene, it was a do it yourself scene, there was a oneness between the audience and the artists," Howie Klein said. "There was no, 'we're the artist and you're the audience and there's this impenetrable wall.' That was what we were against. With Journey and Led Zeppelin there was this wall that you couldn't cross over. But it was the opposite in the punk scene. Anyone could start a band."

It was common for audience members to turn up onstage. Debora Iyall attended many Mab shows before founding Romeo Void, who eventually scored two hits, including the sneering "Never Say Never," and the same was true of Eric Boucher who was a fan in the audience before he appeared on the Mab stage fronting the Dead Kennedys as Jello Biafra. Klaus Flouride, East Bay Ray and Biafra formed the DKs in June of 1978; a month later they played their first show at the Mab opening for The Offs and Negative Trend.

Biafra said in one interview that Dirksen "stuck his neck out and had the sense to make the shows all ages, which allowed me to get the Dead Kennedys off the ground, since I wasn't 21 when we started."

In another interview: "It [the Mabuhay] meant the world," Biafra told Michael Stewart Foley, Professor of American Political Culture and Political Theory at the University of Groningen in the Netherlands and author of the book, "Dead Kennedy's Fresh Fruit For Rotting Vegetables." "It meant seeing some of the greatest music you'll ever see in your life, blisteringly loud, three feet away from you, and you can watch the sweat drip off the guitar strings while you bounce off people ... that was a big adrenaline rush, just all the people bouncing off each other."

The Mabuhay was where "we were all joined together as punks," Penelope Houston, 18 at the time and lead singer/lyricist for The Avengers, told Foley. "I just registered that I was a punk in a world that wasn't punk. ... Whether we were male or female, black or white or Mexican of queer or Asian or whatever, we were all just punks, and we were all joined together in that way, There was this great feeling musically, as well as how you looked, you could do whatever you wanted. You just made it up."

Other notable bands that played the Mab: Black Flag, The Dils, Rank & File, Silvertone, Screamers, the Damned, the Descendents, Blondie, Devo, Jim Carroll, the Ramones, Situations and Tuxedomoon. And there were many more

When the Sex Pistols came to San Francisco in January1978 and played for the last time (until they reformed to cash in decades later), the three opening acts were all Mabuhay regulars: The Nuns, The Avengers and Negative Trend (who never made it to the stage).

The punk scene, including the Mabuhay, spread a DIY message throughout the world. It led to the proliferation of independent record companies like Klein's 415, Biafra's Alternative Tentacles and Bob Biggs' Slash, Xeroxed fanzines and punk magazines like Jean Caffeine's New Dezezes (San Francisco's first punk zine) V. Vale's Search & Destroy, Brad Lapin's Damage and Ginger Coyote's Punk Globe, and the alternative network of performance spaces and clubs. I believe that DIY idea carried over years later to the Internet (it certainly inspired me to start an internet magazine, Addicted To Noise, in 1994), to the widespread self-publishing of books and, most recently, Facebook live streaming, which lets anyone have the power to broadcast video worldwide.

Today, there are videos and audio recordings of early Mabuhay performances on You-Tube by bands including UXA, The Dils, The Avengers, The Sleepers, The Mutants, Negative Trend, Flipper and the Dead Kennedys (in particular, seek out Mindaugis Bagdon's 17 minute film, "Louder, Faster, Shorter," and an audio recording, "Miner's Benefit Compilation," also on YouTube). Additionally, studio recordings by Crime, the Avengers, the Sleepers, UXA, Flipper and others can currently be heard on YouTube.

Since the club shut its doors in 1986 (and by then the San Francisco punk scene was dead) its reputation has only grown, and more than 40 years after the first shows there, the Mabuhay lives on in ways that are obvious and sometimes not so obvious.

In 1987, Sonic Youth included a cover of Crime's 1976 recording, "Hot Wire My Heart," on their album Sister.

In 1990, the year Bikini Kill formed, the band covered The Avengers' 1977 song, "The American in Me," which The Avengers frequently played at the Mabuhay. Bikini Kill not only became the major Riot Grrrl band, inspiring thousands of young women to form bands or assert themselves in some way, but had a major influence on Sleater-Kinney, who remain popular to this day.

In 1991, Chris Isaak, who once led a band called Silvertone that played the Mabuhay, scored a Top 10 U.S. hit with "Wicked Game." The guitarist who wrote the spooky guitar hook that opens the song is former Avengers' bassist James Calvin Wilsey; after The Avengers split up in 1979, Wilsey worked the sound board at the Mab and taught Isaak guitar parts leading to Isaak asking Wilsey to join his band.

When Nirvana played "Smells Like Teen Spirit" on "Saturday Night Live," January 11, 1992, Kurt Cobain wore a hand drawn Flipper t-shirt. Both Cobain and Nirvana bassist Krist Novoselic named Flipper as an influence, as did Jane's Addiction's original bassist Eric Avery. Flipper's classic debut, Album - Generic Flipper, was first released in 1982; it's currently available in MP3 and streaming formats, as are Flipper's other studio albums and live recordings. There is also a DVD, "Flipper: Live – Target Video 1980-1981," currently available.

In 1994 a Swedish band, Sator, covered The Nuns' song "No Solution," which reached #2 on the Swedish charts. In 2006 The Nuns' debut album, Nuns, recorded in 1980 without guitarist Alejandro Escovedo, was reissued. It is currently out of print and used copies are selling for $65. The Nuns' first record was a three song EP released in 1979 on 415 Records; two of the songs, "Decadent Jew" and "Suicide Child," were recorded live at the Keystone Palo Alto in March1977; it is currently out of print.

In 1995, punk artist Winston Smith, whose collages appeared inside or on the cover of such Dead Kennedys' albums as Fresh Fruit For Rotting Vegetables and Let Them Eat Jellybeans, had one of his collages, "God Told Me To Skin You Alive," used for the cover of Green Day's hit album, Insomniac.

In 1996, a compilation album, the less an object, with all of The Sleepers' recordings including all the songs on the group's amazing 1978 "Seventh World" EP, was released. The Sleeper's gifted singer, Ricky Williams (who was also Flipper's first singer and is credited with coming up with that band's name), died of a heroin overdose on November 21, 1992.

In 1997, The Avengers' singer/lyricist Penelope Houston and Green Day's Billie Joe Armstrong wrote and recorded a song, "The Angel and the Jerk," which was used in an episode of "Friends" and appeared on the 1999 Friends Again soundtrack. Houston and

Armstrong also recorded The Avengers' song, "Corpus Christi," with lyrics by Houston, which appeared on Houston's 2003 album, Eighteen Stories Down. The compilation album, Avengers, made up of singles recorded in 1977 and demos produced by former Sex Pistol Steve Jones in 1978, was first released in 1983 and was rereleased in 2010; another compilation album, Died For Your Sins, including studio and live recordings, was released in 1999. The Avengers' live set at Winterland opening for the Sex Pistols in January 1978 can currently be watched at YouTube.

In 2001 Dils Dils Dils, which compiles the group's singles and live tracks, was reissued on CD; it was first released on vinyl in 1991.

In 2004, UXA's first album, Illusions of Grandeur, was reissued. It is currently out of print.

In 2005, a reformed version of Crime headlined the Road To Ruins festival in Rome. A compilation album, Murder By Guitar, was issued in 2013 and is currently available in vinyl, MP3 and streaming formats.

In 2006, a book of Bruce Conner's 1978 Mab photographs, "Mabuhay Gardens," was published in Germany in tandem with a show in Dusseldorf of those 53 photos. In 2007, the Berkeley Art Museum acquired a set of the photos and in 2008 exhibited them in conjunction with a film/video series at the Pacific Film Archive: "Louder, Faster: Punk In Performance."

In 2007, the Dirk Dirksen/Damon Molloy-produced documentary on The Mutants, titled "Mutants: Forensic Report," was released on DVD. The Mutants one and only album, Fun Terminal, was reissued in 2004. While the CD version is out of print, an MP3 version is currently available, and it can be streamed at Spotify.

In the March 8, 2010 issue of the *New Yorker*, a short story, "Ask Me If I Care," by novelist Jennifer Egan was published. A portion of the story takes place at the Mabuhay, Egan's characters listen to The Mutants, Negative Trend, the Dead Kennedys and The Nuns, and Dirk Dirksen gets a mention. That story is also a chapter in her 2011 book, "A Visit from the Goon Squad," which won a 2011 Pulitzer. The book also won a 2011 National Book Critics Circle Award.

The Bruce Conner retrospective, "It's All True," included a room devoted to his 1978 Mabuhay photos. That exhibit was shown during 2016 at the Museum of Modern Art in New York and at the San Francisco Museum of Modern Art. In 2017, the exhibit traveled to the Museo Nacional Centro de Arte Reina Sofia in Madrid. Conner's Mabuhay photos were seen by thousands of people who had previously never heard of the club.

The first major showing of Conner's work in Southeast Asia took place in 2018 at multiple venues. One of the events, held halfway around the world from 433 Broadway on March 3, 2018 in Bataan, Philippines was a "Mabuhay Gardens Punk Party."

Michael Goldberg is a novelist, editor, photographer, digital music pioneer and animal rights activist. He hung out at the Mabuhay in 1978 and his interview subjects included Flipper, Crime, The Nuns, Black Flag, Patti Smith, Frank Zappa, Nicholas Ray, Captain Beefheart, Lou Reed, John Cale, the Sex Pistols, the Clash and The Ramones. He was a Senior Writer and Associate Editor at Rolling Stone magazine for a decade. He founded the first web music magazine, the award-winning Addicted To Noise, in 1994. He was a Senior Vice-President at the SonicNet music site. His novels include True Love Scars (2014), The Flowers Lied (2016) and Untitled (2017). Kerouac biographer Dennis McNally wrote of Goldberg's fiction: "Kerouac in the 21st Century." A collection of his music features and interviews will be published in 2019.

Poster by Roger Reyes

4 **Society Dog**
Fried Abortions
Revenge

5 **Silvertone**
Arkansas Man
Algo

6 **3rd Annual Record Chart Party Benefit:**
Dead Kennedys
Minor Threat
Youth Brigade

7 **Peterbilt**
Fabulous Titans
07080
Bar Wars Ballet

8 **SVT**
Barry Beam
Baby Buddha

9 **Ovenmen**
Fried Abortions
War Zone
Central File

10 **The Tanks**
Wilma
Red Asphalt
GOD

11 **The Adaptors**
Silhouette
The Sheets

12 **The Weoundz**
X-Mas Eve
The Ghouls

13 **Peterbilt**
Chris Harburger
Golden Gate
Jumpers

14 **Rhythm Riot (formerly Two Tones)**
Spiders
Elements of Style
Bar Wars Ballet

15 **The Verbs**
Undersongs
Bob

Bay Area Outrageous Beauty Pageant

16 **Valkays**
The Spectacles
Vauxhall
The Vandals

17 **The Authorities**
Bob & the New Hearts
The Farmers

18 **Social Unrest**
Crucifix
The Breakouts
The Freels

19 **Lance Lyric**
X-Men
Bad Attitude

20 **Sic Pleasure**
Impatient Youth
Fall of Christianity

21 **Das Blok**
Swinging Madisons
Der Lifers
Bar Wars Ballet

22 **Eye Protection**
Swinging Madisons
Mr. Clean
Bay Area Outrageous Beauty Pageant

23 **Punk Globe**
3rd Anniversary Party:
VKTMS
Breakouts
Bar Wars Ballet

24 **KPFA Benefit Party:**
Dead Kennedys
Social Unrest
Church Police

25 **Dirk's Birthday Party**

Poster by Marc Olmsted

Poster by Anomymous

The Spiders
The Tanks
The Renegades

26 Bob & the New-
hearts
Nocturnal Emis-
sions
Silence

27 Drastic Plastic
Memorial Party:
The Contractions
Wilma
Abortions
Red Asphalt

28 Red Rockers
B Team
Varve
Bar Wars Ballet

29 Black Flag
Toxic Reason
Saccharine Trust
7 Seconds

30 Black Flag
Toxic Reason
Sic Pleasure
Overkill

31 Zoo-Z
New Boots

SEPTEMBER 1981

1 Varve
The Tanks
Dubbles

2 MX-80 Sound
Translator
Arkansas Man
Red Asphalt

3 The Innocent

4 Snakefinger
Bob
Films
Jayne Doe

5 SVT
Surface Music
Parental Guid-
ance

6 Social Unrest
The Appliances
War Zone
Jayne Doe

7 Bob
Neutrinoz
Lifers
Parental Guid-
ance
Minus 1
God

8 7 Seconds
Revenge
The Idiots
Blistering Agent

9 KUSF Benefit:
Quiet Room
Half Church
Happy Death
Dynamatons

10 X-Mas Eve
Speed Boys
The Tanks
God

11 Silvertone
The Spoiders
The Ghouls

12 Eye Protection
Mojo Frenzy (fo-
merly
Sweet Tommy)

13 Ruen
The Retorts
Nonchalants

Poster by Roger Reyes

25 The Lewd
Flipper
Crucifix
Bar Wars Ballet

26 Pope Paul Pot
VKTMS
Revenge
Anti L.A
Bay Area Outrageous Beauty
Pageant

27 Bonamics
Wanderlust

28 Golden Gate
Jumpers
Hard Attack
The Pastels

29 Arkansas Man
Minus 1
Red Asphalt
Ibbilly Bibilly

30 The Hostages
Algo
Ravage
Bad Attitude

OCTOBER 1981

1   The Undead
Revenge
Domino Theory
Los Olividados

2   Das Blok
Cruel Tones
Red Squares

3   Flaming Groovies
Impostors
Red Squares
Bay Area Outrageous Beauty
Pageant

Nominal State

14 Donny Snow
The Sheets
The Ironics
Matchheads

15 X-Men
The Job
Blake Quake
Night Shark

16 Wilma
GOD
The Renegades
Central File

17 Hit'n'Run

Meantime
Harvey
Angst

18 The Punts
Varve
Elements of Style
Bar Wars Ballet

19 The Verbs
BTeam
TBA

20 Magnetos
The Act
AKA
5th Column

21 White Silence
Church Police
Wild Boys

22 Social Unrest
War Zone
The Undead
The Uptights

23 Parental Guid-
ance
Zoo-Z
Vauxhall
Noble Barrister

24 Chris Harburger
Silhouette
The Farmers

I first met Dirk Dirksen at a meeting in my apartment on Masonic Avenue and Haight Street in San Francisco. I had just directed a play for the Straight People's Theater called "Heaven Grand in Amber Orbit," written by Jackie Curtis of "Walk on the Wild Side" fame (Jackie was just speeding away, thought she was James Dean for a day…). Dirk had just started at the Mabuhay Gardens, and was wanting to book the play for the club's "Dinner Theater." The Mabuhay Gardens was, after all, a Philipino restaurant, and we were to entertain the dinner crowd before 10 pm, when the place would turn into a three-band-per-night club for emerging punk bands.

The next time I saw him, he was leading the owner, Ness Aquino, through the front door of the club. I'm on stage, with members of the company, erecting the set for the opening night of our play, and Dirk says, "See, Ness, that's the energy I want in here." We played many shows and did a lot of work on the club in those early days. While we were there, we took out the low kitty-litter ceiling above the stage, allowing for a lighting system to be installed; built the first 8-foot extension to the

Photo shows the background curtain, ceiling and lighting before being removed by Alan Curreri. The preformers are the band Novak.

stage; and ripped out several layers of lath and plaster to reveal the beautiful brick wall at the back of the stage, enhancing the ambience of the club for sure.

At the same time as this, I was the janitor of the club. I'd either go early in the morning to clean up, or go to the show in the evening and clean up after the club closed in the wee hours of the morning. Mostly the cleanup consisted of sweeping up trash cans full of popcorn (the staple diet of every Mab patron), which was thrown all over the club nightly, almost ceremoniously (better popcorn than beer bottles, I suppose); wiping down and repositioning the tables and chairs, getting rid of the bottles, cleaning the bar, the office, the kitchen, the dressing room, the floors; and, oh yes, the bathrooms. Oh, the bathrooms! Toilets not flushed, sure. Puke in the bowl, sometimes. On the seat, floor and walls, yeah sure, par for the course. There is, however, one special time that I remember: imagine several smashed bottles in all bowls in both bathrooms, crap and puke on top of the broken glass in all bowls, and then, of course, in the ladies' room there was a stall that had runny diarrhea 5 feet up the wall, with a lovely pair of pink, diarrhea-soaked panties hanging from the door frame.

Hey, I didn't take it personally. I just cleaned it up.

Alan Curreri

4 The Retorts
  Ruen
  Noble Barrister
  Hit'n'Run

5 The Subz
  The Outskirts
  The Authorities
  Nominal State

6 Non-Chalants
  Parental Guidance
  Angst
  The Act

7 Kid Gloves
  Tyrant
  The Works

Poster by Anomymous

8 Benefit for Eastern
  Front:
  7 Seconds
  Sic Pleasure
  War Zone
  Stark Hotel

9 Silvertone
  Top Jimmy & the
  Rhythm Pigs
  The Ghouls

10 The Spiders
   The Innocents
   Varve

11 Red Seven
   Alternate Learn-
   ing
   Ravage

12 Minus 1
   Toy Soldier
   Final Thrust

13 Tattoo

14 Social Unrest

   Crucifix
   Police State

15 The Hostages
   Der Lifers
   The Tanks

16 The Woundz
   The Tanks
   Black Athletes

17 Eye Protection
   Barry Beam
   Lifers
   Young Republi-
   cans

18 Ginger's Birth-
   day Party:
   Revenge
   The Renegades
   Mannequin
   Urban Assault

19 Human Jukebox
   Benefit:
   Ravage
   Ibibbilly Bibbilly

20 Blake Quake
   Bad Attitude
   Monickers
   Bob & the New-
   hearts

21 Minus 1
   Parental Guid-
   ance
   Harvey

22 Wilma
   GOD
   Laughing Black
   Happy Death

23 B Team
   Clocks of Pardise
   Half Church

24 T.S.O.L.
   Minute Men
   Saccharine Trust

25 T.S.O.L.
   Social Unrest
   War Zone
   The Uptights

26 Counterparts
   Vauxhall
   Soldiers of Fortune
   The Insects

27 The Farmers
   Zoo-Z
   Power Source
   Ruen

28 Lance Lyric
   Kid Gloves
   Final Thrust

29 The Weirds
   Bay Area Outra-
   geous Beauty Pag-
   eant 4th Annual
   Revue & Contest

30 SVT
   Top Jimmy & the
   Rhythm Pigs
   The Authorities
   Bar Wars Ballet

31 VKTMS
   Top Jimmy &
   the Rhythm Pigs
   Channel 3

job

11/5 mab 443 broadway W/ CALLING ALL GIRLS, CENTRAL FILE 10:30
11/11 berkeley square 1333 university W/ COUNTERPARTS, NOBLE BARRISTER & THE ABSOLUTES

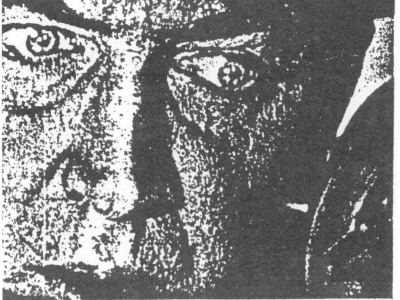

Poster by Anomymous

NOVEMBER 1981

1 Innocent
The Renegades
Blake Quake & the Tremors

2 Plastic Medium
Bonimics
Angst
Donny Snow & the Flakes

3 The Outskirts
The Subz
The Valkays

4 The Undead
Naked Lady Wrestlers
Vengeance
The Uptights

5 Central File
The Job

Calling All Girls

6 Chrome Dinette
The Verbs
The Pastels

7 Flamin' Groovies
Impostors
Bad Attitude
Bay Area Outrageous Beauty Pageant

8 Radio Free
Fang
The Cells
Andy Just & the Defenders

9 Head On
The Tanks
Hit'n'Run

10 Vauxhall
Los Olividados

Wild Boys

11 Perv Magazine Party:
Translator
Fried Abortions
Blake Quake & the Tremors
Cent File

12 The Lewd
Legionnaires
Disease
Crucifix
Domino Theory

13 Contractions
Elements of Style
Night Owls

14 Fabulous Titans
Rhythm Riot
X-Men

15 Red Seven

The Outlets
Ibbilly Bibbilly
Bent Nails

16 Wild Boys
The Subz
White Silence

17 Night Sharks
Ruen
Blake Quake
Dark Side of Pop

18 Noble Barristers
Beluga Whale
Farmer

19 Black Flag
Meat Puppets
The Tanks
Lorelei

20 Black Flag
Flipper
Meat Puppets

21 Eye Protection
Peterbilt
Surface Music
Young Republicans

22 Bob & the Newhearts
Ruen
The Act
Donny Snow & the Flakes

23 Creep Magazine Benefit:
7 Seconds
Central
File
Los Olividados

24 Minus 1

197

Angst
Counterparts
Final Thrust

25 Ruen
Vauxhall
Bob & the New-
hearts

26 Harvey
Jayne Doe
Sheets

27 The Lewd
Social Distortion
Toxic Reason
Vengeance

28 Head On
Tungz
Kid Gloves
Bay Area Outra-
geous Beauty
Pageant

29 Swinging Pos-
sums
Bad Attitude
The Relay

30 Nonchalantz
Unawares
Los Olividados
Pariah

DECEMBER 1981

1 Final Thrust
Prisoner
Tungz

2 Crucifix
Toxic Reasons
Revenge
Los Olividados
Fang

CONTRACTIONS
ELEMENTS OF STYLE
NOV 13 FAB MAB W/ NIGHTOWLS

Poster by Bobbie Hopkins

3 Impatient Youth
Half Church
Deprogrammers

4 The Verbs
The Innocent
Blake Quake &
the Tremors

5 7 Seconds
Fartz

6 Deprogrammer
Mindsweeper
Ruen
Power Source

7 Sagittarius Party:
Tattoo
Hard Attack
Sluts a Go Go

8 Benefit for Anti-
Gun Control
Chrome Dinette
Eye Protection
No Sisters
Pop Smear

9 Tanks
A Happy Death
Angst

10 Lifers
Quiet Room
Minus One
Matcheads

11 VKTMS
Silvertone
Impatient Youth

12 China White
D.I. (formerly
the Adolescents)
Channel 3

13 Private Party

14 Dead Kennedys
Toxic Reasons
Fried Abortions
Angst

15 Dead Kennedys
Crucifix
Church Police
Los Olividados

16 Cruel Tones
Swinging Possums
Central File
The Counterparts

17 Impatient Youth
Swinging Possums
X-Mas Eve
Ribsy

18 Eastern Front
Benefit

19 Eye Protection
Der Lifers

20 No Data

21 Plastic Medium
Outskirts
Radio Free
Bonamics

22 Central File
Insect Idol
Sheets
Authorities

23 Harvey
Parental Guidance
Andy Just & the
Defenders
Red 7

24 Skid
White Walls
White Silence
Night Shark

25 The Spiders
Tattoo
Central File

26 Wasted Youth
Circle One
The Fix
Modern Warfare

27 The Fix
Modern Warfare
Godhead
Los Olividados

28 Angst
Cells
Darker Side of Pop

29 Punk Globe Party:
Swinging Pos-
sums
Ghouls
Bad Attitude
Vauxhall
Counterparts

30 Head On
Ruen
The Tungz

31 Silvertone
Rhythm Riot
Swinging Pos-
sums

JANUARY 1982

1 New Year's Day
Party

2 Minute Men
Effigies
Descendents
Lorelei & the
Torpedos

3 Cells
Sir Blub
Outlets
The Fringe

4 Hans Naughty
Ruen
Bees
Bonimics

5 No Data

6 Golden Gate
Jumpers
White Silence
Drivers
Nominal State

7 Wild Boys
Carnage
Plastic Medium

8 Spectacles
Authorities

9 Contractions
Wolvarines
Subz

10 No Data
11 No Data
12 No Data
13 No Data
14 No Data
15 No Data
16 No Data

WOLVERINES
LIFERS

SATURDAY
FEB 6

MABUHAY
GARDENS

Poster by Anomymous

17 Lazy Boys
Outlets

18 Peter Dayton
Beluga Whale
Borneo

19 Counterparts
Vauxhall
Comboo

20 Finders
Dickheads
Radio Free

21 Rhythm Riot
Lifers

22 Aldo Nova
Audio
Hans Naughty

23 B-Team
Xmas Eve
Paris Working

24 Bad Attitude
Hard Attack
Match Head

25 Naked Lady
Wrestlers
Olividados

Carnage
Pariah

26 Eric Blakely
Parental Guidance
Red 7
Ruen

27 Blake Quake &
Tremor
Phantom Limbs
Brevity
Fring

28 Surface Music
X-Men
Farmers

29 Rhythm Riot
Harvey
Combo

30 Translator
Hostages
Arkansaw Man

31 Verbs
Mr. Clean
Violators

Dirk was having a very bad week, the production facilities water heater went out and the Audi was in the shop, so I offered him the loan of my '67 LTD, w/ ultra-un-power steering and brakes, thinking at least it would be useful if not enjoyable. He was supposed to pick it up one particular evening, but upon returning home from the Lennon studio, after hanging out w/ close friends inc. Der Dingle & some Mutants, he felt too tired to pick up the car and told me he'd do so the following day; later that morning we all cried, because, Dirk was, no more.

I didn't personally meet Dirk during the golden late-70s and early-80s. His partner Damon Malloy was a director of the public access program, Doghouse, I (& Heather McCollom) were involved with, in the late eighties, and he invited Dirk to an episode we needed an audience for. He must've been somehow watching the monitor, though I don't see how, since it was facing the anchors instead of the audience, but when his CU came, he just happened to be picking his nose, I mean really digging, and digging it, staring into the camera with a demented gleam. Much later, I was walking home from Canned Foods when someone in an elegant, yet amazingly decayed BMW stopped in the middle of the street, beckoning me heartily. I opened the door and it was Dirk. He said they wanted to work w/Heather and I, in finishing one of our video projects. He and Damon took us out for lunch at an apparently long forgotten motel restaurant by the beach, that I couldn't believe actually existed, and we decided to put together the Best Of Doghouse. This, instead of doing the post-production of a feature we'd shot, thinking it'd be much quicker and easier to start w/that and see how working together would work. It ended up taking Heather, Damon and I two-plus years, diligently looking through each episode, considering every shot and editing material from the about 25 programs. When we showed Dirk the masterpiece he agreed it was one, while pointing out that there were so many copyrighted musical performances embedded in the final product us naifs overlooked, that even if the budget allowed for us to hire someone to spend weeks getting all of the clearances, which it wouldn't, we couldn't afford to pay for just one anyway. So we owe Dirk (and Damon) The Moon, but neither of 'em ever gave us the least grief and continued to invite us over. We have yet to finish our feature, but we both got to know Dirk (and Damon) so well, and want to shout it from the Transamerica Pyramid's point, how lucky we were to be on the receiving end of so much of his priceless, loving, fascinating sarcasm. I saved some of Dirks' phone messages, because they were the most wickedly-brilliant pieces of humor I'd ever experienced, and Denise Demise agreed they were uncommonly mad, playing some of them at the Friday Dirkfest. Damon told me that Dirk didn't hold back w/ the clients either, giving them the full force of his sharp, diesel-powered wit and that many of 'em left, never to return, feeling completely humiliated. Such was Dirk's unwavering allegiance to his unique, hard core, philosophy.

Davell Swan

The Pope Is Dead — Dirk Dirksen (1937-2006

The mutants gathered at his grave to burn the flame and light the cave. Jello was served at his request before the world heard of his punk rock test. He took the rejects and gave them all names, sent their critics to the astral planes. An uncle, a brother a father, a friend — how many of us did he raise in the end?

And if not for him our din would not be known. He gave us a stage, a place to call home — without his wry smile and discerning eye we'd have been aimless with nowhere to fly .

He gave us purpose in a purposeless world, chaperoned a generation, put his money where his mouth was in the punk vocation, challenged my reasons for playing guitar and encouraged the madness in his theater bizarre

He had the ability to turn you on to yourself, a hard core ringleader, a magic little elf.

He could make you or break you, but he wasn't that mean: anyone who wanted could be in his scene; you just had to be there to know that he did care.

He cared about each and every nut ball, in fact, he enjoyed them all. He applauded your success and rescued us from boredom. When all of us were poor and no one could afford him, he would still let you in with a crooked grin and a strange remark, always tongue in cheek. "I provide music seven nights a week," he used to tell me. Nobody did that then or now. He knew every con, every trick in the book, but he'd let you go on sinker, line and hook, and hang your self publicly if that's what it took, to get the attention that you think you needed.

All the fruits of your glory come from plant that we seeded, one by one by one by minus one.

D.C. Alberts © November 2006

■ ■

Dirk to the Rescue!

A regular at the all ages Gilman street project in Berkeley, I must have been either too young or too lazy to go to the Mab when Dirk was an MC, but I knew Dirk through my work with Kathy Peck of HEAR. Dirk was always helping us, especially with video shoots for PSAs. A few times we had arranged to be backstage at LIVE 105 concerts to get footage of the artists saying things like "Wear your Damn Earplugs!" and what not. I thought everything was all set ahead of time, our credentials would be at the door, we had a room set aside, etc. Well, with the craziness of the event, and everyone running around, things fell through and we didn't have our passes, or it was too loud to shoot and we needed to move, or artists weren't being fed our direction. Any number of things went wrong and Dirk came to the rescue. He knew people- even people who he had beef with that he got to set aside differences in order to help out HEAR. Of course that didn't keep me from messing things up further, but what can I say, I was young and inexperienced.

Thanks Dirk!, Cousin Isaac

FEBRUARY 1982

1 Cells
  Differenz
  Fit

2 Darker Side of Pop
  Subz
  Tsuketanai

3 Cliff Field
  Ravage
  Ibbilly Bibbilly

4 Tyrant
  Kid Gloves

5 Dickheads
  Swingin' Possums
  Radio Free

6 Wolvarines
  Lifers
  Minstrels
  Outskirts

7 5th Anniversary
  Party:
  Trixx
  Sheets
  Minus 1
  Ghouls
  Rayon

8 Babette's B Party
  Timmy & Special
  Guests

9 Mohawks
  Angst

10 I.C.U.
  Scapegoats
  Schemetix
  Model Strikers

11 Tanks

Varve
Farmers

12 VKTMS
  The Lewd
  Fang

13 S.V.T.

14 Flamin' Groovies
  Cruel Tones

15 Beluga Whale
  Powerhouse
  South O Market

16 Jokes
  Fungo
  KIH JOY

17 Punk Globe
  Birthday Party:
  Barry Beam
  Vauxhall
  Sluts

18 Skid & White-
  walls
  P.G.
  Sirens
  Ambulance

19 Silvertone
  Mondellos
  Screaming Urge

20 B People
  Wolvarines
  Screaming Urge

21 Executives
  Soldiers of For-
  tune
  Nominal State

22 Monday Night
  Blues

Couresty Dirksen Archives

23 Mardi Gras Cos-
  tume Party:
  P.G. (?)
  Biological Hazard
  A.K.A.

24 North Mission
  Association Ben-
  efit:
  Varve
  The Looters

25 Cruel Tones
  Harvey
  Anger

26 Flamin' Groovies
  Vauxhall

27 Heavy Metal
  Night:
  3-D
  Audio
  Hans Naughty

28 Bad Attitude
  Ruen

MARCH 1982

1 Monday Night
  Blues

2 The Differenz
  Lazy Boys
  Alternate Learning

3 Sinners
  Silhouette
  Ruen

4 Combo
  Mr Potato Head
  Model Strikers

5 Innocent
  Quiet Room
  I.C.U.

6 **Dickheads**
Finders
Spectacles
Bad Attitude

7 **No Data**
8 **No Data**
9 **No Data**
10 **No Data**
11 **No Data**

12 **VKTMS**
Violators
Bar Wars Ballet

13 **No Data**

14 **Golden Dragon**
Toy Soldier
Aftermath

15 **Amanda Hughes**

16 **Parental Guidance**
Manx
Exttra Terrestrial

17 **No Data**

18 **Wilma**
Katherine
Pops Smear

19 **Mojo**
Cruel Tones
Soul Agents
Parental Guidance

20 **Max Volume**
& the I.L.W.
I.C.U.
Calling All Girls

21 **Addiction**
Golden Dragon
Stereotype

22 **Beluga Whale**
& guests

23 **Philator**
Devon La Crosse

24 **Love Circus**

25 **07080**
Soldier of Fortune

26 **Hostages**
Thump Thump
Thump

27 **Silvertone**
Feeders
Radio Free

28 **Men in Black**
Lazy Boy
Predators

29 **Beluga Whale**
Power House

30 **Mr. Potato Head**
Extra Terrestrial
Wizzard

31 **Parental Guidance**
Ku Ku Ku
Master Grell

APRIL 1982

1 **Moonlighters**
Skids
Whitewalls
Mohawk

2 **VKTMS**
Max Volume
Naked Lady
Wrestlers

Paris Working

3 **Jerry Sikorski &**
the American
Patrol Band
Cruel Tones
Swinging Possums

4 **Pyramid 181**
Wraith
Junior Executives

5 **Beluga Whale**
Red Brtigade

6 **07080**
Dark Side of Pop
I-World

7 **Bad Attitude**
Dimes
Blue Angels

8 **Ruen**
Felix Gulpa
Brevity

9 **Impostors**
DC4
Harvey
Beluga Whale

10 **Hard Attack**
Differenz
Combo
Erik Blakely

11 **Timmy**
Innocense
Page 1

12 **Beluga Whale**
Kingfish

13 **Erik Blakely**

Cliff Fields
Mono

14 **Paris Working**
Ibbilly Bibbilly
Devon La Crosse

15 **Harvey**
Night Shark
Extra Terrestrial

16 **Silvertone**
Vauxhall
Soul Agent

17 **Lifers**
The Show
Sinners
Dimes

18 **Parental Guidance**
Bar Wars Ballet
Trixx

19 **Beluga Whale &**
Guests

20 **Love Circus**
Dave Baby
Fat Ladies

21 **Sinners**
Allies
Katherine

22 **Ravage**
Sing Sing
Deadly Rein

23 **Silvertone**
Impatient
07080

24 **Earl Zero**
Isawan
Ruen
Dark Side of Pop

My Dirk stories would consist of the good, the bad, but never the ugly. I always liked Dirk, & could never understand those people who didn't.

So here we go with the good. It takes place when the Wicked Witch of the West known as Feinstein was ruling & ruining our fair City. She had succeeded in closing down almost all of the punk clubs in SF, but the Mab was still struggling along.

The Witch was in the process of ridding OUR fair City of the vermin (which was mainly us & also the homosexuals until she realized what a faux pas THAT was & started kissing their collective asses instead. Its never stopped bothering me that they went for it.)

So apparently Dirk had been having trouble with SF's Finest. So this one nite, a slow week nite, like a thousand others before it, I was hanging out near the speakers, bopping to the between band music & slugging back a beer, as was my wont. My eyes were roaming around & happened upon a fracas near the door. Dirk was escorting (in no uncertain terms!) 2 punkettes out to the street. So what. I didn't know them, & had no burning desire to make their acquaintance. So imagine my surprise when I see Dirk making a beeline straight for me. My brow furrowed. I was wondering "What the Hell?!" when Dirk started talking over the music right into my left ear.

"I'm really sorry I had to do that," says he. "The cops have been here every night checking ID's. I'm just trying to keep this place open".

I wondered why he was explaining all this to me. Granted, we'd known each other for years, but really only to say "Hey.", & such. Then I realized that he thought I was underage as well. I always was pretty little.

Anyway, so here is Dirk standing there staring at me as if waiting for some form of absolution. So I said, "That's okay," & sort of waved my beer bottle at him in some sort of sign of solidarity. Apparently he was satisfied. He smiled his Dirk smile & waddled away.

I was left with my perplexity & my empty beer bottle. I went to the bar.

Also remember in the very early days they used to feed us sometimes. We would come early, before the club opened & there would be these huge warming dishes full of spaghetti. We'd pig out. Of course, being punks, we never had any money & free food was always a gift from the gods.

I don't know if that was Dirk though, it might have been Ness.

See Ya! Luv,, Roxanne

■■

I remember that I wanted fame. Fortune would have to wait and did. Our band had broken up. It was many years later and Dirkson was making (finishing) a kind of documentary about our band the Mutants. I told him, "It was about time. Up till now you have made us feel like step children that showed up drunk for dinner. Yeah," I said, "You could have done better by us".

I looked at the portraits of bands taken at the Mab. They lined the long hallway that led to the editing room. They were impressive. Crime, The Nuns, Avengers, Dead Kennedys, Offs, VS, every band that ever played at the Mab was there, immortalized and hanging like the art pieces they were. But not a single photograph of the "Mutants" to be seen, anywhere. " Say Dirkson if you like our band so much how come you don't have our picture hangin up there? "

He replied, " I knew you were coming over so I took it down".

Later on, in the editing room, mounted on the wall behind Damon who was editing the Mutants documentary, there it was, our portrait, taken in the glory days.

Fritz Fox

■■■■■■■■■■■■■■■■■■■■■■■■■■■■■■■■■■

I can't remember the year or many of the details…not surprising considering my altered state at the time (I think it was peyote and cognac that night). But I do remember vividly that Dirk defended my honor in a way that was, you know, so Dirk.

It was at the Mab, of course. And the band was the Sleepers. Well, maybe I wasn't drunk enough, but I thought they sucked and said as much to Dirk and whoever else was standing next to me. Turns out one lug got really pissed off that I would DARE say

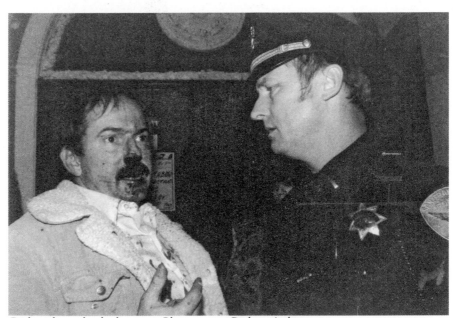

Dirk with another broken nose. Photo courtesy Dirksen Archives

such a thing about his favorite band and started getting aggressive and calling me a slut and worse. Dirk would have none of such talk to a lady in HIS establishment and told him to shut up and behave. Not a chance.

I don't know exactly how we all ended up outside, but it must've been something seeing Dirk and one or more young punks rolling and flailing towards the door, people scrambling to get out of their way. The fight got real good right there on Broadway with a crowd of onlookers cheering Dirk on. Several guys were on him and he's hitting back with all his might. I'm screaming and trying to pull them off, freaked out that they're going to really hurt him. Others pitched in and helped finally end the rumble.

And how was Dirk after all this? Well, he got up grinning from ear to ear, blood dripping down his face, nose broken (again) and his glasses bent in a hilarious way…one lens 'way down on his cheek and the other in the opposite direction on top of his head. But he looked like he'd just had a great time. In my eyes, he was a true hero and gentleman who stood up for a woman and for free speech. May he and his crooked nose rest in peace.

By Vicki Rosen

25 Suspex
Golden Dragon
F.D.R. (?)
East of Eden

26 Beluga Whale
Peer Pressure
East of Eden

27 Big Mac

28 Men in Blsck
Minus 1
The Twist

29 Radio Free
Rodiction
Velveeta

30 Silvertone
Norman Salant
New Critic

MAY 1982

1 Mojo
Bar Wars Ballet
Thump Thump
Thump
Trixx

2 P.R.I.
Hi-Voltage
Felix Gulpa

3 Beluga Whale
Kingfish

4 New Hearts
Erik Blakely
Phil in the Blank

5 El Buen Tiempo

6 New Critic Record
Party
Surface Music

Sharp Young Men

7 Silvertone
Swinging Pos-
sum
Driver

8 Jerry Sikorsky
Swinging Pos-
sum
Driver

9 Love Circus
On Ramps
Peer Pressure
Guerillas

10 Beluga Whale
Kingfish

11 Specimen
Manx
Silent Partner

12 Winter Hawk
Soul Agent
Devon La Crosse

13 Blue Angels
Bar Wars Ballet
Trixx

14 Silvertone
Katherine

15 Dickheads
Mr. Clean
Cameltones
Extra Terrestrial

16 Sentinel
Ronnie Ray Guns

17 Beluga Whale
Kingfish

18 The Employees

Brevity
Year-to-Date

19 Minus 1
Dimes
Hi-Voltage

20 Sinners
Cliff Fields
Erik Blakely

21 Hard Attack
Naked Lady
Wrestlers
The Twist
Stingrays

22 SVT
Sing Sing
Erik Blakely
The Nicolettes

23 Musician's Jam
& Auditions

24 Stingray
Kingfish

25 Jester
Silent Partner
Flint

26 Swinging Pos-
sum
Soul Agent
Driver

27 Manx
Dark Side of Pop
Velveeta

28 Finders
Parental Guid-
ance
The Twist

29 Rayons

Dimes
Sinners
Extra Terrestrial

30 The Impostors
Bad Attitude
New Hearts

31 Closed

JUNE 1982

1 Katherine
Manx
House of Pants

2 Bad Attitude
Sine Wave
Felix Culpa

3 Head On
Power Source
The Fit

4 Erik Blakely
Love Circus
Year-to-Date

5 Innocent
Quiet Room
07080

BAM Magazine July 13, 1984
by Suzanne Stefanac

Outside the On Broadway before the final show, featuring the Dead Kennedys and The Mutants. Photo: Stanley Greene © 1984

An Era Remembered

The gardens where punk rock blossoms

By ANA SANDOVAL
Ledger Staff Writer

"Welcome to the almost legendary, somewhat famous...Mabuhay Garbage,"

So went producer Dirk Dirksen's introduction of his theater the Mabuhay Gardens, which houses many of San Francisco's punk bands.

Punk and New Wave music have swept the nation. With the arrival of England's Sex Pistols, punk has become more than a music, it has become a way of life.

It includes radically-cut, jet-black hair; safety pins through the ears; black leather; torn jeans; and spike heeled shoes, not to mention three chord, decible-driving music.

Many surburbanites venture to the Mabuhay and other punk theaters to see the "freaks" or dress in their own leathers for the night. Many are "closet punks" who listen to the likes of the Ramones or the Sex Pitsols without letting friends or parents know.

One punk from the Concord area, dressed in a ripped T-shirt and safety pins, said his friends might disown him if they heard he was going to the Mabuhay.

Punk is thought of as a savage music bred with violence and distruction. Dirksen sees it as theater. He and his partner Miller began producing shows at the Mabuhay as an outlet for those who "want to make a statement to the public."

The Mabuhay is a Filipino restaurant owned by Ness Aquino. It is also an outlet for other performing arts, such as dance and drama, produced by Dirksen.

Preferring to call it avant-garde music, Dirksen said punk does not have one main philosophy.

"It is a diversified as any other theater," he explained. But he admitted it is a high-energy, high-aggression performance.

He said the music is an interaction between the performers and the audience. The Mabuhay purposely doles out almost three barrels of popcorn a night in straw baskets to patrons.

"This way they can either eat it or express their feelings about the performers," Dirksen said.

And they do frequently — by hurling baskets upon baskets at the bands. Once during one of Dirksen's introduction a beer bottle was thrown, hitting him squarely on the shoulder.

"People shouldn't have such blinders, (to the performers) but they're baboons in every crowd." he replied.

Punk to band members is "just music," said Jeff Olener, lead singer for one of San Francisco's more famous bands The Nunns.

"We're an original band, no ties, no copies, some influences, that's all," he explained.

The group, together for two years, is currently on an East Coast tour which includes New Yorks' biggest punk outlet, CBGB's.

The Nunns members include, Olener and Richie Dettrich on vocals, Jennifer Miro, Aljandro Escovedo, and Pat Ryan.

Brooklyn-born Olener said the band doesn't worry about how great they sound musically. They are just trying to make people unhappy.

"We bring out the pain, the more pain you have the more you can see the light," he said.

He explained the group got its start when they rented out the Mabuhay for $75. "If we never rented it, it would have never happened. It would still be a Filipino restaurant.

Dirksen somewhat disagrees.

"It is ludicrous to say the place made the Nunns or visa versa. We have a strong relationship. Not one person did anything," he said.

Before leaving, the Nunns built up a following of their own. They packed the Mabuhay full for their final Bay Area concert.

They, along with psychologists, believe punk is a little like primal therepy. Audiences sit through ear-blasting concerts reacting to the music in varying degrees. Like other types of music, some sit without moving, others shake a leg or tap a foot.

Others openly dance 'The Pogo,' a punk dance, bouncing around like rag dolls.

They scream obscenities, sing along, or in the case of the East County punk rock group the Gourds, they laugh.

...nd) charged up the crowd. Photo: Stanley Greene © 1984

...long with a whole ...n nights a week, ...hold a mike could ...: Mab. To be sure, ...re of shoddy psy- ...lf-indulgent flail- ...: The Mutants and ...nedys found fertile ...ch to develop their ...us. Two years ago, ...with the Mab and ...the On Broadway. ...ves on again. Tele- ...love, will get most ...se days. He will be ...me strata of artists ...en under his quirky ...e relieved to know...

...mies, will go on as usual. Dirk and his crew will probably still arrange the Hooker's Ball as well as the Bike Messenger's Ball. There will definitely be a few benefits and free concerts this summer as well.

A broad spectrum of individuals has been touched by the On Broadway. Some gripe about Dirk, some grovel, others wonder what will fill the void. Freedom of speech and/or noise is still Dirk's *sine qua non* and the community is richer for his perseverance.

DIRK DIRKSEN — *curator of idiosyncratic art*

I haven't changed my philosophy. Now I'm just going to pay more atten...

R.I.P. ON BROADWAY

That's right, the end of an era has arrived. Dirk Dirksen's famed punk palace ceases to be after Saturday, June 16th. You can bet the goodbye bash will be a smash . . . Ness Acquino, who owns the Mabuhay downstairs, will be taking over and remodelling the upstairs for a dance club. Claims Ness: "Dirk has lost credibility. You can't run a big club with local bands; you get 100 people in there and it doesn't look like you have anybody there." Could be. We DO know that, since On Broadway opened, its stage has held almost 11,000 band concerts, totalling over *55,000* individual performers . . . Dirk will channel his energies into documenting the local rock scene with his cable video showcase "Dirk Dirksen Presents." The last ten days of On Broadway's live shows will be videotaped; the bands include Canada's **D.O.A.**, England's **Exploited**, Boston's **Freeze**, NY's **Kraut**, and our own **MDC, Tales of Terror, 45 Grave**, plus more. Dirk: Mazel tov.

Mabuhay Uber Alles
Remembering San Francisco's punk playpen
with impresario Dirk Dirksen

IN 1977 the 200-seat Mabuhay Gardens at 437 Broadway in North Beach was it, the launching pad for local bands Flipper, the Nuns, Crime, the Dead Kennedys, and Chris Isaak, as well as the first San Francisco venue to book Devo. Blondie, the Dammed, and many others. The Mab was the birthplace of and, some would say, the best showcase for West Coast punk.

The Mabuhay Gardens was the brainchild of local impresario Dirk Dirksen. Today, the 53-year-old former promoter looks about as unlike the archetypal punk-rock promoter as can be imagined. Sitting among walls of videotapes and computer gear in his tiny Pacific Heights apartment, Dirksen is bookish and deliberate, choosing his words with great care. Despite his notorious history of lunacy at the Mab, he looks more like a tenured history prof at UC Berkeley than the man who used to wear ludicrous stage attire and berate a room full of post pubescent punks.

Whereas other promoters and club owners from the nascent punk era, like Hilly Kristal at CBGB, were relatively behind-the-scenes guys, Dirksen was an in-your-face confrontational type both on the phone and on the Mab stage.

"He'd come out with this penis on his nose," recalls Denise Demise, one of the Mab's former stage managers. "He'd start abusing the bands and audience. One year Bill Graham had Dirk hosting the Bammies, and Dirk wore that silly contraption after Graham had asked him to be at least sort of serious."

Kent Wallace, former leader of the Spectacles, believed Dirksen's motives were different. "He'd give you an earful of abuse, but it was to thicken your skin. He used to grief us out on the phone, like, 'Why should I book you?' Once ! sat in his office and watched him do this to other bands. He was winking while he was dissing this other band."

From its beginning, the Mabuhay Gardens was bound to he a venue for absurdity, and Dirksen was •bound to bring it there. A veteran of Straight television production in Hollywood, Dirksen had done game shows like Rocket to Stardom and Your Name's the Game, a call-in bingo show hosted by "Smiling" Jack Smith-

"I had to fire him from Your Name's the Game because he just wasn't getting over," Dirksen says. "Anyway. Jack had so much plastic surgery his face was locked into a permanent smile. When I canned him, he was crying but couldn't stop smiling."

Dirksen got sick of the L.A. grind and in the early 1970s relocated to San Francisco. "At the time, there was no place for experimental theater," Dirksen recalls. "In 1974 I brought Les Nicolettes (to Mabuhay Gardens). They did parodies of movies and pop songs, and (they had been working) at the Mitchell Brothers Theater." The Mabuhay at that point was a Filipino supper club featuring island show bands that were brought in by the owner. Ness Aquino. "By the time Ness paid airfare and expenses to these acts, like these Filipino Elvis impersonators, there was no money left," Dirksen says.

In post-hippie San Francisco, Les Nicolettes' irreverence and satire brought out a mixed crowd. 'There weren't any punks yet, really," Dirksen says.

What became the San Francisco punk movement at the Mab was a strange brew of ex-hippies, beats, and wigged-out suburbanites. What codified the S.F. punk uniform was a CBS late-night broadcast of the Sex Pistols from England. "One week after that it was all leathers and safety pins," Dirksen says.

Dirk and the famous dick nose. Photo by Jill Hoffman

The Mab's first strictly musical performer was a former Canadian stripper by the name of Mary Monday. "She was every kid's dream." Dirksen recalls. "Mary did this kind of S/Mish glam-rock thing and filled the place. Word got out, and these new punk bands like Crime and the Nuns started asking for gigs."

The multicultural split between the Filipino clientele and the North Beach wackos produced some interesting moments. "Ness asked me to produce this show on Channel 20 for Amapola, a Filipino star, and on it, we would have some of the bands who played the Mab," Dirksen says. "One time, before the Nuns were slated to appear. Ness hadn't done his homework, so he tells the TV audience that there was gonna be this gospel act on. The Nuns them-selves break into 'Suicide Child.' I don't know what the people watching must have thought."

As 1977 rolled around, the Mab became San Francisco's leading punk venue. "There were people having sex in the bathrooms, doing drugs there as well," Demise says. The Mab was essentially a late-night club, with the bands performing between 11 p.m. and 2 a.m.

"There was a theater upstairs that had plays" Dirksen says. "There could be no noise downstairs before 11. So when a guitarist would hit a loud chord, the promoter would come down and threaten to sue. Once, the Street Punks accidentally set off one of their flash pots during a performance and the smoke filtered upstairs. The fire department came, closing Broadway for hours."

"It was a zoo," Dead Kennedys drummer Bruce Slesinger recalls. "I'd see people climbing on the stage from every angle, crashing into my kit, covering Biafra win spit, tearing his clothes off. He never stopped singing, though. It was insane."

Like moths to light, the new order descended on Dirksen's playpen. "Bowie, Iggy—once we even had Redd Foxx in there," Dirksen says. "1 didn't think you should have all the same kind of stuff all night — it became dull — so I'd put hippie bands on with punks, especially to rile people. Once, we had this early show that was eight comedians and a play. Well, the play was by this paraplegic named Frank Moore who brought all these girls on stage as emema-bag-wielding nurses as part of the act. Well, all these tourists who'd wandered in for a cheap Filipino meal were subjected to this, and it created a real stir. Flea from the Chili Peppers was there and told me later that he'd been tripping on acid, and after seeing this he had decided to gel into theater."

Dirksen is full of tales of eccentrics who passed through the Mab's doors. "Nico was a real case." he says. "She was a bit touchy, but when we got to this boutique in Sausalito, she lit up, like, 'I must have that dress to perform in tonight.'"

Some local acts had attitudes, too. "Crime were a bitch to get on stage on time," Dirksen says. "So I'd get up there and chide them, saying, 'And now the rich and famous rock stars: Crime.' " Part of the lunacy was because Dirksen provided the crowd with barrels of free popcorn to prevent more dangerous missiles from hitting the stage. "The power-pop Readymades used to really get showered in it," he says "This singer, Gloria Balsam, would sing 'My Dog Fifi' and get buried in it. When the Ramones first played the Mab, Robin Williams opened, and he got corned off the stage too."

In 1981 the Mab moved into the larger upstairs space at the On Broadway theater. In the years that followed, Dirksen's original vision of "anarchy within the boundaries of the Mab's four walls" turned foul much in the same way that the hippie movement went sour at Altamont. Crazy theater became ugly reality.

"I've had my nose broken at least six times, my ankle twice ."he says. "I've buried 64 friends from drugs, murder, suicide, AIDS. I remember going from Ricky's {of the sleepers} funeral to Buck Naked's {lead singer of the Bare Bottom Boys} in the same day.

On top of growing internal problems at the Mab, middle management at the SFPD wasn't friendly to the club. "They didn't like the fact that we'd done benefits for Harvey Milk's causes," Dirksen says. "One night there was a massive bust—27 people got hauled away. [Then SF Sheriff candidate] Mike Hennessey almost got arrested, but he was in line at the time, so he was spared. When Feinstein became mayor, it was nothing but trouble."

San Francisco punk beacons the Dead Kennedys were the band to bring the era of the Mab to a close. "I ran Biafra's mayoral campaign in '79" Dirksen says. "We had slogans like 'I'll Kill Myself if He Doesn't Win,' and Biafra had ideas like making businessmen wear clown suits between nine and five, establishing a Board of Bribery, free Muni, some really provocative stuff."

But the last D.K.s show at the On Broadway in 1984, available on videotape through Target Video, shows a dying scene. (There have been numerous efforts to revive the room in the '90s, but Dirksen says he has nothing to do with them.) While Biafra harangues the crowd endlessly, the bridge-and-tunnel crowd laps up his shtick like honey. At the video's end, Dirksen ascends to the stage for the last time to assault the crowd with one last "Go home, get outta here," which is how he closed every Mab show much the same way "Greensleeves" closes every Fillmore show,

"I might as well have been talking to myself," Dirksen says. As always, no one was listening.

Johnny Angel

DIRK FEST

a tribute to the "Pope of Punk"
coPresented by H.E.A.R. AND KUSF RADIO

LINE UP

THURSDAY, JUNE 7TH @ SLIM'S

Emcees V. Vale and Spencer

Pearl Harbor and the Explosions

Toiling Midgets

The Lewd

The Sea Hags

The Rubber City Rebels

The Symptoms

Ron Jones spoken word artist with
Megan Bierman and Maia Scott

DJ Denise Demise

Film shorts by Karl Hinz

FRIDAY, JUNE 8TH @ GREAT AMERICAN MUSIC HALL

Emcee, Jello Biafra

The Avengers

SF Mutant Non-Allstars with
Naomi Ruth Eisenberg

The Contractions

The White Trash Debutantes with the
fabulous Jon Gries

No Alternative with Chip Kinman of the
Dils and Rank and File

Dana Alberts

DJ Denise Demise

Film shorts by Karl Hinz

Special Guest Ness Aquino, the original owner of the Mabuhay Gardens restaurant which Dirk helped transform into the "Fab Mab" providing a much needed outlet for "outspoken ideas" in Dirk's words.

DIRK DIRKSEN MEMORIAL FUND + AUCTION

June 2007 — hearnet.com/auction Proceeds will help to pay for Dirk's *final expenses and resting place*, to set up the *Dirk Dirksen Memorial Fund*, and for the *preservation of his rare archive* of videotaped performances, photos, posters, and other punk memorabilia.

the Auction Includes these Items and more Original *Winston Smith Dead Kennedys artwork* for WINNEBAGO WARRIOR • *Dead Kennedys "california über alles" single* autographed by East Bay Ray • *Original lyrics, vintage setlists, posters, photos* and more from VKTMS, including Nyna's "C" Harp used on recording of Downtown. • Autographed vintage *Tubes* posters and album art. • *Vintage PUNK photos* by: Chester Simpson, James Stark, Ruby Ray, F Stop Fitzgerald, Bobby Castro • *Autographed drumheads* by artists performing at the Dirk Fest • Artwork by *Mark Mothersbaugh* from Devo • *Autographed Vintage Contractions LP* "Something Broke"

Send donations of $ or autographed music memorabilia, artwork, music, music instruments to:
H.E.A.R., 1405 Lyon St. San Francisco, CA 94115. Phone (415) 409-3277 or email hear@hearnet.com.

Dirk Dirksen Memorial Fund Paypal at hearnet.com/auction • Funds from the auction and concerts go to benefit the Dirk Dirksen Memorial Fund

THANK YOU SPONSORS

H.E.A.R. — Hearing Education and Awareness for Rockers, Inc. hearnet.com *KUSF radio* kusf.org *Punk Globe* punkglobe.com *Lennon Studios* lennonstudios.com *Dirk Dirksen Memorial Auction* hearnet.com/auction *Haight Ashbury Music Center* haight-ashbury-music.com *Winston Smith's Artcrimes* winstonsmith.com *Craig Pop Artist* craigpopartist.com *John Seabury* johnseabury.com *David Denny Audio Consulting* daviddenny.com *Dirksen-Molloy Productions* outspokenideas.com *RE/Search Publications* researchpubs.com *Daniel East* danieleast.net *Future Sonics* futuresonics.com *The Counter Culture Hour* researchpubs.com *Barry Simons – Your Music Attorney* yourmusiclawyer.com *Firehouse Kustom Rockart, Co.* firehouseposters.com *Fuzzmonster Records* fuzzmonster.com *Mike Dingle* dinglestick.com *Drinks with Tony* drinkswithtony.com/dirkdirksen.html *Bobby Imsolucki* imsolucki.com *Unity Foundation* unityfoundation.org *Mack's Hearplugs* hearnet.com/shop/index.shtml *Jai Jai Noire Digital Films* jaijai.com *Great American Music Hall* gamh.com *Slim's* slims-sf.com

Interview with Kathy Peck by James Stark, June 24, 2009

James: How did you get into a band and getting your first gig at the Mab and that process.

Kathy: Summer of 1979, The Contractions (Mary Kelley-guitar, Debbie Hopkins-drums, Kathy Peck-bass) had begun rehearing at a practice space on Folsom Street in San Francisco. That was where we met the Offs and the Dils. The Offs took us under their wing and they encouraged us to go to the Mab and see Dirk about getting a gig. We got all excited, had photos taken and got ready for a show at the Mab. Then, Dirk cancelled the show. So, we ended up doing our first show in Anita Kitses' attic with the Offs because of the Mab cancellation. After that the Contractions got a buzz going and played a lot of shows at the Mab. I think a lot of the guy bands liked us because we were different and Dirk was always looking for a different opener and we were kicking ass.

Kathy Peck. Photo by Fstop Fitzgearld

James: How did your relationship evolve with Dirk since it started out on a bad note.

Kathy: We all use to go to the Mab to see the bands; throw salty popcorn at each other, pogo dance in front of the stage to all the outrageous acts, hang out, fall in and out of love, hide out in the rickety upstairs graffiti- ed backstage rafters and gossip in the girl's bathroom, which was the big social hub. It didn't even have a toilet in it after awhile. The Mab was fun. Equal rudeness for all! I look back on that time like it was our punk rock high school. Because of Dirk, The Mab was where we all learned to play our instruments and become musicians and artists. I can just hear him on stage sardonically announcing a new act, "And now here they are… the Go Go's attempting to play their instruments."

Like I was saying, we began getting gigs at the Mab opening for bands like the Dead Kennedys, SVT and Crime. Then slowly we were able to headline. It seemed very tough and competitive at the time. So, we had to really be good. Maybe, it's because there was always and still is a stigma about girl bands as musicians playing their instruments. Dirk's ability to see that we were a good band period was a big help.

I remember one night at the Mab. The Contractions were playing. It was my birthday and they wheeled out this huge 5 tiered cake onto the stage, right in the middle of our set and everybody stopped playing. All of a sudden Dirk popped out of the cake in a tutu with the dick nose singing happy birthday. Wow. I couldn't believe that, Annette Jarvie (our manager), my band-mates and friend Rebecca Kmeic had talked him into doing it. And, then everyone hid it from me until that moment. That was the moment when I just fell in love with Dirk and he became my life long friend and mentor.

James: When did you develop a kind of business or closer relationship with Dirk?

Kathy: Dirk just became my best friend. It just evolved, Dirk was like my WC Fields dad. Very funny and great with the sarcastic wit that cut both ways. Dirk was very sharp and could figure things out in an exact formula that he would write out for you. He taught me how to be a tough negotiator as opportunities presented themselves to me and the H.E.A.R. foundation (Hearing Education and Awareness for Rockers, Inc.) along with our H.E.A.R. board of directors of course. Our first video, Can't Hear You Knocking (Flynner Films 1990) went out to about 20,000 school districts and was the first hearing conservation video to be shown in the US high school curriculum through Active Physics Textbooks, The National Science Foundation and The American Association of Physics Teachers. Dirk and Damon's Dirksen Molloy Productions presided over all of H.E.A.R.'s educational film distribution and editing and archives of TV interviews and H.E.A.R. documentaries, as well as production of H.E.A.R. Public Service Announcements.

Dirk was very influential in keeping me going. His advise was always; stick to what you are doing, go to work every day and just do a little bit. If you can't do a lot, do a little bit. I had an accident and hurt my back,

Mutants and audience at Great American Music Hall. Photo by James Stark

unable to work along with dealing with my hearing loss and running H.E.A.R. I could barely walk for awhile and he would say, "Hey, you'll get better or give a funny snide remark" He helped pull me out of it. Dirk was awesome. Dirk use to come over to the house and help train me on how to give insulin shots to my diabetic Chihuahua, Choo Choo. Dirk's pet name for my dog was "Satan's Assistant".

James: After Dirk's passing you became involved with the memorial, how did that come about?

Kathy: When Dirk died, Denise (Denise Demise Dunne) and Damon (Dirk's partner, Damon Molloy) were the ones who found Dirk at his flat on California Street. This totally shocked my being when I got the call from my friend and music attorney, Barry Simons about Dirk. I immediately called Dirk's flat and Denise answered the phone saying, "I knew you would call, Kathy." It was unbelievable that Dirk had passed away in his sleep because I had just seen him. He had just been at the Mutants show at Lennon Studios. He had gone upstairs where the Contractions were rehearsing and said hi to me. Before that we had gone out to dinner at the House of Nan Kang's in North Beach after V. Vail's Pranks Re/ Search Publications book release party at the San Francisco Art Institute. After dinner when we were going back to the car which was several blocks away and uphill, Dirk wanted to walk back. But, I said, "No, We're going to take a cab to the car." I could see he was tired. We all knew he had a history of a heart condition. Several years ago he had bypass surgery. Dirk wasn't in the best of health. His body in the end just couldn't take it and it gave out. But, you would never know it; he loved life and thought that everyone had a chance to express themselves. Onward and Upward!

Dirk's wake at the Treat Street house was packed with people. Dirk's sister, Marli, (Marie-Luise Dirksen) a retired National Institute of Health (NIH) scientist and Dirk's favorite beloved nieces, Carla (Teaser) and Cynthia (Ernst), Oliver (Carla's little son so full of life and love) Damon and streams of friends, neighbors, and punk rockers who brought food

Dirk Dirksen with Ted Falconi at the Filmore. Photo by Chester Simpson

and paid their respect. Marli didn't know punk rock and asked Klaus Fluoride of the DKs to explain it to her. Marli knew that Dirk was involved in punk rock clubs, "The Mabuhay Gardens and the On Broadway" as a promoter but, she didn't know the extent and the importance of Dirk's place in punk history and how Dirk's legacy was important to our music community. It was kind of overwhelming for her. I knew Marli through Dirk and had a good relationship with her. The last time I saw her before I was in Washington DC, as co-founder of H.E.A.R. – Hearing Education and Awareness for Rockers, I was on the public subcommittee for the formation of The National Institute on Deafness and Communication Disorders and stayed at her home. Marli was so helpful to us all. She was able to dig right in. We wouldn't have even been able to claim Dirk's body if she hadn't come to San Francisco.

Dirk's funeral was a larger gathering a few days after the wake at a chapel in the Mission district. Denise had worked with Marli and Damon on the arrangements and I helped with putting together a photo-montage of Dirk's life at the funeral ceremony. The Contractions and Ricky Sludge provided the music, Ron Jones prepared a eulogy about Dirk's life and his charitable work with the Rec Center. Dirk's sister Marli talked about his life growing up in Germany during the war playing and pretending in the bombed out ditches. The late Bruce Connor read his spoken word about Dirk as the Pope of Punk, followed by Winston Smith, Dana Alberts, Officer Bob Geary, Jennifer Blowdryer, East Bay Ray, Penelope Houston and many others confessing how Dirk had helped them on their way.

The family wanted the services to be mellow. They wanted it to be about Dirk's life. People got to see the whole Dirk picture. People from the punk rock side didn't know about his involvement with kids, the disabled and those in need; like the children's kitchen at Mission Rec Center where Dirk taught the neighborhood kids cooking classes and came up with his infamous taco sauce and spaghetti recipe and The Janet Polmeroy Recreation Center where Dirk and Damon worked with Ron Jones filming dance recitals and water ballet with blind and disabled talent. The Rec. Center people and others didn't

Avengers and auddience at Great American Music Hall. Photo by James Stark

know about Dirk's time at the Mabuhay Gardens as the " Pope of Punk". It became a convergence of a lot of different aspects of his life. It was also about Dirk's relationship with a neighborhood single mom and her son, Patti and Ian Davis and how Dirk was their friend and mentor. Dirk was always there with a bag of groceries if someone needed it because he and Damon worked with the local food bank to help provide for others. Dirk was busy all the time. I don't know how he did it all with a smile and a wisecrack.

After the funeral we all went to Carole Lennon's and Jimmy Crucifix's place to relax, watch early films of Dirk at the Mab shot by Karl Hinz and just reflect.

"DIRKFEST"

A memorial concert needed to be planned. I talked to Marli and Damon and the family about putting on "Dirkfest". I had this feeling that I should take hold of this and just do it, because I've done so many H.E.A.R. benefit concerts with Dirk over the years. However, I knew it would be a tremendous effort to produce with no budget. Then Dawn offered to host the event for Dirk at The Great American Music Hall. Dawn Holiday, Dennis Juarez, Ted Hatsuhsi and the staff at the Great American and Slim's have always been a tremendous support to all of us in the Bay Area music community. And the bands were just awesome with their response as well as all the great volunteers who helped to put it on. We needed to raise money quickly, there was a deficit, there were medical bills, final expenses, securing the archives and transition for Damon and paying for Dirk's burial plot at the San Francisco Columbarium. I just took a big bite out of it and made it happen with the help of so many others willing to lend a hand.

The stage set designs were created by Craig Pop Artist (Craig Krestan) assisted by Sun Ku and David Kirkpatrick. There were two different color schems: Cool colors for Slims and hot colors for Great American Music Hall.

Craig Pop Artist at work and his designs.

Photos curtesy of The Studio of Craig Pop Artist

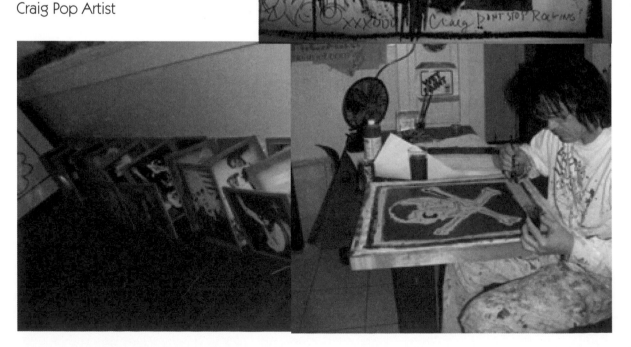

Poster by Wiston Smith

Poster by John Seabury

talked to him about my plans for a memorial show for Dirk. He told me he wanted to MC. This was my start, contacting people at the wake. It wasn't only contacting the bands and musicians. It was about getting in touch with people who were part of the audience, the people who had gone to the Mab, the Mab staff, the photographers, the artists and all the friends who knew Dirk. Most of the bands I talked to were really interested; of course everybody wanted to play. But, I thought this could become an opportunity to go back in time… punk rock time that was the music history that came out of the Mab. It would be hard to find the early bands. Not everybody could do it for one reason or another and, there were some things that were out of my control in deciding who was going to play or even who was getting in. One of the amazing things was finding several early bands and musicians who had not played together for years with their original members.

　　Our friend, Craig Pop Artist (Craig Kresten), created all of the large set designs of different skull and cross bone color schemes for each night working with his assistants Sun Ku and David Kirkpatrick. To us the vibe of the event was just as important as the music, a total experience if you will. I contacted the early Mab photographers, James Stark, Ruby Ray, Bobby Castro, F Stop Fitzgerald, Chester Simpson, and others to contribute to "the Wall of Shame" that Craig constructed to be viewed during the show. People could just go up to wall and see hundreds of photos of Dirk and also find themselves in the photos from back in the day performing with their band or, just being in the scene. It was about everybody who had that connection with Dirk that made it an event that went beyond the usual reunion. I hoped reminiscent of a time at one night at the Mab to honor Dirk.

　　Winston Smith original image of the two punk kids that turn into a skull was used for the DirkFest black and white T-shirt. The Dirkfest posters were just fantastic. Winston created a poster of his "Last Super" with Dirk as the Pope of Punk surrounded by punk rockers for the Saturday night Dirkfest show at The Great American Music Hall. Artist and musician John Seabury created his infamous drawing of Dirk wearing the dick nose for the poster for Friday night Dirkfest show at Slim's. Fire House, (Chuck Sperry and Ron Donavon), silk screened printed a numbered edition of the posters for us. Some of the posters were hand signed by the artists and by the bands.

Dirk Program and with thanks to bands and volunteers

Great performances. Incredible energy. Biafra striding across the stage giving an early acerbic history of Dirk and the Mab bands. We ended up doing 2 nights The Great American Music Hall sold out Saturday so, we added Friday night at Slim's.

At Slim's MC Spencer opens the night with spoken word artist and playwright, Ron Jones with Megan Bierman and Maia Scott, then a great tight set by The Symptoms followed by the bombastic Rubber City Rebels, Sea Hags, and the high ripping energy of The Lewd. Then an unbelievable ex-

DJ Spencer Coppens with Craig Pop Artist's backdrop at Slim's. Photo Randy Seanor

plosive return of two awesome historic punk bands The Toiling Midgets and Pearl Harbor and the Explosions with Pearly Gates.

Next night at the Great American Music Hall. Wisecracking Denise Demise was DJ for both nights. Dana Albert opened up with a poem about Dirk and his band Minus One, followed by then a rare appearance of No Alternative with Johnny Genocide joined by Chip Kinman from Rank and File and the Dils, then a wild set by The White Trash Debutantes with Ginger Coyote, my band The Contractions performed a rare appearance, then because Sally from the Mutants could not play Dirk's memorial, their guitarist Brendan Earley renamed the band, The Mutant All Stars with Naomi Ruth Eisenberg performing violin and to top off the night The Avengers with Penelope Houston with an appearance by Jello Biafra joining at the end of the night with an encore of "Money".

Not to forget Stage Manager Mike Dingle, Bill McCarthy, Victoria Wesson, Lou and Kay, Jessica and all of the other great volunteers and media folks. Dirk Fest I believe helped to encouraged many of these great artists to get back together and do stuff. It was like the whole engine of the original SF Punk scene got ignited again that night for Dirk. And not to mention some punky stuff happened, too.

Dirk Dirksen memorial service held at Valente, Marini, Perata and Co. on Saturday December 2, 2006.

Jennifer Blowdryer

Penelope Houston. Avove and East Bay Ray, Below

Mary Kelly, Kathy Peck and Ricky Sludge.

219

SAT DEC 2: DIRK DIRKSEN MEMORIAL SERVICE

11AM-1PM, 4840 Mission St/bet. Russia-Geneva, San Francisco

Sunday night, Nov 19, 2006, after attending a rehearsal of the Mutants at Lennon Studios in San Francisco, Dirk Dirksen went home and died in his sleep. He had had quadruple bypass heart surgery in 1990 and the prevailing opinion is that he died of a heart attack or a stroke.

But while he was alive, Dirk Dirksen, to quote Winston Smith, "changed the world!" Almost single-handedly he made the early beginnings of Punk Rock possible in San Francisco, by providing an all-ages, low-admission-charge venue where anybody could play - once, at least. Wannabe performers had to submit a "3-song demo tape," a photo, and brief description, and almost nobody was rejected. He suffered 7 broken noses, a broken ankle, an above-elbow replacement and various internal injuries while fending off deluded humans who mistakenly equated "Punk Rock" with violence--a notion implanted by corporate media, the enemy of authentic cultural evolution everywhere.

A Celebration
of the Life of
Dirk Bernhard Dirksen

August 25, 1937 – November 20, 2006

From 1974-1984 (or was it 1986?) Dirk curated thousands of shows at the Mabuhay Gardens, 443 Broadway, and the upstairs On Broadway Theater. Several obituaries have appeared in corporate media, but we think they contain errors.

Introduction: Ron Jones

Song: Deep Sleep
Words and music by Mary E. Kelley
Musicians: Mary Kelley, guitar and vocals
Debbie Hopkins, percussion

Damon Molloy
Marie-Luise Dirksen
Christina Ernst
Carla Tesar
Kathy Peck
Denise Demise Dunne
Bob Geary and Brendan O'Smarty
Patti Davis
Ron Jones

Open Mic: Share your memories of Dirk for 2 minutes or less

Closing Song: Down in the Valley (traditional)
Kathy Peck: Vocals

Down in the valley, valley so low
Hang your head over, hear the wind blow
Hear the wind blow, love, hear the wind blow
Hang your head over, hear the wind blow

Silent reflection

For example, the S.F. Chronicle's Joel Selvin (and Michael Goldberg, in a separate article) stated that the Ramones (and Iggy Pop) played the Mabuhay Gardens, but to the best of our knowledge, this never happened...almost every other U.S. Punk Band did, however. If anyone has the exact date(s) of these alleged concerts, please forward to us, and we will report in the next newsletter.

Dirk Dirksen Place (Mab Alley) Memorial Plaque Drive
The City of San Francisco to honor Dirk Dirksen

My GAWD! The Punks are back... White Smoke for the Pope of Punk...

After almost three years of constant pressure and perseverance Dirk Dirksen Place is a reality.

The City of San Francisco has authorized the street naming of Dirk Dirksen Place at the former Rowland Street location. For those of you who don't know, Rowland Street is the alley next to the original Ness Aquino's Mabuhay Gardens location at 443 Broadway Street in North Beach where Dirk was the ringmaster of scene. With help from so many from the Punk Community and friends of Dirk Dirksen and Ness Aquino, guided by the outstanding support of then San Francisco Board of Supervisors Tom Ammiano and Aaron Peskin we purchased a memorial plaque

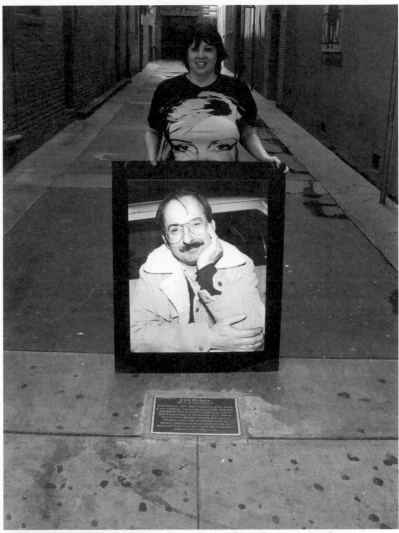

Kathy Peck standing in Dirk Dirksen Place. Photos by James Stark

Dirk Dirksen
SHUT UP, YOU ANIMALS

Dirk Dirksen (1937 - 2006), ringmaster of the circus of the creatively inspired and the willfully deranged, presided as Pope of Punk over nightly excursions into living theater on the premises 1974 - 1984 at Ness Aquino's Mabuhay Gardens, previously a Filipino supper club. He opened the lid on society's garbage can of new talent to look for truth and beauty that gave rise to San Francisco's counter-culture music scene.

and installed it at the Dirk Dirksen Place location with full honors by The City of San Francisco honor the "Pope of Punk" Dirk Dirksen and San Francisco's Counterculture Music Scene that he and Ness Aquino presided over. The Memorial Plaque and street naming drive was presided over by executive director/co-founder of H.E.A.R. and Contractions bassist, Kathy Peck.

221

The Pope Is Dead -- Dirk Dirksen (1937-2006)

The mutants gathered at his grave
to burn the flame and light the cave.
Jello was served at his request
before the world heard of his punk rock fest.
He took the rejects and gave them all names,
sent their critics to the astral planes.
An uncle, a brother a father, a friend --
how many of us did he raise in the end?

And if not for him our din would not be known.
He gave us a stage, a place to call home --
without his wry smile and discerning eye
we'd have been aimless with nowhere to fly .

He gave us purpose in a purposeless world,
chaperoned a generation, put his money
where his mouth was in the punk vocation,
challenged my reasons for playing guitar
and encouraged the madness in his theater
bizarre.

photo credit: http://www.mulleian.com

He had the ability to turn you on to yourself, a hard core ringleader, a magic little elf.
He could make you or break you, but he wasn't that mean: anyone who wanted could be in his
scene; you just had to be there to know that he did care.

He cared about each and every nut ball, in fact, he enjoyed them all.
He applauded your success and rescued us from boredom.
When all of us were poor and no one could afford him, he would still let you in
with a crooked grin and a strange remark, always tongue in cheek.
"I provide music seven nights a week," he used to tell me.
Nobody did that then or now. He knew every con, every trick in the book,
but he'd let you go on sinker, line and hook, and hang your self publicly if that's what it took,
to get the attention that you think you needed.

All the fruits of your glory come from plant that we seeded, one by one by one by minus one.

D. C. Alberts
© November, 2006

222

FAB MAB

THE VERBS

with: THE NOISE

TUESDAY JULY 22

SILVERTONE

FAB MAB
THURS. 24
SAT. 26

CHEEZEHEADS RETURN

From the wild forests of British Columbia...

THE POINTED STICKS

are returning to your fair state for more dancing, more rocking, more mindless fun!

available soon at these fine venues

Oct.11,12 Mabuhay, S.F.
Oct.17 Blackie's L.A.
Oct.18 HongKong Cafe, L.A.

THE NEXT

TUES. JULY 3

MABUHAY gardens
443 Broadway San Francisco
956-3315

A DIRKSEN-MILLER PRODUCTION

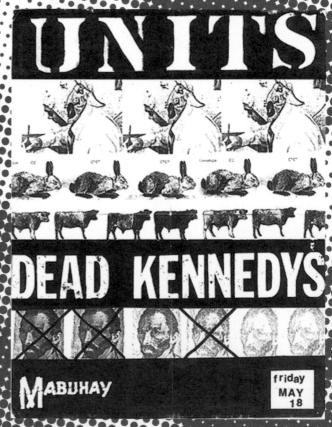

NIPS

Feb. 12 and 24
Mabuhay Gardens

Feb. 17
Deaf Club

S.A.G.

ANIMAL THINGS

W/ THE MUTANTS

SAT. OCT. 3   AT THE MAB

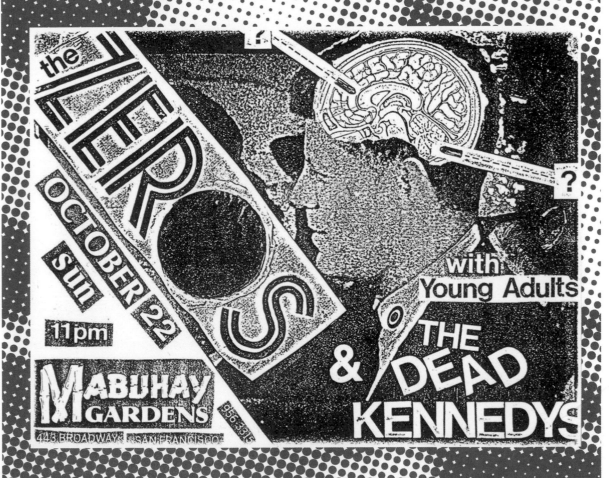

the ZEROS

OCTOBER
SUN 22
11pm

MABUHAY GARDENS
443 BROADWAY   SAN FRANCISCO
956-3315

with
Young Adults

& THE DEAD KENNEDYS

230

New Year's Spectacular Sun. dec 31 • 8:30 pm

VIP$

A DIRKSEN-MILLER PRODUCTION

MABUHAY
Gardens

photo: James Stark

DIRKSEN-MILLER PRODUCTIONS FRONT DESIGN

AFTER **BAMMIE**
FAB **MAB**ie
p a r t y

AFTER The FARCE Go To The REAL ThiNg

the **ROOMATES**

the **LEWD**

WRONG BROS.

TUE. MARCH 25

FAB MABUHAY MAB 11:00

THE **"MUTANTS
OFFs** AND **AXZUM**

FRI.12TH. **11P.M. mabuhay s.f.**
956-3315 443 BROADWAY

THE METROPOLE **NUNS**

FRIDAY FEB. 24

MABUHAY

BOREDOM DOWN

TREND

231

ALSO PUBLISHED BY LAST GASP

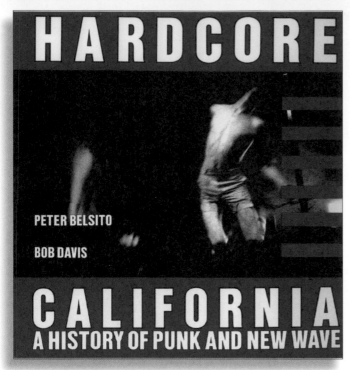
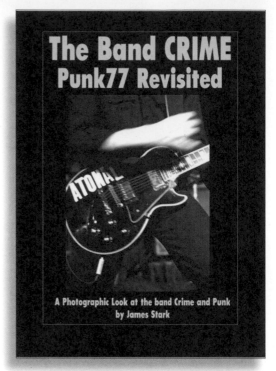